GOODENOUGH ON THE BEGINNINGS
OF CHRISTIANITY

Number 212
GOODENOUGH ON THE BEGINNINGS
OF CHRISTIANITY

edited by
A.T. Kraabel

GOODENOUGH ON THE BEGINNINGS OF CHRISTIANITY

edited by

A.T. Kraabel

Scholars Press
Atlanta, Georgia

GOODENOUGH ON THE BEGINNINGS
OF CHRISTIANITY

© 1990
Brown University

Library of Congress Cataloging-in-Publication Data

Goodenough, Erwin Ramsdell, 1893-1965.
  Goodenough on the beginnings of Christianity / [edited] by A.T.
Kraabel.
  p. cm. -- Brown Judaic studies ; no. 212)
  Articles originally published 1925-1968.
  Includes bibliographical references and indexes.
  ISBN 1-55540-503-7
  1. Christianity--Origin. 2. Church history--Primitive and early
church, ca. 30-600. 3. Bible. N.T.--Criticism, interpretation,
etc. I. Kraabel, A. Thomas. II. Title. III. Series.
BR129.G59 1990
270.1--dc20   90-38390
                                                       CIP

Printed in the United States of America
on acid-free paper

For

O.W. Qualley

Born March 9, 1897
Died December 8, 1988

A member of the Luther College community from 1912 to 1988

Table of Contents

Acknowledgements

The editor expresses his thanks to the following copyright holders for their permission to reprint the articles in this volume, as follows:

"In Memoriam" and

No. 11   *Religions in Antiquity. Essays in Honor of Erwin Ramsdell Goodenough,* ed. Jacob Neusner. (Leiden, 1968: Brill) ©1968. Used by permission of the editor, Jacob Neusner.

No. 1   *Harvard Theological Review* 1925, vol. 18 ©1925

No. 2   *Journal of Religion* 1940, vol. 20 ©1940. Used by permission of the University of Chicago Press.

Nos. 3-5   *Journal of Biblical Literature* 1945, vol. 64 ©1945

No. 6   *Journal of Biblical Literature* 1952, vol. 71 ©1952

No. 7   *The Age of Diocletian: A Symposium, 1951* (New York, 1953) ©1953 by The Metropolitan Museum of Art

No. 8   *Jewish Quarterly Review* 1956-7, vol. 47 ©1957

No. 9   *Harvard Theological Review* 1964, vol. 57 ©1964

No. 10   *Studies in Luke-Acts.* Edited by L.E. Keck and J.L. Martin. ©1966, 1980 by L.E. Keck and J.L. Martin. Used by permission of the publisher, Fortress Press.

Bibliographic Notes

The first section below corrects and completes the bibliography which I contributed to the Goodenough memorial volume (Neusner, 1968). The listing here simply replaces everything in the 1968 bibliography from 1966 forward. (Goodenough's annual reports as the editor of the *Journal of Biblical Literature* from 1935 through 1942 are listed in my introduction to his Presidential Address to the Society of Biblical Literature, item 9 below.)

Second is a list of reprintings of Goodenough's works. Except for the last two entries, items here are in order of the date of original publication.

The third section gives bibliographical details for the works which I drew upon for my contributions to this volume. One other project, not available to me, should be brought to the reader's attention: Prof. Eleanor Bustin Mattes of Lexington, Massachusetts, has begun to prepare a new biography of Goodenough with the cooperation of the Goodenough family. The publication date and the publisher of this work are not determined at this writing.

Throughout this volume I refer to the works of Goodenough by short title, and to other works (on list III) by the author's name and the year of publication.

Morton Smith's memorial minute on Goodenough is reprinted, lightly edited, from Neusner, 1968. Variations of the same text appeared in *Numen* 12 (1965) 233-235 and *History of Religions* 5 (1966) 351-352.

I.

1966

"The Perspective of Acts," in *Studies in Luke-Acts, Essays Presented in Honor of Paul Schubert*, eds. L.E. Keck and J.L. Martyn, Nashville, Abingdon Press, 1966, 51-59.

"The Greek Garments on Jewish Heroes in the Dura Synagogue," Philip W. Lown Institute of Advanced Judaic Studies, Brandeis University, *Studies and Texts:* Volume III, Biblical Motifs, ed. Alexander Altmann, Cambridge, Harvard University Press, 1966, 221-37.

1967

"A Historian of Religion Tries to Define Religion," *Zygon* 2 (1967) 7-22.

1968

Jewish Symbols in the Greco-Roman Period ("Bollingen Series XXXVII"), New York, Pantheon Books, 1968, vol. 13: *Indexes and Maps With the Author's Corrigenda and Comments for the Preceding Volumes.*

"Paul and the Hellenization of Christianity" with A. Thomas Kraabel, in *Religions in Antiquity. Essays in Memory of E.R. Goodenough,* ed. J. Neusner, Leiden: Brill, 1968, 23-70 (Studies in the History of Religion, XIV).

1969

"Life Purpose in View of the Past," in *Studies in Language, Literature, and Culture of the Middle Ages and Later,* eds. E.B. Atwood and A.A. Hill, Austin, The University of Texas, 1969, 385-98. (Rudolph Willard Festschrift).

1971

"Dura-Europos" (with M. Avi-Yonah), vol. 6, 275-98 and plates 1-9 (between 300-01), and

"Symbolism, Jewish (In the Greco-Roman period)," vol. 15, 568-78, in *Encyclopaedia Judaica*, Jerusalem, 1971.

II.

The Theology of Justin Martyr (1923) – Reprinted by Philo Press, Amsterdam, 1968.

The Politics of Philo Judaeus, Practice and Theory. (1938) – Reprinted by Georg Olms Verlag (Hildesheim, 1967).

Toward a Mature Faith. (1955) – Reprinted by University Press of America, Lanham, Maryland, 1988, with an introduction by William Scott Green. Brown Classics in Judaica Series.

An Introduction to Philo Judaeus. (Second edition, revised, 1962) – Reprinted by University Press of America, Lanham, Maryland, 1986, with an introduction by Jacob Neusner. Brown Classics in Judaica Series.

The Psychology of Religious Experiences. (1965) – Reprinted by University Press of America, Lanham, Maryland, 1986, with an introduction by William Scott Green. Brown Classics in Judaica Series.

Goodenough on The History of Religion and on Judaism. Edited by Ernest S. Frerichs and Jacob Neusner. Brown Judaic Studies 121. Atlanta: Scholars Press, 1986.

Jewish Symbols in the Greco-Roman Period. Abridged edition. Edited, with a foreword, by Jacob Neusner. Bollingen Series. Princeton: Princeton University Press, 1988.

III.

Bruneau, P.

1982   "Les Israelites de Delos et la juiverie delienne." *Bulletin de Correspondance Hellenistique* 106:465-504.

Buckley, W.F.

1951   *God and Man at Yale.* Chicago: Henry Regnery.

Eccles, R.S.

1985   *Erwin Ramsdell Goodenough: A Personal Pilgrimage.* Chico CA: Scholars Press.

Esler, P.

1987   *Community and Gospel in Luke-Acts. The Social and Political Motivation of Lucan Theory.* Cambridge UK: Cambridge University Press.

Feldman, L.

1986   "The Omnipresence of the God-Fearers." *Biblical Archaeology Review* 12:58-63.

Gager, J.G.

1986   "Jews, Gentiles and Synagogues in the Book of Acts." In Nickelsburg 1986, pages 91-99.

Georgi, D.

1986   *The Opponents of Paul in Second Corinthians.* Revised edition. Philadelphia: Fortress.

Grant, R.M.

1983   "Homer, Hesiod, and Heracles in Pseudo-Justin." *Vigiliae Christianae* 37:105-109.

1987   "Goodenough, Erwin R." *The Encyclopedia of Religion,* Mircea Eliade, Editor-in-Chief. New York: Macmillan Publishing Company. Vol. 6, pages 76-77.

Hanfmann, G.M.A.

1983   *Sardis from Prehistoric to Roman Times.* Cambridge MA: Harvard University Press.

Horsley, G.H.R.

1983   *New Documents Illustrating Early Christianity. A Review of the Greek Inscriptions and Papyri Published in 1978.* North Ryde, N.S.W. Australia: Macquarie University.

van der Horst, P.

1989   "Jews and Christians in Aphrodisias in the Light of Their Relations in Other Cities of Asia Minor." *Nederlands Theologisch Tijdschrift* 43:106-121.

Kraabel, A.T.

1981   "The Disappearance of the 'God-fearers'." *Numen* 28:113-126.

1984   "New Evidence of the Samaritan Diaspora has been Found on Delos." *Biblical Archaeologist* 47:44-46.

1985   "*Synagoga caeca.* Systematic Distortion in Gentile Interpretations of Evidence for Judaism in the Early Christian Period." In Neusner and Frerichs, 1985. Pages 219-246.

1986   "Greeks, Jews, and Lutherans in the Middle Half of *Acts.*" In Nickelsburg 1986. Pages 147-57.

1989   [Review of Watson (1986), Esler (1987) and Sanders (1987)]. JBL 108:160-163.

Meeks, W.A.

1983   *The First Urban Christians.* New Haven: Yale University Press.

Meyers, E.M.

1987   [Review of Eccles 1985]. *Journal of the American Academy of Religion* 55:146-48.

Negev, A.

1978   "The Greek Inscriptions from 'Avdat (Obada)." *Studii Biblici Franciscani, Liber Annuus* 28:87-126, plates 7-24.

Neusner, J.

1968   *Religions in Antiquity. Essays in Memory of Erwin Ramsdell Goodenough.* Edited by J. Neusner. Leiden: Brill. Studies in the History of Religion, XIV.

Nickelsburg, G.

1986   *Christians Among Jews and Gentiles. Essays in Honor of Krister Stendahl on His Sixty-Fifth Birthday.* Edited by G.W.E. Nickelsburg with George W. MacRae, S.J. Philadelphia: Fortress. [=*Harvard Theological Review* 79.1.3].

Räisänen, H.

1983   *Paul and the Law.* Tubingen: J.C.B. Mohr (Paul Siebeck), 1983. WUNT, Vol. 29. Reprinted Philadelphia: Fortress, 1986.

Reynolds, J. and Tannenbaum, R.F.

1987   *Jews and God-Fearers at Aphrodisias: Greek Inscriptions with Commentary.* Cambridge Philological Society Supplementary Volume 12. Cambridge UK: Cambridge Philological Society.

Robert, L.

1978   "Maledictions funeraires grecques, I: Une epitaphe metrique au Piree." *Comptes rendus de l'Adademie des Inscriptions et Belles-Lettres.* Paris. Pages 241-269.

Sanders, J.

1987   *The Jews in Luke-Acts.* Philadelphia: Fortress.

Sandmel, S.

1968   "An Appreciation." In Neusner, 1968. Pages 3-17.

Watson, F.

1987   *Paul, Judaism, and the Gentiles. A Sociological Approach.*
              Cambridge UK: Cambridge University Press.

White, L.M.

1987   "The Delos Synagogue Revisited: Recent Fieldwork in the
              Graeco-Roman Diaspora." *Harvard Theological Review*
              80:133-160.

Preface

I

Erwin Ramsdell Goodenough was born in Brooklyn, New York on October 24, 1893. He died in Cambridge, Massachusetts March 20, 1965. He spent nearly 40 of the years in between on the faculty of Yale University, teaching history at first; later he would be a member of a half-dozen Yale departments at once.

There are several accounts of his life and career. The most important is his autobiographical *Toward a Mature Faith* (1955). The memorial volume *Religions in Antiquity* (1968), edited by Jacob Neusner, includes a brief account by Morton Smith, reprinted below, and a more extensive "appreciation" by Samuel Sandmel.

The biography by Robert S. Eccles published in 1985 provides the most detail. Like Sandmel, Eccles was a doctoral student under Goodenough; his work is more a tribute than an analysis (Meyers 1987), but it is still helpful in at least three ways. It offers a detailed review of Goodenough's career, provides extensive summaries and paraphrases of Goodenough's major and minor writings, and publishes excerpts from important private letters and other materials from the Goodenough papers in the Yale University Library.

Goodenough's personal values and his scholarship were closely related; understanding either greatly helps to clarify the other. With no area of his work is that more true than with what is presented in this volume.

II

Twenty years after Goodenough's death, in prefaces to the reprint of *An Introduction to Philo Judaeus*, and to the book of essays edited by himself and Ernest Frerichs (1986), Jacob Neusner summarized the importance of Goodenough's contributions to three areas of study: the material evidence for the Judaism of the Greco-Roman period, Philo, and the history of religions. Neusner makes it clear that Goodenough's work in any one of these would be the equivalent of a credible career for many writers – but Goodenough worked brilliantly in the three simultaneously.

What is often forgotten, however, is that Goodenough's first area of interest was none of those for which he is best known. Rather it was the beginnings of Christianity. His first scholarly publication was his still-cited and reprinted 1923 monograph on Justin Martyr. And that concern never left him: his final project, the one which occupied his last day of writing, was about earliest Christianity and its Hellenization. He had originally intended his work on that topic to be the culmination of his career and also, I suspect, of his own personal quest.

It is not hard to reconstruct the basic outline of what he would have written about early Christianity. There are many hints in the essays reprinted here, and in his other writings. He and I talked about little else when I worked for him. And Eccles (1985:170-71) reprints a letter of October 11, 1958 to Mircea Eliade which gives a rather detailed plan. It would have moved through four major concerns:

I.   The various forms of Judaism at the beginning of the Common Era, including early rabbinic Judaism, the Dead Sea scrolls and the apocryphal literature.

II.   The Hellenization of Judaism, and the great importance of that phenomenon for the story of Christianity. The letter to Eliade provides one listing of the sources he would use: Philo, "the hellenistic group of synagogues" and the other archaeological evidence presented in *Symbols,* and finally the "early Christians mentioned in *Acts*," many of whom Goodenough believed were originally hellenized Jews (Eccles 1985:170).

III.   "The tremendous impact of Jesus as an historical person" (Eccles 1985:170).

IV.   "The obviously different way various early Christians interpreted" that impact (Eccles 1985:170).

As is clear almost from his earliest writings on, Goodenough attributed the great variety in the forms of New Testament Christianity not so much to internal evolution within the early Christian movement as to two other factors: the differences in pre-Christian background and piety brought to the new faith by the earliest generations of

Christians, and the diversity in the audiences the first Christian missionaries faced. To point to a "religious evolution" which might have taken place within the Christian movement in the decade or two between Jesus and Paul is not sufficient to explain the great differences of emphasis between their messages. And even three or four decades of development cannot begin to account for the many divergences between the content of Paul's letters and what *Acts* will say about him.

Goodenough's approach has a great deal to recommend it, and helps to explain his continuing value for the study of the religions of the Greco-Roman world. But it also causes significant discomfort to more traditional interpreters because of the way it elevates the importance of external factors in the development of earliest Christianity. Goodenough's understanding of how Christianity grew attributes more to the formative power of religious and social contexts, less to the new religion's own internal dynamic.

III

Perhaps "he had dallied too long on the preliminaries." Samuel Sandmel was speaking as much for himself as for Goodenough when he attributed that judgment to Goodenough after their last meeting two weeks before Goodenough's death (Sandmel 1968:15). In one sense the conclusion is a correct one. How much more could Goodenough have said about the beginnings of Christianity if he had had longer to live, or if he had given more time to it and less to those other areas of research!

But the fact of the matter is that there was already more than enough publication about the New Testament by other scholars. As Goodenough himself said more than once, more of the same would not have been much of a contribution. Goodenough had a different angle on the New Testament, and that was just because of his other research and writing. The data he took seriously, particularly those of Greek-speaking Judaism, few others were considering important yet. And what later was to establish his reputation world-wide – the interpretation of Jewish material evidence from the Greco-Roman world – was still an unknown field. Not only had it been up to him to formulate its methodology. He also had to assemble many of the artifacts. Much of what constitutes "Jewish symbols" would not be so accessible to us now, were it not for the trips he took, the letters he wrote and the colleagues he queried.

On the New Testament and early Christianity he wrote the essays here reprinted – and very little else. His main contribution to this field would be his editorship of the *Journal of Biblical Literature* (JBL) from

1935 to 1942, not the things he published about Christianity there and elsewhere.

But in the comments on early Christianity scattered throughout the *Symbols* and his other writings, he was signaling the way he thought the study of early Christianity should be taking. Occasionally he wrote more global pieces – such as Nos. 2, 3, 6, 7 here – which made more obvious the direction he intended to follow once he finished all the *prolegomena.*

The *magnum opus* was never completed. What he had once thought of as a study equal in extent to the *Symbols* themselves (Eccles 1985:85) became, in plan, a single volume after he became ill. Even that was unattainable; the last essay in this book is all that remains of that effort.

As he prepared for this project, Goodenough knew that he would almost have to begin over if he were to write credibly. His systematic knowledge of critical New Testament studies derived from his graduate school days (Sandmel 1968:6-7, Eccles 1985: 173-74). When I began to work with him, my chief task was to try to bring him up to date as rapidly as possible. He worked at it heroically in the last weeks, and some of what we talked about is there in the footnotes at least. It never really made it to the body of the essay.

IV

Besides, there were other things on his mind as his time grew very short. When I first met him, he had inscribed a copy of *Toward a Mature Faith* and given it to me. The last chapter, "Personal Again," a kind of *credo,* is chiefly about prayer, or rather about Erwin Goodenough praying. Ten days before his death I asked him about that. "I still pray," he said, "but I no longer live on prayer as I used to." His situation was different now: "I am part of the cosmos...Religion is searching. That's what scientists live on. We have no right to expect peace; there is none."

It was an idea I had already read in the page-proofs of volume 12 of the *Symbols:* "The deeper religious spirits know that true religion lies in the search for the end, not in its attainment" (*Symbols* 12:74). On those same pages of the *Symbols* he was working with the Apostle Paul, and there again is repeated the parallel he often drew between personal religion and the life of the scholar. It was an ideal of great power as he embodied it.

The developing essay on the New Testament he turned over to Krister Stendahl to see through to publication. The rest of his writings he placed under the care of his literary executor, Jacob Neusner.

Goodenough had prepared a list of his "more important articles," and he added to it the last year before his death. He thought they might be reissued some day. They are noted in the 1968 bibliography, and many of them have been reprinted either in the Frerichs-Neusner volume (1988) or in this one.

Goodenough hoped for immortality, at the very least the kind of immortality proper to any great scholar. In the Woodbridge East Side Burying Ground in Woodbridge, Connecticut, his memorial carries the inscription he requested: "The scholar is dead but scholarship lives on." It identifies him as "Professor of History of Religion" at Yale. It bears no symbol at all.

Decorah, Iowa
May 17, 1990

In Memoriam

Erwin Ramsdell Goodenough was born in Brooklyn, New York, in 1893. After attending Hamilton College he went for two years to Drew Theological Seminary and then to Garrett Biblical Institute, from which he received the bachelor's degree in theology in 1917. He then studied for three years at Harvard, where he was much influenced by the teaching of George Foot Moore, and for three years at Oxford, from which he received the D.Phil. in 1923. In that year he returned to the United States as instructor in history at Yale, where he remained, becoming Assistant Professor of History in 1926 and Associate Professor in 1931, then Professor of History of Religion in 1934, and John A. Hoober Professor of Religion in 1959. On his retirement from Yale in 1962 he spent a year at Brandeis University as Jacob Ziskind Professor of Mediterranean Studies, and settled in Cambridge, where Harvard placed at his disposal an office in Widener Library. Here he continued his research until his final illness.

During his work for his first published book, *The Theology of Justin Martyr* (1923), he came to the conclusion that many hellenistic elements of early Christianity were probably derived, not directly from the pagan world, but from the already hellenized Judaism through which Christianity first spread abroad. Almost all the rest of his scholarly works were devoted to the study of this hellenized Judaism, which figured largely in all of them and was the primary concern of the *The Jurisprudence of the Jewish Courts in Egypt* (1929), *By Light, Light: The Mystic Gospel of Hellenistic Judaism* (1935), *The Politics of Philo Judaeus, with a General Bibliography of Philo* (1938), *An Introduction to Philo Judaeus* (1940), and the monumental *Jewish Symbols in the Greco-Roman Period*, of which the publication began in 1953 and was completed, by publication of the thirteenth volume, in 1968.

In these works Goodenough set forth a picture of hellenized Judaism which may be seen as complement and counterpart to Moore's classic picture of rabbinic Judaism. But while Moore's work was the careful analysis and description of a well-recognized body of written sources, Goodenough's work required the collection of a vast body of archaeological material hitherto scattered through thousands of publications, museums, and private collections, some of it unrecognized, most of it neglected, and almost all of it misinterpreted. With the presentation of this material, the volumes of *Jewish Symbols* necessitated a profound revision of previous notions of hellenistic, and also of rabbinic, Judaism. From now on, wherever the Judaism of the Greco-Roman world is seriously studied, Goodenough's work must be used as one of the major sources.

This great scholarly achievement was recognized by grants from the Bollingen Foundation (whose magnificent publication of *Jewish Symbols* is a credit to our country), by degrees from Garrett, Yale, the Hebrew Union College, and the University of Uppsala, and by membership in the American Academy of Arts and Sciences. It was, however, only one aspect of Goodenough's career. He was always an active participant in many scholarly organizations in this country and abroad. From 1935-42 he edited the *Journal of Biblical Literature* and he was long the representative of the Society of Biblical Literature to the American Council of Learned Societies (ACLS); from 1947-58 he was President of the Connecticut Academy of Arts and Sciences; he was a member of the councils of the International Association for the History of Religions and the World Union for Jewish Studies, and of the Committee on the History of Religion of the ACLS. In this last role he played a large part in the organization of The American Society for the Study of Religion and was its first President.

Along with this activity in historical studies, he was also deeply concerned with contemporary religious problems, a concern which derived from his upbringing in a household of intense Protestant piety. Because of this he was always anxious to determine the valid and enduring elements of religion and to redefine religious life in the light of scientific discoveries, particularly in the fields of physics, psychoanalysis, anthropology and sociology. He was much involved in the Institute for Religion in an Age of Science, and was a member of its advisory board from 1956 on. At Yale he gave generously of his time in counseling students with religious problems, his home was always a center for discussion of religious questions, and his own beliefs were summed up in his book, *Toward a Mature Faith* (1955).

All these achievements live on. What is lost to us, and what we mourn, is the personality – the wide learning, the extraordinary combination of clarity and profundity, the candid recognition of the limitations of his learning and of the suppositions required for his theories, the warmth and intensity of his life.

Morton Smith

1

The Pseudo-Justinian "Oratio ad Graecos"

1925

In 1925 The Theology of Justin Martyr *had been out for two years and the publication of* By Light, Light *was still a decade in the future. This essay on the* Oratio ad Graecos *of Ps.-Justin, Goodenough's first scholarly article, provides a bridge from the first book to the second. It is about a work of "Justin," but most of it is devoted to Greek-speaking Judaism, here represented chiefly by Philo.*

As soon as this essay was published, Adolf von Harnack quickly wrote a review of it, and of Goodenough's criticism of Harnack's own work on the Oratio. *As a result Goodenough modified his own position when he discussed the* Oratio *again in* By Light, Light. *There (page 299) he wrote: "When the article was written I had not recognized the Mystery and its ramifications in Philo, and so missed a good deal of the implications of the* Oratio." *He withdrew the suggestion that Paul had drawn on the* Oratio *in his letter to the Galatians. But he maintained the essentials of his thesis as he rewrote the article in* By Light, Light *299-305.*

In a recent treatment of this text (Grant 1983), Robert M. Grant agrees with Harnack that the Oratio *is Christian and that it draws on Galatians. However, Goodenough's position has much to recommend it if it is accepted that the supposed parallels to Galatians are standardized commonplaces, the position he comes to in* By Light, Light *298. The crucial chapter*

1

five (translated on 3-4 below) is the point at which the Oratio *comes closest to anything like Christian references. Goodenough asserts that, on the basis of that evidence, the* Oratio *"would not have been recognized by a Greek as referring to Christianity at all" (page 11 below). The Syriac translator of the* Oratio *must have agreed, for he felt it necessary to supplement the text in order to make the link to Christianity unmistakable (pages 10-11 below, cf. By Light, Light 305).*

Following this story from the 1923 monograph to this article (1925) to By Light, Light (1935) provides a remarkable picture of a young and growing scholar "in transition," moving not only from one position to another but really from one scholarly field to the next. Goodenough was determined to master Greek-speaking Judaism. His reason for that was clear: it would help him to understand more completely the emergence of Christianity, and to chart is earliest directions. But already in 1925 he was so far into Philo that it is not surprising that he never successfully completed the return to the original subject, the beginnings of Christianity. With the possible exception of no. 3, none of the other articles reprinted in this volume will be as technical and full of scholarly detail as this early effort. (See also Eccles 1985:62.)

Erwin R. Goodenough, *Harvard Theological Review* **18 (1925): 187-200**

The "Oratio ad Graecos" is to be found in the third volume of Otto's "Corpus Apologetarum Christianorum," and in Harnack's "Die pseudo-justinische Rede an die Griechen."[1] It represents itself as a defence for turning from the religion of the Greeks to the religion of the Logos, and presents its case most vigorously. The document opens with the traditional denunciation of the immoralities of the Greek gods and heroes, a purely Greek polemic which was begun at least as far back as Xenophanes. To this subject the author adds nothing, but presents an excellent epitome of the usual arguments. He then discusses the current way of living among the Greeks, and says that he rejected it with loathing; he justifies his opinion with a half-dozen vivid statements about Greek practices. From commenting upon the Greek religion and morality he turns in contrast to describe with equal pithiness the high moral and spiritual character of his new faith, exhorting his former associates to find the same peace and exaltation which the change has

---

[1]Sitzungsberichte, Berlin Academy, 1896, p. 634 ff.

meant to him. The writer has remarkable power of going to the heart of what he discusses.

The document depends entirely upon its own testimony for its date and classification. Only one manuscript copy came down to us, that in the Codex Argentoratensis (burned in 1870), in which the Oratio received an impossible ascription to Justin Martyr, corresponding to a work of similar title ascribed to Justin by Eusebius. There is, indeed, in the statements of the Oratio about the Logos, a close resemblance to some of Justin's ideas; but that Justin was capable of saying so much to the point in so small a compass is inconceivable. With this evidence for authorship discredited, there is no further tradition whatever to help us in identifying or dating the document. Harnack has investigated the date, and decides that it could not well be later than 240, because, as he ingeniously points out, paederasty is mentioned by the author as a shameful practice, but not as a breach of law. In this way it would have been alluded to until 240, when for the first time a law was instituted against this vice. At the same time Harnack alleges that the conception of the Logos is so advanced as to make an earlier date than 180 unlikely, and consequently he thinks that the date of the document falls between 180 and 240. With this Bardenhewer agrees. That the document is not later than 240 is made probable by Harnack's suggestion; but that the Logos-passage could not have been written before 180 is not so convincing. To this passage I will try to show that Harnack has not paid sufficient attention.

So far as the first four chapters of the Oratio are concerned, in which the immoralities of the Greek gods and of the Greek manners are set forth, they might have been written by a convert to almost any philosophic sect at any time after the third century B.C., and need not detain us. The last chapter, the fifth, is the only one in which positive remarks are made about the writer's own faith. It reads as follows:

> Henceforth, ye Greeks, come and partake of incomparable wisdom ($\sigma o\phi\acute{\iota}a$), and be instructed by the divine Logos, and learn to know the incorruptible king, and recognize his heroes who never slaughter whole nations. For he, our captain, does not desire strength of bodies and beauty of forms, nor the haughtiness of high birth, but a pure soul fortified by holiness. And indeed the divine Logos has ceaseless care over us, and teaches us both the passwords of our king and divine deeds. Oh thou soul which has been permeated with the power of the Logos! Oh trumpet of peace in the soul torn by conflict! Oh city of refuge from terrible passion! Oh teaching that quenches the fire within the soul! This instruction does not make us poets, it does not train us as philosophers, nor as skilful orators, but when it has been learned, it makes mortals become immortals, human beings gods, and from earth leads to the realms beyond Olympus. Come ye, and be instructed. Become as I am now, for I was like you. These things

captured me, the divine inspiration of the instruction, the power of the Logos. For as a skilful snakecharmer makes the terrible serpent creep out of its hole, and puts it to flight, so the Logos drives from the recesses of the soul the terrible sensual affections: first lust, through which every horror is born, enmities, strifes, envy, intriguing, anger, and such like. So when lust has gone forth the soul becomes serene and calm. And when the soul is relieved from the evils that flow about its neck, it returns to him who made it. For it must be restored whence it departed.[2]

The first and most striking fact about this fine description of the power of the Logos to release the soul from the tyranny of the lower nature is that it contains no hint of Christ, or any syllable that is distinctively Christian. And yet, so far as I have been able to ascertain, this obvious point has never been noticed. Found with Christian writings, its Christian character has gone unchallenged. It is this matter which I wish particularly to discuss.

At first sight the Logos-passage, and with it the whole document, might well appear to be the product of any of the late Platonic or Eclectic mystics, for it fits in perfectly with the Logos-ideas of both Plutarch and Cornutus. But the general tenor of the Oratio is against this. The Eclectics never, to my knowledge, set off such an antithesis as is here made between the gods of Greece and the Logos. They rather sought to find the Logos in mythology by allegorizing the ancient myths. So, to say nothing of the Hermetic literature proper, the identification of Hermes and the Logos was a common device of the Stoic "adaptation" of mythology. Cornutus says expressly: "And, as it happens, Hermes is the Logos, whom the gods sent us from heaven, making, of all living creatures on the earth, man alone to be rational."[3] It is hardly necessary to quote from Plutarch. His identification of Osiris with the Logos, for instance, is a familiar example of his attitude toward popular mythology. Even Plato, fiercely as he denounced the gods, and peremptorily as he banished Homer from his Republic, preserved in the Timaeus their purified replicas as intermediate deities.

The presumption, then, from the sharp contrast of the gods and the Logos is that the document did not come from the pen of a pagan philosopher. But another school of thought, hellenistic Judaism, did scornfully reject the mythology of the Greeks for a pure devotion to the Logos. To the Jews in the Diaspora the legends of the immoralities of the gods were of course particularly distasteful. They preached openly

---

[2]The translation is made from the text as printed by Harnack.
[3]Cornutus, c. 16 (ed. Lang, p. 20), following the text as altered by E. Krebs, *Der Logos als Heiland im ersten Jahrhundert*, Freib. i. B., 1910, p. 34, n. 2.

that such mythology must be rejected before a true knowledge of God was possible. So, for instance, Josephus reproaches the Greeks for ascribing "sodomitical practices to the gods themselves," and representing that "the gods married their own sisters, contriving this apology for their own strange unnatural lusts."[4] In another passage Josephus refers to Plato's expulsion of the gods from the Republic.[5] The polemic against Greek mythology in the Oratio is thus quite compatible with the spirit of hellenistic Judaism. Unquestionably, in preaching against polytheism, the Greek reproaches against mythological immorality would be as handy a weapon for hellenistic Judaism as they proved later for early Christianity.

But more positive evidence for the nature of the Oratio is to be found in the Logos-passage itself. Here the soul of man is represented as a divinely pure creation which is sunk to the neck in evils. It is subject to sensual passions, whose affections produce states in the soul which change its fundamental nature, essentially pollute its pristine purity, and hence estrange it from Him who made it. Only one thing can change this tragic apostasy. Man must appeal for help to the divine Logos, and listen to its instruction. As one does so there comes to him a mystic knowledge with active power of its own to chase the evils of sense from the soul. Like enchanted serpents the sins creep forth and go away. The conflict of spirit is stilled by a trumpet of peace, the fire of the soul is quenched. No information is given which will make one wise in worldly wisdom, but the mystic password by which man rises beyond humanity and himself becomes divine. For by its nature the soul must necessarily return to Him who made it, if it is to be freed from sensual slavery. In such a restitution, and so alone, is peace to be found. The Logos is a city of refuge, where the pursuing passions cannot follow; it is an incorruptible king, whose presence in the soul drives out all sin.

The figure of the Logos as a city of refuge undoubtedly has its source in Judaism rather than paganism. The word φευγαδευτήριον used in the Oratio is the familiar Septuagint word for cities of refuge, and these cities were taken by Philo as the basis for one of his most beautiful Logos-passages. In his treatise "De fuga et inventione" (§§91 ff.) Philo has a fine description of the mystic purification of the soul. The soul, he says, must strip off from itself its base affections, first the body, then the λόγος προφορικός (speech), in order that the λόγος κατὰ διάνοιαν (reason) alone may be left. Thus freed, the highest part of man can in purity embrace true Being (τὸν μόνον ὄν) "in such a way that it can not be separated." Philo now changes the figure, and

---

[4]C. Apion, ii, 275, ed. Niese; cf. ii, 242 ff.
[5]*Ibid.*, ii, 256.

represents this liberation of the highest part of the soul as a flight to the cities of refuge. "These," he says, "are very beautiful and well-walled cities, the best possible refuge for souls worthy of eternal salvation" (§ 96). The six cities are all explained as being powers of descending value from the first city, which is the divine Logos. There were three cities provided on each bank of the River Jordan by the law. Those on the Canaan side, where the majority of Israelites lived, were of course more readily accessible to an unfortunate person hotly pursued by avengers. These three, therefore, are explained by Philo as places of refuge from the rougher passions, adapted to the majority of men, whose lives are lived on a low plane and hence have little reserve with which to meet bodily temptations. Such people need immediate help. The first city on the Canaan side is thus explained by Philo to be the negative injunctions of the Jewish law, which is the part of the Jewish system most easily understood. Even the most ignorant man can be controlled by specific prohibitions. It is still on the lower plane, but one step in advance brings to the positive injunctions of the Torah, which he calls the second city, and one step farther still to the third city, where man finds refuge from the sins of his life in an experience of God's tender mercy. All three of these cities, or refuges, are so close to all men as almost to touch their daily lives. But across the great divide of life, which separates between an animal and a reasonable way of living, is a refuge from animal temptation in the activity of the mind. To Philo this was graphically illustrated by the cities of refuge beyond the Jordan accessible only to the few permanent residents of the other side, men who lived habitually contemplative lives, and to those whose passions harassed them so slightly that they had time to get over to the other side. The first city of refuge here Philo explains as being the kingly power of the Logos, by which he seems to mean a mystic apprehension of the divine majesty, which must result in a compelling fear of God that will overpower all evil desires. Higher than the majesty is the next city, which is represented as being a mystic apprehension of the creative power of the Logos, which Philo here says is the power commonly called God by Moses. For an apprehension of that creative power which out of its own goodness has made the world, including man, will awaken not fear but a spontaneous love for the author of our being. Philo does not here use the phrase, but he has in mind the recognition of the fatherhood of God as a more exalted experience than the recognition of his kingliness or majesty, and suggests the powerful effect upon a man's life which the apprehension of God's fatherhood must exercise. But all these five are lesser manifestations of the Logos, the mind of God, which is the sixth city. Greater than the majesty or love of God, or the merciful provisions of the law, is the mind itself of God. "Therefore," says Philo, "Moses urges him who is able to run swiftly, to stretch out without stopping for breath to the most exalted divine Logos, who is the source of wisdom, in order that by drawing from the flowing source he may win the prize of eternal life instead of death."[6]

It seems plain that in making the cities of refuge to be a symbol of experience of the Logos, the author of the Oratio could only have been drawing upon hellenistic Judaism.

Another figure of the Logos in the Oratio is found in the representation of the Logos not as a place of refuge but as a power coming into the soul of man and cleansing him from evil. Does man himself, in hellenistic Judaism, have to be able to run to the inaccessible sixth city in order to find the Logos and experience its power, or does the Logos meet the seeker half way? It is first to be noticed that in the Oratio the Logos comes to man, and charms and drives from his soul by a mystic power all the sins and passions of the senses, but apparently only after he has himself turned to the Logos. There is no prevenient grace in the Oratio, for it is the clear implication of the spirit of the exhortation that only when man of his own will leaves his sins and turns to the Logos can he hope for any help from the Logos.

We have but to turn a page in Philo from the passage I have just been citing to find a similar representation of man as needing only to forsake his will for sin and seek the Logos, in order to have the Logos come and drive out sin from his life entirely. Here Philo is still discussing the cities of refuge, and now he takes up the additional element that a fugitive must remain in the city until the death of the high priest. This Philo interprets by shifting his ground. The high priest is of course identified with the Logos. From Philo's point of view the question is how long we may remain in the city of escape from the life of sense. He answers that we may remain until the high priest, the Logos, dies. The death of the Logos, he explains, is the departure of the Logos from the soul, for of course, properly speaking, the Logos cannot die. But

> so long as this most sacred Logos lives and survives in the soul, any involuntary error (change) is powerless to return into it; for the Logos has by nature no share in any sin, and is incapable of contamination

---

[6]§ 97. One familiar with Philo will recognize that in this passage Philo is adapting to the Old Testament account of the cities of refuge his famous doctrine of the descending powers of the Logos as described in Quaest. in Exod. ii, 68; Harris, Fragments of Philo, p. 67. Paul's race to the goal in Phil. 3, 13 finds here a striking parallel.

from it. ...For if by the vigorous indwelling of the Logos sin was dispossessed, so, when the Logos departs, sin by all means comes back in. For the blameless high priest, who is a reproof (ἔλεγχος) of sin, enjoys from nature the elect honor that a slip of purpose never finds place in him. Wherefore it is right to pray that that should live in the soul which is at once the high priest, king, judge, and reproof, who having been elected to jurisdiction over the whole of our minds is never put to shame by any of those led in for its judgment (§§ 117 f.).

Philo has badly mixed his figures here, but the sense is sufficiently plain. Before the incorruptible purity of the Logos, which comes into a man who wishes to turn from sin, all sin vanishes ashamed. As Philo says further on in the same treatise, the Logos nourishes the soul, illuminates and sweetens it (§§ 137, 139). The author of the Oratio and Philo thus agree in believing that if a man will turn from his sin and pray to the Logos, the Logos will answer by coming to live in his soul. Once in the soul, the presence of the Logos is so sweetening and illuminating that sin dare not remain or try to enter. Indeed, when thus blessed by the Logos, a man cannot fall even into slips of purpose, unless the Logos first be dismissed from the soul. The passages in Philo and the Oratio are in perfect agreement as to the function of the Logos, and in their attitude toward it. But further comparison shows a still more detailed resemblance.

For the Logos is represented in the Oratio as a captain, στρατηγός, that is, as our leader in the struggle with evil. With this figure goes that of the Logos as having ceaseless watch over us. Both figures are military. Philo wrote similarly about the divine help which is ready to assist men in the struggle of life:

> Again, when you see in the wars and disasters of life God's merciful hand and power (χεῖρα καὶ δύναμιν) hovering over you and defending you, be silent, for this ally (βοηθός) has no need of assistance in the fight. And the witness of this fact is the statement of the Holy Scriptures, "The Lord will fight for you, and you shall be silent" (Ex. 14, 14). So if you see the legitimate offspring and first-born of Egypt being destroyed (Ex. 11, 5), that is, lust, pleasure, pain, fear, iniquity, frivolity, and riotous living, then be silent in awe, shrinking before the fearful power of God, "For," say the Scriptures, "not a dog shall move his tongue, from man down to the beast" (Ex. 11, 7). Which is to say that it is not fitting that the doglike tongue, with its howling and barking, should vaunt itself, nor should the man in us, the dominating mind, do so, nor the bestial creature, the senses, when the ally comes wholly from outside and of his own accord to shield us, after that which is peculiarly ours has been destroyed.[7]

---

[7]*De Somniis*, ii, 265-267.

Philo here speaks of the χεῖρα καὶ δύναμιν of God and does not specify the Logos. But in this δύναμις anyone familiar with his writing will recognize the divine Logos. In representing the Logos as a military aid, the Oratio is thus quite in accord with hellenistic Judaism.

Still another figure of the Oratio is that the Logos is a doctrine, of automatic power to help the soul. The conception is clearly that which gnosticism and the mystery religions had in common, that of a saving knowledge epitomized in passwords. The conception was early taken into Christianity and finally used with great force by Clement of Alexandria. But that it had long before been assimilated by hellenistic Judaism has, I think, been clearly demonstrated by Friedländer in his dissertation entitled "Der vorchristliche jüdische Gnosticismus" (Berlin, 1898). I refer to only two passages in Philo, not mentioned, I think, by Friedländer, one where Isaac with only one wife and no concubine is contrasted with Abraham who had both Sarah and Hagar. Abraham, Philo explains, represents here one who had to supplement his inadequate grasp of divine things (Sarah) by turning to earthly wisdom (Hagar). But Isaac was satisfied with Rebecca because she was at once virtue and a divinely given knowledge, which needed no completion in concubine arts, whose offspring are bastard doctrines.[8] In another passage Philo says that true doctrine, ὀρθὸς λόγος, comes to man not by seeking in the wells of the earth (human science), but as a blessed shower from heaven of divine knowledge, which not only waters the best vegetables growing in the soul, but is itself a rain of manna coming ready to eat, saving man from starvation in the desert.[9] The manna is of course the Logos as well as the ὀρθὸς λόγος. So, in representing the Logos as a saving knowledge, the Oratio is again quite in accord with hellenistic Judaism.

Directly suggestive of hellenistic Judaism is also the identification of σοφία with the Logos.

The list of sins of the flesh in the Oratio is a typical hellenistic Jewish borrowing from Stoicism. Lietzmann[10] has noted over two dozen such lists in Philo, besides lists in the Wisdom of Solomon and 4 Maccabees. One such I have already quoted.

The Oratio closes with a striking statement of mystical consummation: "And when the soul is released from the evils which flow about its neck, it returns to him that made it. For it must be

---

[8]De congressu quaerendae eruditionis gratia, 34 ff.
[9]A free paraphrase of Quod deus sit immutabilis, 152 ff. From Hans Windisch, Die Frömmigkeit Philos, Leipzig, 1909, p. 31, n. 5.
[10]Handbuch zum Neuen Testament: Römerbrief, pp. 34 f.

restored whence it departed." The author may mean here either the mystical consummation in this life, or he may be referring to what happens at death to one whom the Logos has purified. For though the Logos can and does purify the soul, yet so long as man is in the body he is still surrounded, if no longer permeated, with fleshly evils. It needs no demonstration to point out that this was the usual heaven looked for in hellenistic Jewish literature from the Wisdom of Solomon on. While the Palestinian Jew and after him, with some modification, the Christian looked for a resurrection of the dead, and an immortality in company with his beloved body (for of this love the Palestinian Jew was not ashamed), the hellenistic Jew more usually expected at death to be freed from the filthy prison of his body, and to return to an eternal consummation of mystic communion with the Logos, or with God himself.

So while I find no literary parallelism to indicate that the author of the Oratio used Philo as a direct literary source, the parallelism of ideas is certainly very close. According to both writers the Logos is $\sigma o \phi \acute{\iota} a$, the military conqueror and protector in the soul's warfare, an incorruptible king, a city of refuge from sin, a power whose pure presence in the soul drives out all sensual desire, and a mystic knowledge which is itself empowered to overcome evil; both look for release after death to effect a return to the soul's spiritual source. Clearly the author of the Oratio must have been trained in a hellenistic Jewish school. But was he also a Christian? As I have pointed out, there is no mention of Christianity, and I can find no shred of specifically Christian thought. In second-century Christian documents, as for example in Justin, the same philosophy of life presents itself, mixed with many foreign elements, but (what is most important) in the process of syncretization with the conception of Jesus as the Son of God. Had the Oratio been written by a Christian, the point brought out in such an exhortation to former Greek associates as we have here would have been the identity of Jesus Christ with the Logos which can thus transform the soul.

Harnack, in speaking of the Logos-passage, compares it to Clement of Alexandria's Logos.[11] As is well known, Clement's Logos is avowedly developed directly from Philo's writings. In one respect, however, Philo's Logos is distinguishable from Clement's, namely in Clement's repeated insistence that the Logos was incarnate in Christ. Indeed, in the Syriac recension of the Oratio which Harnack has discussed in detail, the one essential difference between the two documents has not been noticed at all by Harnack, namely, the fact that the author of the

---

[11]Sitzungsberichte, Berlin Academy, 1896, p. 646.

recension is obliged to supplement the original with the statement that he is turning from Greek mythology specifically to Christianity. As I have pointed out elsewhere,[12] the distinguishing difference between hellenistic Jewish and Christian apologetic is that hellenistic Jewish apologetic takes the Logos as needing no demonstration, and centers its attention upon monotheism, while Christian apologetic pays less attention to monotheism, because it had to face the reproaches of all who understood the Greek Logos-doctrine, that in identifying the Logos with Christ it was simply talking ignorant nonsense. So the Oratio, as an explanation to Greeks for becoming a Christian, answers not a single question that the Greeks would have raised, and indeed it would not have been recognized by a Greek as referring to Christianity at all. As an explanation, however, for becoming a "God-fearer" in a Philonic synagogue, the document is consistent and admirably pithy.

It seems to me then plain that we have here not a Christian document at all but the speech or letter of some Greek convert to hellenistic Judaism addressed to his former associates. That throughout the Diaspora many such converts found in Greco-Jewish mysticism a haven which nothing else could offer them is well known. That many of them were God-fearers who accepted the ethics and mysticism of hellenistic Judaism without its legal code and circumcision is equally familiar. It would rather be surprising that the writings of these people (for some of them must have written) should have completely disappeared, than that a document from such a source should now be discovered.

Thus far I have ignored one very important aspect of the Oratio. In the brief Logos-passage there are apparently two direct though unacknowledged quotations from Paul's letter to the Galatians. The first is, "Become as I am, for also was as you," γίνεσθε ὡς ἐγώ, ὅτι κἀγὼ ἤμην ὡς ὑμεῖς, which corresponds exactly to Gal. 4, 12, except that all manuscripts of Galatians lack ἤμην. Again, a few lines below this sentence in the Oratio is the list of sins from which the presence of the Logos frees the soul: "Enmities, strifes, jealousy, factions, wraths, καὶ τὰ ὅμοια τούτοις," which again corresponds exactly to a part of Paul's list of the works of the flesh in Ga. 5, 20; 21, ending like Paul's list with καὶ τὰ ὅμοια τούτοις. Here some literary dependence is unmistakable.

The significance of the similarity becomes still more striking when the context in Galatians is studied. Paul has been urging the Galatians to stand fast in their new liberty in Christ, which he has won for them in freeing them from slavery to the στοιχεῖα, the elements of this

---

[12]In my *Theology of Justin Martyr*, Jena, 1923, pp. 139-142.

world, which, he insists, are not gods in the proper sense at all. The argument of Lietzmann[13] seems to me conclusive that Paul is here classing the Jewish feasts, set according to movements of heavenly bodies, with heathen worship of the stars as gods. He is urging the Greek Christians not to turn to Jewish rites, because such a change would be essentially but a reversion to their old worship of the gods, while Paul has been leading them to a pure worship in the Spirit of Christ. True freedom is to be found only by walking in the Spirit, whereby we may cease producing the fruits of the flesh to produce the fruits of the Spirit. Therefore become as I am, Paul urges, who was once as you are. The entire argument in the latter part of Galatians is thus very similar to the fundamental plea of the Oratio, while the two verbal parallels make it clear that the connection was direct.

The question then which must be decided is whether Paul used the Oratio, or the author of the Oratio used Galatians. I am convinced that Paul used the Oratio, for while his argument is entirely consistent as an adaptation of an older hellenistic Jewish argument as found in the Oratio, it is inconceivable that a Christian would use the argument of Galatians, as he must have done were the Oratio a Christian production. If the Oratio is a Christian argument based upon Galatians, the author for some reason has carefully rejected all mention of Christ to return to a non-christian Logos doctrine. He has introduced specifically hellenistic Jewish imagery to describe the Logos in a purely Philonic fashion. He has taken a part of Paul's list of the works of the flesh, but omitted Paul's beautiful list of the fruits of the Spirit, though this would have fitted strikingly with his argument. On the other hand, if Paul is using the Oratio, he has christianized it, and adapted it to fit a group of people threatening to go over to Jewish legalism. He has supplemented the list of the works of the flesh in the Oratio, and balanced it with the fruits of the Spirit. The saving Logos has become the Spirit of Christ. That is to say, if Paul was using the Oratio we have a natural and intelligible adaptation for Christian purposes of some ideas which he found in an hellenistic Jewish document. If the author of the Oratio was a Christian who knew Galatians, the way in which Galatians is used is inconceivably forced and artificial. The only conclusion which the two documents seem to me to permit is that Galatians is later than the Oratio, and that Paul knew it and used both ideas and phraseology from it.

A *tertium quid* would be that the Oratio is an hellenistic Jewish document, but written after, and using, Galatians. But hellenistic Judaism seems to have been thoroughly disorganized by the preaching

---

[13]Handbuch zum Neuen Testament: An die Galater, 1910, p. 246.

of Paul. For while we have mention of σεβόμενοι in Josephus,[14] there is no indication that after the spread of Christianity Judaism presented itself to outsiders in any such form as is to be found in Philo and the Oratio. The clash with Christianity shortly led the Jews even to reject the Septuagint, which had come to be the symbol alike of hellenistic syncretism and Christianity, and to supplement it by new and more literal translations. We have no trace or hint of a post-christian hellenistic Judaism, and such a group must be invented if it is to be the background of the Oratio. We are thus driven back to our dilemma between an author of the Oratio who was a Christian and used Paul, but eliminated all trace of Christianity from his argument so as to produce a purely hellenistic Jewish document, and on the other hand one who was an hellenistic Jew writing a treatise later used by Paul.

If I am right in taking the latter alternative, there remains the question of date. I should incline to set the date in the first fifty, perhaps the first twenty-five, years of the Christian era, though it might have been written earlier. The author seems to represent an advanced stage of hellenistic Judaism, which it is difficult to put much before Philo and which was probably nearly contemporary with him. With no external testimony a closer dating would be entirely arbitrary.

---

[14]Antiq. xiv, 110 (Niese). Cf. Schürer, Jewish People in the Time of Jesus Christ, II, ii, pp. 314 ff.

2

The Fundamental Motif of Christianity

1940
> *Nygren's* Agape and Eros, *here reviewed by Goodenough, was a work of great influence in Europe and North America at the time of its publication. Among those in the denominations of "the reformers," as Goodenough calls them, it is still an important study. Two emphases in this review are vintage Goodenough: the defense of the piety of "the pagans" of the Greco-Roman world, and the stress on religion as something personal, not conceptual, at its base.*
> *Personal too is the idea that Jesus himself is the "fundamental motif" of Christianity, rather than any principle, even the principle of agape. The Christology presented by Goodenough here is considerably more orthodox than he himself was thought to be. (See also Eccles 1985:114.)*

Erwin R. Goodenough, *The Journal of Religion* **20 (1940): 1-14**

Christian scholars do nothing more important than when they recurrently ask themselves this question: Is there a basic doctrine of Christianity, a single idea which has been consistently central throughout Christian history, a Grundmotif which, underlying all the variety of Christian experience, gives it unity and distinctiveness?

The problem has been reopened in a most interesting way by Anders Nygren in his work, *Agape and Eros*, the last volumes of which have recently been published.[1] It is an elaborate and learned, but always readable, work which students of Christianity cannot afford to overlook. It comes from a Swedish scholar, representative of a school whose methodology, we are told by P.S. Watson, the translator, in the Preface to the second volume, is "motif-research...an enquiry directed to discover the 'fundamental motif' of any given outlook or system of thought,....that factor in virtue of which a particular outlook or system possesses its own peculiar character as distinct from all others." Such a methodology must appeal to all students of history who are interested in more than the anti-quarianism of curious facts. Its elaboration here shows how the method takes us at once into the heart of problems, but at the same time the book makes all too clear the dangers of the method when it is not used with the greatest caution. The result is an enormously stimulating work, but with accurate statements and inaccurate or overdrawn ones so intermingled as virtually to destroy its historical value for the untrained reader. It is an interesting example of a book which is on the whole quite wrong because its method is not quite right.

I

The thesis of the book is that the basic contribution of Christianity was its conception of Agape. Agape is the unmotivated love of God for unworthy man, which flows out with no trace of self-seeking from God to bring, supremely in the offering of the Son, salvation to man. It is a creative love in that those who receive it do so not because they are worthy: instead they are newly made into creatures worthy of God's love after they have received it and as a result of receiving it. God does not call the "righteous," for they have the false conception that human moral effort has value in God's sight. This idea, later important in Christianity as what Nygren calls the "Nomos motif," was basic in Judaism, he repeatedly declares, and its rejection by early Christianity was a radical departure. When man has received divine Agape, he will shed abroad to other men the same unmotivated love, loving even enemies, not for his own profit or because they evoke love or because of any "divine principle" within them but because it has become his nature to love as it is God's nature to be Agape and to love.

In contrast is the pagan Eros, which is love based upon self-interest, as Agape had been theocentric. Here God is the Absolute, and love is the way from man to God. Eros is not God's love for men but is man's love of God, his passionate desire to achieve the *summum bonum*. It is

---

[1]London: Society for Promoting Christian Knowledge, 1938.

sublimated sexual passion, mysticism, the craving to be united with the Beloved, in the very highest of all forms. But it is still self-seeking, desire for benefit to one's self, and implies the attraction of the Object, as well as sufficient divinity in man's own nature so that man can recognize the Object's desirability.

The first volume is devoted to elaborating this contrast, to expounding from every angle the complete mutual exclusiveness of the two, to showing how Christianity is, in the New Testament, simply an elaboration of Agape, with only a few faint traces of Eros in the Johannine writings, and how paganism is just as completely Eros to the exclusion of Agape.

One cannot help feeling that Nygren has driven a good thesis into the ground. His choice of New Testament texts for serious consideration is so limited that they become mere proof texts, and even these he does not treat in the round. And while he goes into psychology, very properly, to recognize sublimated sex in the mystic desire, he nowhere attempts, in spite of his promise, to discuss the nature of Agape in the same analytical way. The "love" of Agape is contrasted with the "love" of Eros in that the latter alone has the element of desire. Now, in taking "desire" in any sense from Agape, Nygren seems to be false to the love of God as it appears in the Gospels and in Paul, and to make the word "love" itself synonymous with mercy or benevolence. I am not a psychologist, but what meaning "love" can have without desire, in however sublimated a form, escapes me completely. Certainly, we are on safe ground when we recognize the yearning desire of God's love in the New Testament. The woman sweeping the floor for the lost coin, the love of the shepherd seeking the lost lamb, the cry, "O Jerusalem, Jerusalem, how often would I have gathered you!" lose all their power if the *desire* of God to find and save is taken from them. The New Testament sharply denies that Jerusalem, or man, is worthy of such love: on this we can fully agree with Nygren. But this does not exclude God's desire. Fortunately, most of us know even in the human realm what it means to be loved far beyond any deserts of our own, loved passionately and yearningly. And what is the meaning of John 3:16 if not precisely that the Agape which gave the Son is desirous love, caring infinitely to save man, unworthy as he is, to eternal life?

The Christian attitude to God, in turn, has no "self-seeking" in it, says Nygren, unless it is tainted with Eros. But, except in the scattered passages Nygren uses, that is not the attitude inculcated by Jesus in the Synoptics, by Paul or John. "Seek ye first the kingdom, and all these shall be added," is much more the Grundmotif of the gospel than the passive and selfless motivation Nygren describes. The Beatitudes, "if thou wilt be perfect," the sanctions of the parable of the talents, of the wise virgins, and of many other parables are, to say the least, quite as suggestive of "self-seeking" as is the mystic's trying to lose himself in union with God. Even the command to love our enemies is not addressed to purely disinterested motives. In Matthew it is immediately followed with the explanation: "For if ye love those who love you what reward have ye?" and Luke says directly: "But love your enemies, and do them good, and lend, never despairing; and your reward shall be great, and ye shall be the sons of the Most High." That this appeal to sanctions falls below, directly denies, the conception of Agape as Nygren idealizes and isolates it is obvious; but the fact remains that it represents much more predominantly a New Testament teaching and attitude than does Nygren's Agape. In Paul the struggle to attain the Crown has exactly the motivation of the struggle which Nygren, forgetting Paul's struggle, says is distinctive of pagan Eros (p. 138). That is, the Christian who is purely the passive recipient of Agape without "self-seeking" in his desire for God or divine rewards is as rare in the New Testament as in paganism.

Furthermore, Nygren evades the difficulty that there is much in the New Testament which shows that the recipient of Agape is not indiscriminately selected, but must himself, to get the benefit of Agape, be willing to do his part. Nygren frequently quotes the statement that God sends rain upon the just and unjust, to illustrate the unmotivated, the universal, nature of Agape. But in practice the New Testament shows that salvation does not work out that way. God calls *not* the righteous but the sinner, a verse Nygren often cites, but always in another connection. If God gives rain to both indiscriminately, why does he not also give saving Agape? The only answer is that God can make out of the "sinner" what he cannot out of the "righteous," and this difference can be a matter only of the response which the one gives but the other does not, that is, something inherent in the individual who is saved. The New Testament is full of the necessity of human response to Agape: the mighty works which could not be done in Capernaum; the attitude of Jesus to the Cyrophoenecian woman, to Zacchaeus in the sycamore tree, and to blind Bartimaeus; the refusal of Jerusalem to be nestled; the fact that the father meets the Prodigal Son only when the Prodigal has himself come within sight of home. If the answer to this is predestinarianism, that the power of response is likewise a gift from God to men selected for no merit of their own, a conclusion to which the logic of Agape led Paul and the Reformers, still Agape is selective and not at all the universal thing which Nygren alternately asserts and, by implication, denies.

Nygren does not resort to predestinarianism, and, when he very briefly tries to fit his conception of Agape into the eschatological sayings in the Synoptics, he abandons all he has been defending in Agape:

> Just because Agape consists in complete recklessness of giving, it demands unconditioned self-giving. As a force that creates fellowship it pronounces an annihilating judgment on the self-seeking life, which refuses to let itself be refashioned after the pattern of Agape and spurns offered fellowship. The Coming of Agape decides a man's destiny; the question for him is whether he will yield himself up to be transformed, or will resist, and so encounter Agape only in the form of judgment on his life [I, 75].

Excellent a statement as this is in itself, it belies the character of Agape in the rest of the book. When Agape can be damning judgment, the logic of loving one's enemies as the supreme human manifestation of Agape breaks down completely. Agape, functioning in man, Nygren insists, is to love the enemy with no thought of the enemy's worth, just because Agape is unbroken and uncaused love. But God himself, we see here, gives Agape to all men, but thereby makes the recalcitrant only the more damnable. And Nygren in this passage certainly shows, what he elsewhere emphatically denies, that the man who is saved is not completely worthless, but has a quality which makes him desirable, namely, the power to respond to God's Agape. Again we must choose between predestination, by which God arbitrarily puts this quality into some but not into others, irrespective of their inherent worth, or we must recognize that God is seeking in man an inherent worth, the power of response.

II

Thus, the Agape of God, as Nygren presents it in spite of himself, is a love for all which finds fruition only in the responsive. In such a picture we are getting dangerously near to a sublimated conception of sexual love projected into God himself. That the union of God's love with responsive men results in new birth, and that they in turn must be fruitful, by no means makes the conception less one of projected sexual imagery. If we are tracing Grundmotifs actually to the bottom, we must admit that the Grundmotif of the mystic fertility gods, who offer salvation by fertilizing the suppliant with divine life-force, is quite the same psychologically as this Agape. Recourse to predestinarianism only puts the difficulty off. For if God selects certain ones arbitrarily, without reference to any inherent merit, to give them the responsiveness they inherently lack, still the rest of the pattern follows exactly the same lines. God's creative love is given only to the responsive, though he has first had to make them so, and condemnation, essentially for unresponsiveness, is given to the rest.

One feels driven back to the love of God for Israel in Hosea, where Hosea is commanded to marry an unworthy woman "even as the Lord loveth the children of Israel" (Hos. 3:1): "And I will betroth thee unto me forever" (Hos. 2:19). And surely Christ's love for his bride, the Church, is part of the New Testament doctrine of divine love. Nygren, so far as I remember, nowhere calls Agape an unsexual love as contrasted with the sublimated sex of Eros; but, when he points out the sexual pattern of Eros only, the reader must understand such a contrast to be implicit. Incidentally, Nygren does not point out that Agape is used in the New Testament of ordinary love, even of unworthy love, as well as of ideal love. Not only must husbands have Agape for their wives (Col. 3:19, Eph. 2:4) but the Pharisees are condemned for their Agape of the glory of men (John 12:43), and the unregenerate in general for their Agape of the "world and darkness" (I John 2:15; cf. John 3:19).

When Nygren turns to the pagan world, he discusses only the philosophers. Plato, Aristotle, and Plotinus are regarded, on the whole unexceptionably, as showing the contrast between their unmoved absolutes, whether forms or τὸ ὄν, and the Christian God who takes the loving initiative toward man. Much of this contrast is quite sound. Certainly, there is all the difference in the world between the Christian God counting the hairs of our head and the Unmoved Mover of Aristotle. Just as truly the Synoptics have no hint of the Greek notion that the soul of man is inherently divine and must escape the material to be united with God. But when this is made into a contrast between Christianity and paganism in general, the contrast, so far as Grundmotif is concerned, becomes misleading and false. Nygren recognizes that the gift of the mystery religions to Greek philosophy, beginning at least with Plato, was to color the philosophers' abstractions with a desire for appropriation. It was not enough to describe the Absolute: man must somehow himself experience the Absolute. But the mysteries themselves were no more philosophic in the classic sense than Christianity, and their appeal was precisely the yearning love of their deities for man, their suffering which became the way for man to God. The picture of Isis revealing her loving kindness to the degraded ass, in the last book of Apuleius' *Metamorphoses,* her revelation of the sacraments and how, if the ass complies, she will change him into a being worthy of herself, is one which would have much confused the contrast between Agape and Eros had Nygren considered it.

Thus, when Nygren makes a complete contrast between Christian and pagan motivation, he goes too far. Eros, he says, is a product arising out of man, his love for divine Reality, his desire for it, balanced by his hatred of matter, while early Christian Agape arose in God and was imparted to men. Granted that Eros in this sense was a very important element in paganism, it was very early important in Christianity, if Paul is any representative of early Christianity. He too, as has been mentioned, is straining forward for the Crown; he too is wrestling with his lower nature, from which, like the ass's hide of Apuleius, he cannot be freed except by divine intervention; he, with the Spirit, is groaning for redemption with groanings which cannot be uttered; he is buffeting his body, and striving to walk not after the flesh but the Spirit. Paul does not like the word "gnosis," but the culmination of religion is for him as for pagans to "see face to face" the undistorted vision of God which sees not Platonic reflections but Reality. This passion for perfection of religious experience Paul does not call "Eros," but we are again reminded of Watson's words in describing the method of "Motif-research": "Similar or identical forms and expressions may sometimes conceal totally different motifs, while widely different forms and expressions may sometimes represent the same motif." There are, it is obvious to anyone who knows Paul and the Greeks, striking differences between Paul's religious passion and that of the pagans. But the difference is not accurately indicated in Nygren's claim that in paganism a man himself desires religious experience and strives for it, whereas in Christianity God's Agape picks him up, transforms him, and leaves it necessary for the man only to hold to God in faith while he passes on to his fellows the Agape he has received. If this were the contrast, Paul would belong, in spite of occasional passages, rather than with the Greeks; for, much as he feels that he was at the first a brand snatched from the burning by Agape, his life is thereafter one of passionate struggle to crucify the flesh and walk after the spirit.

III

The danger of "Motif-research" has become sufficiently apparent: there is constant peril of oversimplification. The contrast which Nygren has drawn between the Agape of Christianity and the Eros of philosophical mysticism (not paganism in general) is largely true. There is nothing in pagan philosophy, or in paganism, which can be compared with I Corinthians, chapter 13, or John 3:16. And while the Grundmotif of John 3:16 may be paralleled in the mysteries, one has indeed to go underground to the roots for the similarity, while I Corinthians, chapter 13, remains unique. But when Nygren attempts to make Agape the essential motif of early Christianity and to interpret all early Christianity – its Pauline struggle, its eschatological severity, its final judgment based upon conduct – as elaborations of the Agape Grundmotif, it is obvious that he has failed. Early Christianity cannot be subsumed under I Corinthians, chapter 13, or under the Johannine conception that God is Agape. Nygren is really – in the second volume he almost confesses it himself – a "reformer" (pp. 24-27). His conception of the kind of reformation needed grows out of his idea that Christianity began simply with Agape, that as it developed it became complicated with foreign elements, especially those inherent in Eros, until by the Reformation it was brought back to Agape, but only to become later corrupted with Eros again – a natural, almost inevitable, cycle. In such a statement is disclosed the essential weakness of the reformers, who seem, to those who refuse to follow them, to be interested in some one aspect of Christianity to the point of losing the richness of the tradition as a whole for to put all of Christianity – that is, unadulterated Christianity – into the conception of Agape is to simplify beyond Luther and Calvin, certainly beyond the New Testament.

Nygren's oversimplification becomes increasingly apparent in the later volumes. The Apostolic Fathers mingle Agape with Nomos, the legal Grundmotif of Judaism, he says, and here for the first time Nygren recognizes that the Christian is taught to seek a reward, but notices it as a perversion of early Christian Agape. Justin seems to him much closer to Agape, though Nygren by no means proves his point. The Gnostics, of course, he tosses to the dogs of Eros; Marcion was almost a Christian, Nygren judges, certainly so in his rejection of Nomos, but in his rejection of the resurrection of the flesh, creation by God, and the true incarnation Marcion was on Greek, and hence non-Christian, ground. Tertullian was much too nomistic to have done justice to Agape; and Clement and Origen were so far afield that Origen, Nygren thinks, was rightly pronounced a heretic and not Christian at all, for with Origen Agape was entirely replaced by Eros. Irenaeus was much closer to the truth of Agape, the closest of all writers of the early church, but even Irenaeus spoiled it when he said that Christ came down to men that men might rise to God. This is much too close to Eros! In the Christological controversies, Nygren continues, orthodoxy was really defending Agape against Eros, though even Athanasius and Gregory of Nyssa grounded their personal religions on Eros motivations. Agape and Eros were finally blended by Augustine, Nygren says, in the great doctrine of *caritas:* yet *caritas* is basically man's desire for God and so hellenistic rather than Christian; it is still quest for the Greek *summum bonum.* Augustine's notion of grace, however, was Agape. It was the combination of these two, Nygren tells us, which constituted the medieval synthesis of Agape and Eros. But Nygren sees along with this an even stronger Eros religion given to the Middle Ages by

Dionysius and his successors, for in their writings Eros was supreme in both God and men.

> During the whole of the Middle Ages, Eros had been a living reality – but it was imprisoned in the Caritas synthesis. As perhaps the most important element in this synthesis, Eros had largely moulded the interpretation of Christianity without any one realizing what a transformation of Christianity it effected [II, 449].

But the renewed study of Plato, the Neo-Platonists, and Dionysius, in the Renaissance resulted in the rebirth of pure Eros. Nygren finally treats the Reformation very interestingly as a complementary rebirth of Agape.

As the reader goes through these pages, especially those which describe the early centuries of Christianity, he wonders increasingly what could have kept Christianity together if its Grundmotif so rarely came to even approximately adequate recognition. Why were men ready to die for a Christianity which, as Nygren describes it, actually differed so slightly from Hellenism, and why did Christianity not break into a thousand pieces in the hellenistic environment if its Grundmotif was so rarely and weakly appreciated?

The only answer to this question must be that, however interesting Nygren's account of Agape in its historical vicissitudes, Agape could not have been the Christian Grundmotif if that term is to have any intelligible meaning. For I cannot understand a Grundmotif as anything but the basic factor of some entity's existence, and this, Nygren abundantly demonstrates, Agape in Christianity was not. Surely if the Grundmotif of Christianity is to be found, it must appear not in such an attenuated and broken line as Nygren's Agape but in the common element which all who claimed in any way to be Christian shared and emphasized.

IV

If this point of view is taken, it will appear that the Grundmotif of Christianity from the beginning was not any philosophical or theological conception, for on no such conception was Christianity unitedly emphatic. The actual Grundmotif appears to me to be so obvious that I should hesitate to suggest it if it were not almost invariably ignored. If there was a single basic and motivating principle in early Christianity, it was unquestionably the life, death, and confidently accepted resurrection of Jesus, or, in a word, Jesus himself. In the experience of the early associates of Jesus a new dynamic was released, which was Christianity. From the beginning those who shared in this experience used various "old bottles" of ideology to

account for the experience. There were the Judaistic eschatology and
legalism and hellenistic frames of the most diverse sorts. The dynamic
experience in a specific person burst them all, or, to change the figure,
transformed them all into new compounds. And very early, even from
the first, different pre-existing types of thought were combined, like
nomism with eschatology, along with prophetic conceptions, into a
single complex. The Christian Gnostics tried to take Jesus and his
dynamic power into Gnosis. And soon the hellenistic-Jewish, later the
hellenistic, ideas were used to enrich or supplant earlier explanations.
In this process many new ideas, like Agape, were conceived. But while
different sorts of Christianity advanced different explanations, the
vital and continuous force through every interpretation was not any
single idea but the reality of the experience of God through Jesus, the
certainty of immortality through Jesus, the conviction that, however
the problems of life might be formulated, Jesus' death and resurrection
had solved them. Recognizing this, early Christian apologists faced
paganism and Judaism with their theory of "preparation." It must not
be forgotten that these apologists were confronted not only with a
living Judaism but with a still very vital paganism, and that with
these before them they asserted not that Christianity had a new
ideology but that what of good their neighbors had was fulfilled and
realized in the person of Jesus, the actual death and resurrection of the
Son of God. Early Christians did not agree upon any single new *idea*
which Christianity seemed to them to contribute to either Judaism or
paganism, and for us to try to isolate such an idea, and then to treat it
as the Grundmotif of the early faith, is to invite such failure as Nygren
seems to me ultimately to reveal. To the early Christians who knew
paganism as we can never do, Jesus was a reality, tangible, fresh,
eternal, who accomplished the fulfilment, opened the doors which
before that men could go through only in their fancies. The constant
between all the different forms of early Christianity, let me repeat,
and the only one I can see, is Jesus himself. "That which we have seen
with our eyes and our hands have handled" was the distinctive
message of early Christians to paganism. The vivid reality of their
Savior induced a reality of experience beyond the power of myths to
reproduce or of philosophy to inspire. Coupled with the sublime
ethical teaching of Jesus (itself, Jewish parallels show, a "fulfilment"
of Jewish tendencies), the result was an exemplification, not a mere
formulation, of the ethics of love – an exemplification in the lives of
the followers who had actually "put on Jesus Christ."

The reality of the experience gave Christians not new ideas for
myths but a mythopoeic power lacking in paganism. If it is true that
paganism can be shown to have foreshadowed the basic motifs of

Christian myths of the union of God and man in a new birth, a saving manifestation of divinity to and in humanity, yet it is also true that paganism produced no myth comparable with the first chapters of Luke for power, directness, and beauty. And in pagan myths of the dying and rising God there appears nothing so moving as the story of the journey to Emmaus or the post-resurrection scenes in the Fourth Gospel. No one in his senses would deny that Christianity, rejected and hated by Jews and pagans alike, was a new religion. But the new Christian message was not new in every respect: it was essentially the declaration, based upon the experience, that the God pagans and Jews worshipped in ignorance had been revealed in the resurrection of Jesus. While the pagans were turning to "principles" only thinly personified, the Christians had the vivid person, Jesus their Savior. And in this person their lives were transformed.

Nygren has not failed – he has brilliantly succeeded – in writing a history of Christian Agape. But he has failed in his attempt to make Agape, at any time, the Grundmotif of Christianity, the criterion of true Christianity. His failure is that of anyone who would isolate some one idea in the Christian complex which seems to him to have survival value, in order to make that one idea the focus of the whole. Indeed, quite apart from the question of survival value, the basic motif of Christianity, in the sense of a basic *concept* in Christianity, has never been isolated to the general satisfaction of scholars because no one concept has been central throughout the varieties of Christian experience; in the early period this was even more true than in later periods when Christian ideology had become at least officially standardized. If we are to understand early Christianity, we must ultimately do so not as modern philological or philosophical scholars, but as first-century fishermen on the Lake of Galilee who see through the mists the risen Lord. Philology and historical philosophy, our clumsy conveyances to the past, can be of use to us only in so far as they succeed in bringing our souls back to such places of experience, for understanding of other men, from our own or any generation, is achieved not in the mind but in the heart.

3

John a Primitive Gospel

1945

Goodenough never wrote more ably on the New Testament than the first article below, still frequently cited by students of the gospel of John. (The following serves as the introduction to Chapters 3, 4 and 5) In one sense Casey's debate with him (no. 4) is a classic case of the encounter between form criticism and the earlier documentary approach to the Gospels. One would concentrate on the gospels as wholes, sprung "fully formed from their authors' minds with no developments of consequence between the vents themselves and their being recounted in one of these documents" – as Goodenough caricatures it on the first page of his Reply. The other would stress the pre-history of the various pericopes, as they circulated in the oral tradition – the preaching and teaching – of the earliest Christian communities. The two authors agree at least on a description of the issue, see the summary statement of Goodenough, page 35 below, quoted at length by Casey on pages 63-64 below.

At the same time Goodenough restates familiar themes of his own. He stresses the diversity of Diaspora Judaism and its distance from the better known Judaism of the Roman period, that represented by the abundant rabbinic literature. And he insists that Diaspora Jews attracted to Christianity would have seen that new religion as an answer to human issues as defined by their particular version of Diaspora Judaism.

Christianity could restate its message in new forms very rapidly, he reminds us. Look at the difference between traditional Palestinian Christianity and the letters of Paul, though Paul began to preach and to write no more than a decade or two after the Crucifixion. Paul was not changing "the Christian message" or altering "Christian teachings." He was rather concerned to express the impact of Jesus upon him in ways that made sense to someone of his religious background. The Gospel of John, says Goodenough, is doing something similar. It is not necessary to postulate development within earliest Christianity to account for the differences between the Synoptics (or Jesus himself) and the Gospel of John. These differences are not the result of internal development, but of the diversity within the pre-Christian Judaism out of which the new religion originated. We allow that Paul is early because we have no choice: the dates of his major letters are too firmly fixed. If we assume a pre-Christian hellenistic Jewish background for (the author of) the Fourth Gospel, there is no reason why it could not be early too.

The closing words of the Reply again make the connection between New Testament studies and Goodenough's work on hellenistic Judaism. Goodenough's consideration of "Jewish sacramental and Messianic meals" would be presented in great detail in the various volumes of Symbols. *Chapter 7, "Fish and Bread," and chapter 9, "Wine in Judaism," in volume 12 provide summary statements, with cross references to earlier volumes. See also Eccles 1985:118-22.*

Erwin R. Goodenough, *Journal of Biblical Literature* **64 (1945): 145-182**

In his interesting *Christian Beginnings* M.S. Enslin says of the Gospel of John: "Every critic, whatever his views as to the author, agrees that the gospel cannot antedate the year 100" (p. 448). At the risk of being refused the title "critic" I propose here to show reasons for disagreeing with that consensus of opinion. The Gospel seems to me quite a primitive product from the very early church, though of course nothing indicates any precise date.[1]

---

[1]After writing the following paper I was saved embarrassment by C.T. Craig, who told me of a book I had overlooked, P. Gardner-Smith, *St. John and the Synoptic Gospels*, 1938, where it is argued that Jn is independent of the Synoptics, and for the reason that it was written at least as soon as Mk. I have since read this book with great interest, but find that it duplicates little of my general argument (see below n. 12), and that its suggestions for the origin of Jn, which are not elaborated, are quite different from those which I make at the end of this paper. So with the addition of a few cross-references to Gardner-Smith I am publishing the article much as it was first written. The case on the other side has certainly been repeated often enough.

To present so novel a thesis three steps are necessary. First we must examine the reasons which have suggested the late date; secondly we must consider what positive evidence there seems to be for an early date; and thirdly we must suggest a new hypothesis for the origin of early Christian documents in terms of which Jn might properly be considered early.

I. The Chief Arguments for a Late Date of John

A. The Implicit A Priori

The united opinion that Jn is late has an intangible, usually unstated, basis of judgment, and a series of more explicit arguments. The hidden argument is that Jn must be late because its interpretation of Jesus is so different from that in the Synoptics. Our minds function largely as we attempt to see or construct order in the facts about us. In modern criticism we have found a sense of order in early Christian remains by visualizing first an historic Jesus whose nearest portrait is to be found through a critical study of the Synoptic Gospels. This historic figure we have tried to reconstruct out of Mk and Q primarily, and we can see how in Mt and Lk the story is already growing. We are all especially impressed by the fact that the idea of the Virgin Birth does not appear in what is demonstrably the earliest Gospel of the three, Mk, and that it is also unknown to Paul, who was likewise early. From the simple Galilean peasant, then, we have felt that there was a gradual, and in good part traceable, evolution toward the Second Person of the Trinity, from Mk to the other Synoptics, then to Jn, then to the Fathers of the second century. This sense of an evolving form is something that we have felt to be profoundly necessary if we were to continue studying the early records. So we have set the details in this framework, – and most scholars will fight to keep them there.

Such a reconstruction of Christian thought is by no means modern. It goes back to the second century itself according to Papias and his successors, who dated Jn at the close of the first, or beginning of the second, century.

To the testimony of the ancients we shall return shortly. But at the outset we must understand that this general scheme of the origin of Christianity is entirely a hypothetical creation. It has persisted only because scholars have with amazing unanimity ignored in that connection the fact that the letters of Paul are the earliest definitely datable documents of Christianity (though not necessarily the earliest documents), and that in those letters Jesus is not at all the Synoptic figure, but is, with many differences of detail, generally admitted to be essentially the Jesus of the Fourth Gospel.[2] If, as we must assume, the tradition behind the synoptics was being formulated in approximately the years when the letters of Paul were being written, then it is clear that Christianity had no such periodic divisions in its evolution, but from very early times propagated simultaneously both the Pauline-Johannine and the Synoptic points of view in regard to Jesus. Traditional New Testament scholarship has avoided facing that difficulty by insisting upon the creative uniqueness of Paul, and his sense of isolation from the Christianity of Jerusalem. But if the Synoptic Jesus and the Pauline Christ were not steps of development the one out of the other, but were being formulated at the same time, then all sense of development is at once lost. If Colossians and Romans could have been written by 55 a.d., so far as our knowledge of any theological "development" is concerned Jn could have been written just as early.

We shall consider the origin of Christianity and its documents as the third problem of this study. But we have had to begin with this hidden premise of the lateness of Jn's ideas because the hidden premises are usually the determining ones. So long as a man feels that Jn "could not" have been written before 100 because an earlier date would destroy his whole conception of the evolution of Christianity it is useless to bring other arguments to his attention. What follows is addressed to readers who will freely allow that the date of the Gospel may still be an open question.[3]

---

[2] I need refer for this only to Benjamin W. Bacon, *The Gospel of the Hellenists*, 1933, 316 (hereafter Bacon, *Hellenists*).

[3] The hidden premise has not always, of course, been hidden. So G.H.C. MacGregor, *The Gospel of John*, 1928, pp. xxix f., says that the disputes with the "Jews," and such objections as "He makes himself equal to God"; "Art thou greater than our Father Abraham?"; "Can this man give us his flesh to eat?" come from a "later age." Of these Jesus' attitude toward the "Jews" in Jn is most often taken to indicate that the Gospel is late. See Ernest C. Colwell, *John Defends the Gospel*, 1936, 44-46, where the matter is, in my opinion, exaggerated. That Jn is trying to represent Jesus as not being himself a Jew, as Colwell implies, goes altogether too far. The bone of contention, Colwell rightly says, is that the Jews rejected Jesus as the Messiah and as a divine being: but this issue must have been clear by the time of the Pauline persecutions in Jerusalem, and so we need no late date to explain a group who felt themselves on this ground tragically rejected from Jewry. It was precisely at these two points that Paul seems to have capitulated to Christianity, and as a result felt himself liberated from the Law. Certainly we know of no later controversy by which to date the origin of such a sense of estrangement of at least some Christians from the Jews. These references to "Jews" might have been written during, or at any time after, the Pauline persecution.

B. External Evidence: The Ancient Tradition

The operation of this hidden premise has been powerful in modern criticism of the ancient tradition. The tradition is preserved in Eusebius. In one passage he quotes a single sentence from Papias in which Papias mentions two Johns, one in a list of the disciples, and immediately afterward another called "Presbyter John, the Lord's disciple." Eusebius concludes from this that it was the second or "Presbyter" John who wrote the Gospel. He goes on to say that Papias professed to have heard none of the apostles but only their immediate followers. In another passage Eusebius quotes Irenaeus for the tradition that the disciple John himself lived in Ephesus to the time of Trajan, – a tradition used by many later writers, then and now, to justify the presumption that it was the disciple himself who wrote the Gospel. Both Papias and Irenaeus agree at least in assigning the Gospel to Ephesus; that "John" lived and died in Ephesus, Eusebius also quotes Polycrates and Dionysius of Alexandria as saying.[4]

In addition Eusebius quotes a lost work of Origen to the effect that Jn was the "last of all" the four Gospels, an idea which Origen probably learned from his predecessor in Alexandria, Clement, whose words Eusebius has preserved:

> Last of all John also, aware that the bodily (i.e., external) facts had been revealed in the [other] Gospels, was urged on by his acquaintances [or disciples], and, under inspiration of the Spirit, composed a spiritual Gospel.[5]

There is no evidence to show where Clement in the late second or early third century got that information.

Discussion of this meager evidence has become incredibly complicated. Only the most conservative scholars still cling to the idea that Jn was written by the "beloved disciple" himself, but in the opinion of all the evidence establishes that fact that Jn was written in Ephesus at a late date. The Lakes,[6] to be sure, recognize that the evidence establishes nothing as to place also: they think that the internal evidence, the Logos doctrine especially, suggests Alexandria rather than Ephesus, – a suggestion with no foundation whatever. But even they keep the tradition of the late date without further comment.

---

[4]These statements are all collected by K. and S. Lake, *An Introduction to the NT*, 1937, 275-281, where they may most conveniently be consulted.
[5]From Eusebius *HE*, VI, xiv, 7. See also *ibid*, III, xxiv, 7-14, where it is said that John wrote the Gospel to supplement the other three for Jesus' early ministry which they had omitted. See on both of these Bacon, *Hellenists*,112.
[6]*Introduction*, 53.

All that this evidence has told us is that from Papias on (and Papias is rapidly falling into disrepute as an authority) there was a tradition that John, usually John the Disciple, wrote the Gospel late and at Ephesus. We cannot reject the tradition of authorship on the basis of internal evidence as is usually done without throwing doubt upon the statements of date and place also, and substituting for the tradition as a whole the criterion of internal testimony of the Gospel for and to itself. We must believe the tradition on all three points only as it conforms to internal testimony, not compel the internal evidence to adjust itself to tradition at all.

Similarly direct quotations of the Gospel in early Christian writings are so late that they tell nothing of the date of its composition. Traces of Johannine ideas and phraseology do indeed appear in the writings of the early second century,[7] but they show only that such phrases were in circulation at that time. No certain acquaintance with the Gospel as a whole can be demonstrated until the latter part of the second century, when its apostolicity, and hence acceptance into the canon, occasioned considerable controversy. In any case these references to the Gospel establish only that Jn was in existence in the middle or late second century. As to how long before that time it was written we have only internal evidence for deciding.

C. Internal Evidence

1. Jn and the Synoptics. The starting point for studying the internal evidence has generally been the question whether Jn shows direct knowledge of the Synoptics, and here again agreement of critics is practically unanimous. For while some think that the author of Jn used all three Synoptic Gospels,[8] others that he had only Lk and Mk,[9] and still others that he had only Mk,[10] almost all agree that he at least

---

[7]For this evidence see most conveniently J.H. Bernard *Gospel according to St. John*, 1929, I, pp. lxxi-lxxviii (with cross references there given) *(ICC)*. See also MacGregor, pp. liv-lxii; Edwyn Hoskyns, *The Fourth Gospel*, 1940, I, 105-118; B.W. Bacon, *The Fourth Gospel in Research and Debate*, 1910, 18-28.

[8]Bacon, *Hellenists*, 114; Hoskyns, I, 72-87, concludes that the author of Jn did not have the three Synoptics before him when he composed his Gospel, but had their material and form in his head; H. Windisch, *Johannes und die Synoptiker*, 1926, 42-54; W. Bauer, *Das Johannesevangelium*, 3rd ed. 1933, 246 f. *(Hbdch z. N.T.,* VI); E.C. Colwell, *John Defends the Gospel*, 1936, 7-9.

[9]Bernard, I, pp. xciv-cxxi; B.H. Streeter, *The Four Gospels*, 1936, 393-426.

[10]V.H. Stanton, *The Gospels as Historical Documents*, III. *The Fourth Gospel*, 1920, 214-220.

used Mk and so date the composition of Jn later than Mk.[11] They explain that Jn was composed as a restatement, correction, or supplement (spiritual or factual) to the Synoptic tradition as recorded at least in Mk. The evidence for this conclusion, considering the unanimity with which it is held, is amazingly inadequate. We shall consider here only the arguments for Jn's dependence upon Mk, for that is the point of total agreement, and the general position must stand or fall at that point.[12]

Even these arguments are too elaborate for detailed consideration. I quote Colwell's excellent résumé of the case:

> Jn's outline is Mk's outline; the events of Jesus' career are, with few exceptions, those found in Mk. In both Jn and Mk, John the Baptist is the beginning of the Gospel, and the "baptism" of Jesus is followed by the call of a small group of disciples. In both we find the cleansing of the temple, the feeding of the five thousand, the demand for a sign, the accusation that Jesus has a familiar spirit, the walking on the sea, the entrance into Jerusalem, the anointing in Bethany, the announcement of the betrayer, the prediction of the denial by Peter, the arrest of Jesus at night, the trial before the high priest, Peter's denial, the trial before Pilate, crucifixion between two others, the death and burial, and the discovery of the empty grave. This is too much repetition for a mere supplement. Rearrangement and transformation of the material should not conceal from us the Markan framework upon which the superstructure of the Fourth Gospel is built.[13]

This is a formidable list. We begin, however, so far as seeing evidence in it for the dependence of Jn upon a written and finished Mk, by noting that of the nineteen items listed, thirteen, or all but six, are in the Markan account of the events of Passion Week. For these events scholars, including Colwell himself,[14] are generally agreed that there was a special source upon which Mk drew, so that we have only to

---

[11]R. Bultmann, *Joh. Evang. (Meyer's krit-exeget. Kommentar)* is in course of publication, and the introductory section has not reached us, if it is yet published. The commentary itself, however, nowhere suggests that John is based upon Mk.

[12]Gardner-Smith discusses many more passages than what follows, and with his conclusions I generally agree, though not with his assumption (p. 15 n.) that Mk was written after the fall of Jerusalem. Mk and Jn both seem to me to antedate that tragedy. Gardner-Smith's method, however, is to stress the differences between Jn and the Synoptics alongside the similarities, and so he often seems to belittle the significance of the similarities. The arguments will probably have to be presented a good many times before they are given their full force.

[13]Colwell, loc. cit.

[14]Op. cit., 2.

suppose that the author of Jn had this same source, or a similar one, to take all but six of the parallels from consideration as evidence that Jn was based upon Mk. We then notice that three of the six which are left, together with one Colwell has not mentioned, appear together in the sixth chapter of Jn, a section beginning with the multiplication of the loaves, going on to the walking on the water, then the demand for a sign, and then the confession of Peter. To this block we shall return: but here it is notable that these do appear in a block like the Passion narrative, and that, as with that narrative, they indicate rather a special source for that block common to Mk and Jn, than that Jn must have been based upon the complete Mk. For with the elimination of these two blocks the Markan "framework" for Jn has completely disappeared. The notorious contrast between Jn and the Synoptics is precisely that Mt and Lk are in a Markan framework of which Jn shows no trace, except in that it begins with John the Baptist, and ends, naturally, with the crucifixion and resurrection. We can certainly allow that much of a sense of order to oral tradition.

The argument for the dependence of Jn upon Mk is more usually based upon verbal similarities in the parallels. Bernard[15] has presented the most important of these in a cogent and convenient form, and we may follow his order in considering them.

a. The anointing at Bethany (Jn 12:1-8 and Mk 14:3-9; cf. Lk 7:36-49). The story is a notoriously difficult one, since Lk has a version even more different from the versions of Jn and Mk than these are from each other, and yet with distinct points of verbal similarity to each. Jn and Mk agree that the woman's ointment was $\mu\acute{\nu}\rho o \nu$ $\nu\acute{\alpha}\rho\delta o \nu$ $\pi\iota\sigma\tau\iota\kappa\hat{\eta}s$ $\pi o\lambda\iota\tau\acute{\iota}\mu o \nu$ (Jn reads $\pi o\lambda\nu\tau\epsilon\lambda o\hat{\nu}s$), "of ointment pistic nard very valuable." We do not know what the "pistic" meant here, since it is a rare word, and for that very reason its appearance in the two accounts is all the more striking. Both Jn and Mk record the protest that the ointment could have been sold for three hundred denarii and given to the poor; both have Jesus interpret her act as anticipating his burial; and both record in almost identical words the final saying that the poor are always with us. In addition to these verbal similarities both Jn and Mk put the scene in Bethany, in the week before the crucifixion (although not on the same day of the week). The points of contrast in the accounts are equally striking. Jn puts the incident in the house of Mary and Martha and the newly risen Lazarus, while Mk puts it in the house of Simon the Leper (Lk in the house of Simon the Pharisee). In

---

[15]Vol. I, pp. xcvi-xcix: "Comparison with Mk." On the first incident see also his II, 409-414. Bernard considered these passages sufficient indication that the author of Jn used Mk.

Mk the woman anoints the head of Jesus, in Jn and Lk the feet. In both Jn
and Lk the woman wipes Jesus' feet with her hair (in Lk she wipes
away her tears, and then anoints the feet; in Jn she wipes away the
ointment). In Lk only does the incident occur in Galilee, and is the
woman a "sinner."[16]

To account for the similarities it is usually supposed that the
author of Jn had both Mk and Lk before him, or at least had the story as
told in those Gospels thoroughly in his mind, and that he put together
details from each as he wished.[17] Such a suggestion is based upon the
presupposition that we are dealing primarily with documents, – an
idea which it is one of the real contributions of Form Criticism to have
refuted. We now see that we are dealing primarily not with documents
but with individual pericopes (I refuse to use the pedantic Greek
plural), each of which had its own vicissitudes of transmission. That
the author of Jn wrote this story with Mk and Lk before him, and took
one phrase from one, another from the other, is of all reconstructions the
most artificial. The phenomena of agreements and disagreements in the
stories are those of oral transmission, not of documentary dependence at
all.

For any raconteur knows that he hears identical stories in a great
many forms, and that two things survive most often the wear and tear
of insensitive repetition. The first of these is the catch-words. So the
"valuable pistic nard ointment" and the three hundred denarii would
long survive a total loss of the original place or circumstances of the
incident, or even of the characters involved. Secondly, persons and
places blur behind the persistent power of a striking apothegm. I do not
recall to how many people during the recent political campaign I heard
attributed the saying that Thomas Dewey looks like the bridegroom on
a wedding cake. So two identical apothegms, that the ointment is a
premonition of the burial, and that the poor are always with us,
appear in both Mk and Jn. That is, oral transmission would have
produced exactly the sort of agreements and disagreements as those in
this pericope as told by Jn, Mk, and Lk. On the contrary, one writing
from a written source, and with any sense of loyalty to tradition at all
(which the early Christians had in high degree), would preserve
precisely the names of the characters, and the place and order of events
which are here so divergently presented. The most natural guess is that

---

[16]Mt 26:6-13 is an almost exact reproduction of Mk and need not be discussed
separately.
[17]Bultmann, *Joh. Ev.*, 315, suggests that the story of Jn is told "nach einer
schriftlichen Quelle, die er redigiert"; but that source is, apparently, not Mk. In
his *Gesch. der synopt. Trad.*, 1921, 38, he seems to assume that the Johannine
form of a story would of course be later than the Synoptic.

all three Evangelists told the story as they had it from oral tradition, either directly as they had heard it, or from different papyrus sheets where the oral story had been recorded in various forms.

The history of the story seems to me to begin with Lk's version. With Mk's text of course before him, when Luke came to that story he did not like it so well as another rendition which he had heard or read elsewhere. The story as he preserved it seems the closest of all three to the way in which it was originally told (or happened). In this primitive form the woman is a sinner, which accords with probability since in holy tradition she would tend to become a saint, rather than retrograde into a sinner. As a sinner she naturally wept over Jesus' feet, then wiped them with her hair and anointed them with some ointment she had brought with her. The host, a Pharisee, questioned the propriety of Jesus' allowing her to do this; Jesus answered him and at the end forgave the woman her sins.

In the version of Jn, which seems to me the second in remove, the story is basically changed, though catch-words remain. The woman, now Mary of Bethany, is no longer a sinner and so does not weep, but she still dares pour her ointment only on his feet, and she still wipes his feet with her hair, though it is now absurdly the ointment which she wipes away, not the tears. It is absurd to have her wipe away the ointment because such ointment was designed to be left on the skin, and in her own house it is absurd that she must use her hair rather than a towel for the purpose. A new set of apothegms give point to the story. The ointment becomes of great value, is a preparation for his burial; and that is more important than any single act for the poor.

The version recorded in Mk seems to me the latest form of all, an attempt to clarify the story as it now appears in Jn. The great value of the ointment is retained in exactly the same words, along with the apothegms prompted by it, but the difficulty about the hair and the ointment is removed by having the woman put the ointment not on Jesus' feet but on his head, or hair, and so by omitting all reference to the woman's hair.

That this was exactly the history of the story I do not claim finally.[18] In investigations of this sort we can hope to arrive only at verisimilitude, but I do insist that such a development in oral tradition is far more likely than that the author of Jn constructed his version from the texts of Mk and Lk. For if one disregards all context and simply puts the three versions of the story beside each other, Mk's version seems definitely the latest and most sophisticated. It is very unlikely

---

[18]Gardner-Smith, 48, has a different reconstruction, different because he does not consider the Lukan elements.

that the evolution of the story would be to make the sainted Mary of Bethany into a sinner, or to get the ointment on Jesus' feet and Mary's hair once it had been on Jesus' head, where its "Messianic" character was too obvious to need explanation. The reason why I do not insist upon this reconstruction more emphatically is that stories do have a way of disintegrating as well as of picking up form and coherence, and the whole may have been reversed, and Mk's version have been the earliest. But such disintegration is likewise a process of oral tradition, rather than of literary tradition. In no case does it seem to me that the resemblances can be used as proof that the author of Jn wrote with the text of Mk before him.

    b. A miracle of healing (Jn 5:2-9 and Mk 2:1-12). It is thought evidence of Jn's use of Mk that both these passages tell of the healing of a man who is commanded, "Rise, take up thy bed and walk," and who does so with the command repeated in the narratives: he rose and took up his bed and walked, or went out. The words are of course set in two quite different stories. In Jn the healing is that at the pool of Bethesda; in Mk it is the paralytic borne of four. In Mk the controversy which follows is again about Jesus' power to forgive sins; in Jn it is over the fact that he healed the man on the Sabbath. That the author of Jn liked the phrase as he found it in Mk, and went on to create a totally different setting for it, is a possible hypothesis, perhaps, but one much less likely than that the saying was a beloved tradition from Jesus, and that in popular telling it had become set into two different stories. So with us, as already noted, popular tradition is constantly ascribing an identical aphorism to quite different people and circumstances. This is a phenomenon occurring a hundred times in oral transmission for once that it is deliberately done by an author having a written source before him. The coincidence in no sense is evidence that the author of Jn was rewriting Mk at this point.[19]

---

[19]Streeter, 398, makes much of the fact that Jesus must have said this in Aramaic, and that the identical Greek must therefore reflect literary dependence. Admitting that this is true, it by no means follows that it came to Jn from Mk. Streeter also says that Jn and Mk both use the vulgar κράββατον which Mt and Lk alter whenever it occurs in Mk. This means only that Jn and Mk repeat it in its racy colloquial form, not that Jn must have had it from Mk. But Streeter himself (409) is aware that "Epigrams easily circulate by word of mouth." A similar survival of a phrase in Jn and Mk, but in each case with a different setting, is the "prophet not without honor" of Jn 4:43-45 and Mk 6:4, which Gardner-Smith, 20-22, discusses in much the same way. On pp. 25-27, he treats the incident of the healing quite as I do above.

c. The feeding of the Five Thousand and the Storm on the Lake (Jn 6:1-21; Mk 6:30-52).[20] Here there are indeed a number of striking similarities, even more than Bernard indicates. The "five thousand" appears in both stories; "bread worth two hundred denarii," the five loaves and two fishes,[21] "grass," that they all "sit down" ($\dot{\alpha}\nu\alpha\pi\acute{\iota}\pi\tau\epsilon\iota\nu$), the "broken pieces" ($\kappa\lambda\acute{\alpha}\sigma\mu\alpha\tau\alpha$), the twelve baskets, ($\kappa\acute{o}\phi\iota\nu\sigma\iota$), that the baskets were filled with bread and that fish were also left over, these are all common elements, so many that some sort of literary relation is highly probable, unless the story was conventionalized in the telling as was no other in the NT. The impression is confirmed by the fact that Jn, instead of at once going on to the long discourse of the sacramental meaning of the miraculous feeding, stops to tell of Jesus' crossing the lake, walking part way on the water and overtaking and rescuing the storm-tossed disciples, with the characteristic aphorism in both, "It is I, be not afraid." In the second story the verbal coincidences are not so many that good oral transmission could not have produced them, but the immediate succession of the two stories makes an ordinary oral background for the two by far the least likely guess.

The parallels to Mk in this chapter, we said, continue. Mk (8:1-38) has the feeding of the four thousand as well as of the five. In the second story the numbers are changed so that the mystic seven takes the place of the five and the twelve, as it usually does in early Christian iconography of the baskets. This feeding too is followed by a crossing in a boat (but not of miraculous stilling of the waves, vv. 10 and 13), the demand for a sign (vv. 11, 12), and, after a healing of a blind man which may well have suggested the ninth chapter of Jn, by the confession of Peter (vv. 27-33). The demand for a sign is echoed in Jn 6:30, where, however, a sign is given, the true bread of the eucharist in contrast to the manna of the wilderness: in Mk all signs are categorically refused. In Jn (6:66-71) Peter confesses that Jesus is the Holy One of God who has the words of eternal life, while in Mk Peter says that Jesus is the Messiah (Mt 16:16 adds "Son of the living God"). But here we have a clustering of incidents – as well as verbal parallels – which puts this group upon a different footing from the other parallels (always excepting those in the Passion Narrative); and in

---

[20]Gardner-Smith, 27-36, seems to me to minimize the importance and number of the parallels in this chapter of Jn. I agree with his conclusion that the author of Jn did not have the stories from one of the Synoptic Gospels, but feel, as he does not, the necessity for more than an ordinary "popular story" to account for all the coincidences.

[21]Though the $\iota\chi\theta\acute{\upsilon}\epsilon\varsigma$ of Mk have become "prepared" or "cooked" fish, $\dot{o}\psi\acute{\alpha}\rho\iota\alpha$, in Jn.

conversation C.T. Craig told me that he thought this group made it highly probable that the author of Jn had Mk before him.

As we have suggested above, this is to consider the similarities rather than the general differences between the two Gospels, to use Bernard's phrase in a slightly changed meaning. For if the author of Jn took these from the completed Gospel of Mk it is astonishing that he should have reproduced with great care just this one cluster of stories from a special part of Mk, or this one and the Passion group, and done so with these two groups alone. In these sections, far from reproducing his source, whatever it was, with utter disregard for tradition, the author of Jn has reproduced it in his own words to be sure, but still has done so very faithfully indeed. The conclusion is unavoidable that he may have reproduced so few Markan stories in this way precisely because he had so few to reproduce.

These stories reached him, I am sure, not in the written Mk at all. They probably came to both authors in a written unit, though they may have reached both through a ritualistic rehearsal where the words had become stereotyped because the details all had symbolic meaning in the cult. Mk tells the multiplication story twice, on this explanation, because he has the ritualistic tradition of two communities. But still more probably the ritualistic tradition had itself been reduced to writing, and it was this which both authors had. Actually, as Bernard points out, the sacramental suggestion is strong even in Mk, where Jesus "lifts up his eyes to heaven" in blessing before breaking the bread, while in Jn the rest of the chapter is devoted to the famous eucharistic parallel of bread and Jesus' body. The "sign" has become in Jn, as was noted, the eucharist itself. The sequence of the first two stories, Jesus' walking on the water following the great feeding, is kept by Mt (14:13-33), and lost by Lk (9:10-17),[22] but their evidence here is clearly secondary to Mk. The original sequence of these two stories, it seems to me, may well have had sacramental meaning also, for the point of the sacrament is the miraculous character of Jesus' body, which his ability to walk on the water clearly indicates.[23]

That Jn drew all this material from Mk (or Mk from Jn) or from a sacramental eucharistic tradition, written or oral, to which we shall return, these are alternative solutions of the problem of this group of stories. In view of the general differences between Mk and Jn the least

---

[22]In its place is the stilling of the waves in Lk 8:22-25.

[23]Which Mt emphasizes by telling of Peter's failure to walk on the sea. Bernard's denial (I, pp. xcviii and 185, 186) that Jn's περιπατοῦντα ἐπὶ τῆς θαλάσσης meant that Jesus was walking on the water seems to me very forced. The incident may well have originally been a post-resurrection account, as has often been suggested.

likely solution of all is the one generally accepted, that the author of
Jn took the stories from Mk.[24]

    d. Events at the Last Supper. Even Bernard does not press this as
indicating that the author of Jn is following the written Mk. Bernard's
point here is that the order of events at the Last Supper as told by Jn is
more like Mk (and Mt) than Lk. and that hence the Jn-Mk order is most
probably historical. Apart from this dubious conclusion, the point has
clearly no value for putting the composition of Jn later than that of Mk.

    e. Peter's denials of Jesus (Jn 18:15-18, 25-27 and Mk 14:53, 54, 66-
72). Bernard points out that Peter's three denials of Jesus are described,
in both Jn and Mk, as having occurred while he was waiting in the
courtyard of the high priest, and that both Jn and Mk twice mention
that he was warming himself. "Perhaps Jn here follows Mk while he
departs from the Markan story in other particulars." Bernard goes on to
point out that Jn and Mk record almost identically the question of
Pilate, "Do you want me to release to you the king of the Jews (Jn 18:39;
Mk 15:9). But he himself is forced to conclude: "There is thus a
probability that Jn 18 goes back at some points to Mk 14, 15; but this is
not certain." We can agree with him completely that this is not certain,
for apart from the highly likely supposition that separate passion
narrative sources were in circulation, and in the hands of both
Evangelists, at these points only the suggestive details and aphorisms,
the sort of things preserved in oral tradition, appear in common.

    f. The mocking of Jesus (Jn 19:2-5; Mk 15:16-20). There are many
details in common here, such as the crown of thorns, the purple robe, the
fact that the mocking is done by Roman soldiers (and not by Herod's
soldiers as in Lk 23:11). In this story again, which must have been told
many times before its first writing, the common details are adequately
accounted for if a similar source, oral or written, lay behind Mk and Jn,
and do not at all compel the use of Mk by the author of Jn.

    Bernard closes this section with the suggestion that Jn 12:27, 28, the
cry of agony answered by a voice from heaven, was Jn's rewriting of
Mk's story of the struggle in Gethsemane, and that Jn 20:17 came from
the lost ending of Mk as reflected in Mt 28:9, 10. The arguments in both
cases are two tenuous to need reviewing.

    This is the chief evidence that the author of Jn had Mk before him,
and that Jn must therefore be dated after the completion of Mk.
Evidence for his use of the other Synoptics is much more sparse than
even this. The duplications of Mk in Jn, except in three of the cases, are
merely of passing phrases which prove nothing. The three cases (i.e.,

---

[24]Bultmann, *Joh. Ev.*, 155, argues convincingly to the same point. He suggests
that a "σημεῖα=Quelle" lay behind both Jn and Mk.

the anointing in Bethany, the double pericope of the Five Thousand and the Crossing of the Lake, and the mocking of Jesus) show, however, with what exactness the author of Jn could reproduce a story as it reached him – if it reached him. Over against these few parallels is the total impression of the two books which is that no two men could have told the story of Jesus much more differently than did the authors of Jn and Mk.[25] The most natural conclusion is that a writer who could reproduce stories in such detail as did the author of Jn in these cases, simply did not know the rest of Mk at all. In all probability for these and for the Passion Week in general there was a common (or similar) written source in the hands of both Evangelists. Other similarities between the two Gospels are adequately accounted for by oral tradition.

2. *The Gospel and the Epistles.* One of the most generally appealing arguments for the late date of Jn is an indirect one. The Johannine Epistles, it is argued, were written by the same author as the Gospel, and the Epistles, especially the second and third, have a pastoral tone which suggests later organization, while the way in which they denounce heresies and heretical teachers seems to reflect the heresies and problems of later times. So if the Epistles are late, the Gospel must be late also.

The affinities between the Gospel and Epistles are admittedly close and many. 2 and 3 Jn are so short, however, that nothing can be concluded about their authorship. The Johannine phraseology of both indicates at least that they came from a circle deeply infused with the Johannine way of thinking, but the few lines which each letter offers us establish no more than this.[26] Without definite certification that they were written by the same author as Jn and 1 Jn, which such small anonymous letters by no means provide, they are the tail of the Johannine corpus, and we cannot allow the tail to wag the dog by making them in any sense impose a date upon the Gospel.

1 Jn is much longer and its phrases parallel with Jn are impressively numerous;[27] accordingly the argument that it was written by the author of Jn is much more cogent than for 2-3 Jn. Unquestionably the same man could have written both documents, though I am not fully convinced that that was so. The first Epistle may also have been written by a man saturated with Johannine phrases and ideas. For if Jn

---

[25]This contrast has often been elaborately drawn. See for example Enslin, 438-447; Colwell, passim; E.J. Goodspeed, *Introduction to the NT*, 1937, 296-315.
[26]See Bacon, *Hellenists*, 136.
[27]These will be found most conveniently presented by A.E. Brooke, *The Johannine Epistles*, 1912, pp. i-xix *(ICC)*. Cf. Bacon, *Hellenists*, 359-369; H. Windisch, *Die kathol. Briefe*, 109-111 *(Hdbch z. Nt*, 1930).

was as early as I suspect there must have been in Ephesus or somewhere a center of Christianity which preserved Jn as its Gospel and ultimately forced it upon what seems to have been a rather reluctant Church. In this center the key words must long have been Love, Light, Way, Life, Truth, Logos, the World, rebirth, children of God, abiding in God or Christ. To analyze here the whole list of parallels between Jn and 1 Jn as given by Brooke is impossible. If a center of Christianity be supposed, however, where for years Johannine Christianity was dominant, it seems entirely natural that this phraseology should be reproduced in a letter by a later correspondent. I do not doubt that many pastoral letters from leaders of Christian Science to other believers are as saturated with the phraseology of *Science and Health* as is 1 Jn with the phraseology and message of Jn. The saturation does not imply that Mrs. Eddy wrote all such pastoral letters of Christian Science.

Even if a common author is supposed, however, there seems nothing in 1 Jn which requires a late date, or one later than the Gospel itself. The only details worth discussing in this connection are those of the heresies which 1 Jn denounces, and which are generally taken to refer to heretical movements of the late first or early second century.

The heretical point of view denounced in 1 Jn is essentially the denial that "Jesus Christ came in the flesh" (4:2). 1 Jn 2:22, 23 is much debated. It says only that anyone who denies that Jesus is the Christ is "the liar." What is meant by that seems explained in the next sentence, that the "antichrist" is the one who denies the Son. 1 Jn 2:18 tells us that there were "many antichrists about, presumably of the same sort; and the considerable number of "false prophets" of 4:1 are probably still the same people. It was they who denied that "Jesus Christ is come in the flesh."

These statements are generally taken to refer to the heresy of docetism, especially as presented by Cerinthus in the early second century. It is important to notice just what the passages say. They accuse the heretics of denying that Jesus was the Christ, the "Son" of God the Father, come in the flesh. In the general Johannine cast of the letter, the "Son" must be the Johannine Son, the Logos. Jesus Christ was the Logos incarnate: this was the thesis of the Gospel, and the Epistle tells us that many were rejecting it. Brooke admits that nothing in the Epistle indicates "more precise docetism."[28] Actually nothing indicates any concern with the problem of docetism at all, that is with the reality of Jesus' flesh, or with the relation of the incarnate "Christ" to "Jesus." "Jesus Christ is come in the flesh" is an early statement by a man unaware that a distinction would ever be made between "Jesus" and

---

[28]Op. cit., p. xlv. H. Windisch, *Kath. Briefe*, 127, 128, is just as cautious.

"Christ," or that it would be proposed that "Christ" took up his temporary abode in "Jesus" only to leave "Jesus" before the crucifixion, since divinity could not suffer. The question simply was: "Was Jesus the Son of God, or Logos, incarnate?" To read anything more into these statements violates their primitive looseness. It is to be presumed that as soon as the thesis of the Gospel was announced there would be people who protested, so that if the author of the Gospel wrote the Epistle he might well have done so very soon afterwards.

In the last chapter (5:5-8) another reference to the same docetic heresy is usually identified. One who overcomes the world, that passage says, must believe not only that "Jesus is the Son of God," but that "Jesus Christ" "came" in or through both water and blood, not in or through water only. This Spirit witnesses this, the writer continues, and so the witness is three-fold, Spirit, water, and blood, which three are one. The implication is that there are people who say that Jesus Christ came only in or through the water, not the blood. It is recalled that not only did Cerinthus have "Christ" avoid the crucifixion and its "blood," but that he taught that "Christ" descended into Jesus after the baptism in the form of a dove, and so came in or through the water. Brooke, a model of discretion, goes over all the evidence with great care,[29] and concludes that the "most satisfactory explanation" of the language of the passage is to see in it a reference to these ideas of Cerinthus. But Brooke fails to note that the argument is not how "Christ" came to "Jesus," but how "Jesus Christ" came, and I doubt that the author of the Epistle had ever heard of the distinction.

The verse is again so cryptic that we cannot be sure just what it meant. The basic question is what the author meant by "blood," with the meaning of "water" almost as important. Two explanations seem to me to be possible. In one the reference in both words is to the coming of Jesus Christ, the Logos, to the world, so that the "water" would mean Jesus' baptism, the "blood" his passion. The other would take both words in a sacramental sense, and see the argument as being about the mystic coming of Jesus in baptism and eucharist. A word must be said about each.

According to the first of these, the verse refers to the problem of how the passion of Christ, the "blood," could be included in the work of Christ, his coming to men and his salvation of them.[30] The cross, Paul assures us, was a stumbling block at the beginning, and a large part of

---

[29]Op. cit., pp. xiv-xlix, 131-138, 154-165.
[30]Brooke himself says (p. xlvi) that the point of the passage is to register the view that the passion was not an essential part of the Messianic work of salvation.

his argument was dedicated to showing how the "blood" was an essential part of the work of Christ. Paul finally came to the solution in Col 1 20 when he said that the ultimate reconciliation of man with God was made "through the blood of his cross." Heb, 1 Pt, and Rev agree with 1 Jn that it is the blood of Jesus Christ which cleanseth us from all sin. But the very care given to demonstrating that the death of Jesus was a necessary part of his work indicates that at the beginning this was a point of difficulty. All 1 Jn does in the controversy, if this is the meaning here of "blood," is to take sides with what became the orthodox explanation. The Church has naturally not preserved the attacks upon this position. But there is no reason to suppose that the idea that the Logos suffered and died, the greatest difference between Philo's Logos as presented in the Patriarchs and Jn's Logos, was accepted without protest, or had to wait for Cerinthus to be questioned. From the nature of the case this must have been an early stumbling block to both Jews and Greeks, and hellenized Jews.

If, however, the words "water" and "blood" are here references to Christian sacraments, the reference seems to me to be likewise early. For if these two words are sacramental the "Spirit" would be sacramental in the passage also. The early Christians, according to Acts, were chiefly concerned with conveying the benefit of Christ, if not his being, to believers in the form of baptism and the Holy Spirit. Acts 8 14-17 is the chief passage, where the question arises whether the Samaritan converts had received the Holy Spirit or had only been baptized. When Peter and John discovered that the converts had only been baptized they prayed, put their hands upon them, and "they received the Holy Spirit." The sacramental conveying of the Holy Spirit to all believers in this way was, so far as we know, exclusively a feature of the earliest Church. In these accounts of Acts there is no corresponding interest in what Paul was to call the "cup of blessing," the "communion of the blood of Christ," though this sacrament must quickly have taken its place with equal importance beside the other two. If the "Spirit" and "water" in the passage of 1 Jn are sacramental, the passage would seem to reflect a very early stage when the cup was not being recognized by some as having power to convey the benefit of Christ along with the others. To such people 1 Jn would be saying that the Logos-Jesus came to the world not only in the sacraments of "Spirit" and baptism but also in the eucharist, and that the three sacraments all alike, εἰς τὸ ἕν, unite in bearing witness of that coming.

Whatever explanation of the passage may be the true one, there is nothing in it that requires a late date.

Similarly the eschatological immediacy in which 1 Jn repudiates the heretics is rather early than late. For "it is the last hour," and these heretics, who are antichrists, are final proof of the fact (2 18). We have long associated the passionately immediate anticipation of eschatological triumph with early times: on this basis, largely, do we suppose that 1 Thess is an early letter of Paul. The same argument would incline us to put 1 Jn also early (and the Gospel with its similar eschatological immediacy, as well).

Without stopping to analyze all the rest of the possibly late details in 1 Jn, none of which offers so good a case for lateness as the foregoing, we may conclude that the relation between Jn and the Epistles, whatever it was, can by no means be used as an argument for a late date of the Gospel.

3. *Johannine Ecclesiasticism*. John must be dated late, another argument runs, because it reflects an advanced sacramental position in its references to both baptism and the eucharist, and has a far from primitive conception of the Christian community or Church.[31] Again the argument seems quite without foundation.

As to baptism, Jn 3 3-8, with its reference to being born again in water, is in no way a more elaborate conception than Paul's idea that in the same rite the believer is baptized into Christ's death. Neither explanation needs to be later than the other.

The eucharist in Jn presents more elaborate difficulties, but in the discourse on the eucharist (in the sixth chapter) nothing is said which goes beyond the eucharistic doctrine of Paul. What seems sophisticated and late in John is the extensive use of the Philonic metaphor that the manna of the wilderness was the Logos.[32] This allegory of the manna was possibly a commonplace not original with Philo. Its application to the eucharist was very early, for Paul refers to it in 1 Cor 10 2-4. In this passage Paul, by casual allusion alone, can say that the sacrament of baptism was in fact given to the Fathers in the cloud and in their crossing the Red Sea,[33] while they got the spiritual food and drink (*sc.*

---

[31]This is most succinctly stated by the Lakes, *Introduction*, 61-63.

[32]Material on this in Philo is summarized in my *By Light, Light*, 1935, 208.

[33]This verse is one of the most important for the continuity into Christianity of what I described in *By Light, Light* as the "Mystery of Moses" (see esp. chapters VII and VIII). There I explained what Philo meant when he talked of being "initiated by Moses into the greater mysteries." Yet nothing Philo says carries the idea quite so far as this statement of Paul, which from its cryptic character is obviously an allusion to a commonplace for his readers, that the crossing of the Red Sea was (by allegory but none the less really) a baptism of the Fathers into (εἰς) Moses himself. That his readers could have understood such an allusion is conceivable only if some Jewish exposition of Moses set forth a doublet of the Red Sea and the Well in the Desert, along with manna, and if Moses was therein himself the Logos into *whom* the Fathers were baptized and

which Christians have in the eucharist) through eating the manna and drinking the stream from the rock, which rock and its stream with Philo was the Logos or Sophia, with Paul was Christ. That is, Paul makes it clear that by the barest allusion the Corinthian community would understand that the bread of the eucharist equals the manna, since both are the eating of the Logos. There must have been considerable exposition of that complicated equation such as Jn 6 gives before Paul could have alluded to it as cryptically as he does for the Corinthians. It is natural to suppose that it is the explanation of the eucharist which he himself taught them when he was with them, so that he did not need to repeat it fully in his letter. In contrast there is another story of the meaning of the eucharist which he must tell them in full as though they had never heard it before, the story of the institution of the eucharist at the Last Supper. To this we shall return. Here it need only be emphasized that the eucharist-manna theory of Jn is at least as old as, probably considerably older than, the letter to the Corinthians. Its presence in Jn does not suggest a late date.

If Jn's sacramentalism is not late, neither is its conception of the Christian community, or Church. The only parts of the Gospel which can remotely be construed as references to the Church are the "I am the vine, ye are the branches" of Jn 15 1 ff., the sense of corporateness of the final prayer of Jn 17, and the committing to the disciples of the power to forgive sins in Jn 20 22, 23. Of all three a word must be said.

The vine in this passage, as even Archbishop Bernard recognized,[34] is not the Church but is Jesus himself. The vine is a figure here of the nature of Jesus, that is, we shall presume, it is a Logos figure. It is not that Jesus is the trunk and we the branches: the conception is a much more mystical one, that Jesus is the vine in its entirety, and we are branches in the vine, parts of a greater unit, not whose source but whose totality is Jesus. The figure presented such grave difficulties that, popular as it was in art, the later Church made little or no use of it to describe the *corpus Christianum:* the official figure of the Church is not the vine but Paul's "head and members." For the vine of Jn is actually pure pantheism. Far from representing an advanced stage, it represents a primitive stage where the notions of paganism were being borrowed

---

of whom they communicated. It is precisely this doublet which I discuss in that work at pages 221 f.; while that Moses was both the Logos incarnate, and the one who released the Logos to the Fathers in the manna and the well, seems Philo's central point. The crossing of the Red Sea followed by a scene at a well appears likewise at Dura.

[34]II, 478. He thinks it is a eucharistic reference suggested by the first eucharist just celebrated (according to Paul and the Synoptics). See also Ed. Schweizer, *Ego Eimi*, 1939, 39-43.

without adequate digestion or a full sense of their implications.[35] The great Logos in which we are all members is a Stoic conception, but as presented in the Gospel the vine is the Logos rather in the form of Neo-Platonic emanation than in the Stoic form, since the Logos-vine is not itself the ultimate: God is the farmer cultivating the vine, not himself the vine as he would be to a Stoic. The vine of Jn echoes not so much the Stoic Logos as the adaptation of the Stoic Logos to Platonic thinking for which Philo is proverbial, though in all the multitude of figures by which Philo presents the Logos in this sense in no place does he, so far as I know, say that the Logos as it spreads down from God is a "vine." But in his most explicit single description of this emanation in which all things find their reality, while his figures are usually those of light and a stream, he does refer to the lesser manifestations as growing out (*germinant*) from the higher.[36] The Evangelist may have had the figure from pagans among whom this Logos conception was applied to Dionysus in a sacramental as well as philosophic-mystical sense, but more likely, since his figures had demonstrably for the most part been used previously by hellenized Jews, he had this figure too from such Jews, even though it is not to be found in Philo. In any case it indicates no advanced ecclesiasticism at all, but only the sense of solidarity which the Christians must have had from the beginning, a solidarity and oneness in Christ. It is the kind of figure which the Christian community would have applied to itself before it had Paul's "head and members," rather than afterwards.

The prayer of Jn 17 similarly seems to me not to be late. It is an elaborate exposition, probably the first in writing, of a conception that all are one in Jesus as Jesus is one with the Father. One of the ideas of the chapter is that Jesus as the Son gives to his followers the revelation of God (vss. 7, 8), and this idea we know was at least as old as Q, since it is clearly if briefly stated in Mt 11 25-30=Lk 10 21, 22. This is the only extended "Johannine" fragment in Q, and it has caused great perplexity among scholars who have thought this sort of thinking must be late. All difficulties disappear if we suppose that such ideas in the Church were early. Certainly no one can seriously argue that this

---

[35]Bernard, II, 477, 478, recalls that Israel was often compared to a vine in the OT, and that this is the source usually assigned to the Johannine passage. Although he fails to see the pantheism of the passage he is still quite right in feeling that this is a totally different vine from the tragic vine of the prophets and psalms.

[36]*QE* ii, 68. Philo did not invent this conception of the emanations. See Onatas the Pythagorean quoted in my *By Light, Light*, 20, 21.

Synoptic pericope of Q originated without counterparts or context in the early Church.[37]

More suggestive of later ecclesiasticism is finally the incident in Jn 20 22, 23, where Jesus in an appearance to the disciples after his resurrection breathed upon them and gave them the Holy Spirit together with the power to forgive sins. All commentators at once recall the accounts in Mt (16 19 and 18 18) of the giving of this same power to the disciples, as well as the final commission to baptize in the name of the Trinity (28 19, 20). Again Bernard[38] is right in seeing that the Johannine commission is more primitive than any in Mt, and that the author of Jn could not have known the Matthean form of the tradition. The power of forgiveness may well have been one, as the records relate, which Jesus claimed for himself in his life time, and which his successors claimed from the beginning in his name along with other miraculous powers. It must have been as early a prerogative as the power to baptize which implied it. At the same time, as we have remarked, Acts tells us that the practice of giving the Spirit was early, apparently as early as baptism itself. The explanation that Jesus authorized such power must have been almost as early as its primitive exercise. I see no hint of "later ecclesiasticism" in Jn's use of the tradition.

II. Positive Arguments for an Early Date

A. The Author's Ignorance of the Synoptic Tradition

No more irrelevant description of its character was ever forced upon a document than the current conception that Jn was written to correct or supplement the Synoptics. We have seen that the author can reproduce that tradition as accurately as any one when he wanted or was able to do so. He seems to have reproduced so little of the Synoptic tradition for the reason that he knew so little of it. The author had a stray pericope sheet of the cleansing of the temple, for example, or had heard the story in isolation. He then put it where he did at the beginning of Jesus' career not because he wanted to correct Mk's allocation of it to the end of Jesus' life, but simply because he did not know in the least where it belonged.[39] Much in the Synoptic tradition that would have been of great value to his monumental allegory of Jesus' nature and mission he omits, while he includes such pericopes as

---

[37]A brilliant discussion of the problem was recently presented by T. Arvedson, *Das Mysterium Christi: Eine Studie zu Mt 11 25-30,* 1937.
[38]II, 677-681.
[39]See on this Gardner-Smith, 12-15.

the anointing of the feet and the walking on the water although they have little more value for his purpose than most of what else the Synoptists relate. He omits the one block of material because he happened not to have it, just as he included the other merely because he had it at hand. He was uninterested in gathering such material, and concentrated upon his allegory and creative writing of sermons for Jesus, because like Paul he felt that Jesus' nature, incarnation, death, and resurrection were the essence of the Christian message. So, unlike Paul, he gives a few key events as pretexts for the "I am" sermonizing of his divine Logos, but like Paul it is the one event, the incarnation and victory over "death" or the "world," in which he is interested. Such a point of view seems to me definitely an early one. There is certainly no reason for dating it late in the case of Jn when we know it was early in the case of Paul.

B. The Virgin Birth

Since the incarnation is the central interest of both Paul and Jn it is equally significant, and in the same way for each, that neither of them records the Virgin Birth. In the case of Mk and Paul it is usual to suppose that this event was omitted because they had not heard of it, and their ignorance is taken to indicate that both were written early. The same inference is natural for Jn. Indeed it was the amazing absence of any reference to the miraculous birth of Jesus in the Gospel which provoked an early attempt (beginning apparently in the mid-second century) to alter Jn 1 13 so that it would suggest the Virgin Birth rather than the divine birth of all believers.[40]

It is much more certain that the author of Jn did not know the story of the Virgin Birth, at least as it is told in Mt and Lk, than that either Mark or Paul did not know of it. For Jn (7:41-43) records that when some claimed that Jesus was the Messiah others objected on the ground that Jesus was a Galilean and hence could not be the Messiah since the Messiah was to be born in Bethlehem of the seed of David. The pericope as Jn records it must be quite primitive. It was this objection which was later recorded in Mt as a prophecy specifically of the birth of Jesus. That is, the objection to Jesus on the basis of this prophecy led the Christians to claim that the prophecy had been fulfilled: that

---

[40]For such spiritual birth see my *By Light, Light,* 153-166, 201. W. Bauer, op. cit. 22, briefly reviews the argument about the text, and properly decides for the traditional reading. Bultmann, *Ev. Joh.,* 37, n. 7, says that Jn "deu Gedanken der Jungfrauengeburt nicht nur nicht enthält, sondern (wie Paulus) ausschliesst." On the other side see best T. Zahn, *Komment. z. NT,* IV, *Evang. des Joh.,* 1908, 72-77, 700-703. I should have ignored this point but for the kind prompting of M.S. Enslin.

Jesus had actually been born in Bethlehem of the seed of David, a claim of which we have two versions. It seems impossible that the author of Jn knew these answers, and yet left the objection in the air as he has done. It is much more likely that he had never heard them, and such ignorance we must ascribe to quite an early date in Christian history, in Jn's case as in the others.[41]

C. The Institution of the Eucharist.

It seems equally clear that the author of Jn had no knowledge of the institution of the eucharist at the Last Supper as told by Paul and the Synoptists. The eucharistic discourse of Jn 6 has been mentioned for what seems to me the primitive character of its theology or philosophy as compared with the Pauline story.[42] It seems incredible to me that an author who would have retold in such detail as he did the story of the Passion, and who felt it important to stress as he did the Last Supper, should have failed, had he known it, to rehearse the event which the Church has ever since thought to be the supreme act of the Christ of history, the institution of the eucharist at the Last Supper.[43]

The sixth chapter, with its long insistence upon the necessity of eating the flesh (and drinking the blood vss. 53-56),[44] shows that the members of John's community were devout communicants who believed in the real presence. But they knew only the quite clumsy story of the multiplication of the loaves and fishes to justify their practice, quite clumsy because it made no place for the wine, while it included the soon to be discarded fish as part of the meal. Now the art remains of early Christianity make it highly likely that the early eucharistic observance included fish with the bread and wine, and it has long been suspected that the Messianic fish which the Jews of the time ate, along with the bread and wine which they still partake of with "blessing" in

---

[41]This passage is discussed at greater length, but with the same conclusion, by Gardner-Smith, 38-40.

[42]"I am the vine" of ch. 15 has of course been explained as a eucharistic utterance from early times. Bernard (I, pp. clxvi-clxxvi), who argues that that was its meaning, can still, after reviewing all the evidence, conclude only that such an interpretation "is not modern fancy." W.F. Howard, *The Fourth Gospel in Recent Criticism and Interpretation,* 1931, 150, says outright what most commentators presume about the omission of the eucharist from the Last Supper in Jn: "Silence assumes knowledge in this case." Prejudgment can go no farther.

[43]Bacon, *Fourth Gospel in Research and Debate,* 431.

[44]Colwell, 136, 137, minimizes Jn's concern with sacramentalism, to the point of making the authior reject in this discourse reference to "anything physical." It is one of Colwell's least convincing passages.

a special way, was what lay behind the Christian observance. In so brief an essay there is not space to present or to discuss this evidence.[45] What appears increasingly likely is that on Friday nights, as well as at the major feasts, faithful Jews were eating a Messianic meal, in which they partook of the Messiah in the form of fish, bread, and wine, in anticipation of his coming and of the great Messianic banquet of the future life. This banquet early Christians would have continued, since they were still observant Jews. Only, and this was the great step, since Jesus was now their Messiah, the Christians in partaking of the Messiah were partaking of Jesus Christ himself. Myths are much more apt to be produced by cult acts than cult acts by myths. Christians in this early meal found themselves partaking of Jesus Christ in the blessed elements, and the practice cried out for a definitely Christian justification, arising from an act or command of Jesus himself. Two stories thus arose.

The first story would appear to be that given in Jn. For this the analogy of the miraculous feeding of the ancient Israelites in the desert with manna, and their getting the divine drink from the rock of Sophia or Logos, of which mention has already been made, offered one element. Just why the fish took the place of the rock as symbol of the divine fluid in the new version of the story I cannot say. But Jesus took the place of Moses for the Christians now in a new feeding of the multitude in the desert, and this was a symbol of the new sacrament in which Jesus gave his flesh and blood to his followers, the heavenly food and drink, and made such partaking a general requirement for all Christians. With this, as we shall see at once, was fused another, a Messianic, element.

That this stage in, or form of, the celebration of the eucharist is not purely imaginative on my part is definitely witnessed by the order for the celebration of the eucharist in the *Didaché*. The passage, familiar as it is, is so important that it must be quoted entire:

> IX. 1. And concerning the eucharist, hold eucharist thus: 2. First concerning the cup, "We give thanks to thee, our Father, for the holy Vine of David thy child, which thou didst make known to us through Jesus thy child; to thee be glory for ever. 3. And concerning the broken bread: "We give thanks to thee, our Father, for the life and knowledge

---

[45]The subject has been discussed, but by no means exhausted, by I. Scheftelowitz, "Das Fisch-Symbol im Judentum and Christentum," *Archiv für Religions-wissenschaft* , XIV (1911), 1-53; F. Gavin, *"Berakha and Eucharist,"* in his *The Jewish Antecedents of the Christian Sacraments,* 1928, 59-114. Gavin gives in the notes on pp. 64, 65, a valuable bibliography, from which should especially be mentioned W.O.E. Oesterley, *The Jewish Background of the Christian Liturgy,* 1925, 156-230.

which thou didst make known to us through Jesus thy child. To thee be glory for ever. 4. As this broken bread was scattered upon the mountains, but was brought together and became one, so let thy Church be gathered together from the ends of the earth into thy kingdom, for thine is the glory and the power through Jesus Christ for ever." 5. But let none eat or drink of your eucharist except those who have been baptized in the Lord's Name. For concerning this also did the Lord say, "Give not that which is holy to the dogs."

X. 1. But after you have been filled, thus give thanks: 2. "We give thanks to thee, O Holy Father, for the holy Name which thou didst make to tabernacle in our hearts, and for the knowledge and faith and immortality which thou didst make known to us through Jesus thy Child. To thee be glory for ever. 3. Thou, Lord Almighty, didst create all things for thy Name's sake, and didst give food and drink to men for their enjoyment, that they might give thanks to thee, but us hast thou blessed with spiritual food and drink and eternal life[46] through thy Child. 4. Above all we give thanks to thee for that thou art mighty. To thee be glory for ever. 5. Remember, Lord, thy Church, to deliver it from all evil and to make it perfect in thy love, and gather it together in its holiness from the four winds to thy kingdom which thou hast prepared for it. For thine is the power and the glory for ever. 6. Let grace come and let this world pass away. Hosannah to the God of David. If any man be holy, let him come! if any man be not, let him repent: Maran atha, Amen." 7. But suffer the prophets to hold eucharist as they will.

Here are a number of very important Johannine reminiscences. The cup is the vine, "made known through Jesus thy Child."[47] The bread is broken and scattered "on the mountains."[48] The bread gives "life," "eternal life,"[49] and "knowledge," which again had been revealed in Jesus. In the story in Jn the fragments were gathered together into twelve baskets, and its gathering together in the *Didaché* signified the reunion of the Church, a direct adaptation of a Jewish-Messianic

---

[46]K. Lake, whose translation in the Loeb Classics I am in the main reproducing here, allowed "light" instead of "life" to slip through the printers' hands.

[47]Why "child," παῖς, instead of the Johannine "son," υἱός, I shall not guess. In Jn, as we shall see, the vine is not eucharistic at all. The *Didaché* appears here to be a later adaptation of Jn's earlier conception. For if the author of Jn had meant the reader to understand the eucharist by the vine he would in all likelihood, in view of chapter 6, have said so.

[48]ἐπάνω τῶν ὀρέων. In Jn (6 3) the miracle happens when Jesus had gone "to the mountain," εἰς τὸ ὄρος. In Mk 6 46 Jesus goes to the mountain only after the miracle, as in Jn 6 15. But in Mt 15 29 the feeding of the four thousand takes place upon a hill. Gardner-Smith, 28, thinks of a common oral tradition, but does not consider adequately the possible ritualistic nature of that tradition.

[49]Cf. *Did.* ix, 3 and x, 3 with Jn 6 27, 48-59.

prayer for the reunion of the scattered tribes.[50] The concluding prayer echoes the Johannine idea that they are "filled."[51] The ἐσκήνωσεν of Jn has become κατεσκήνωσας, and Jesus is "tabernacling," through the eucharist, in our hearts; but the allusion seems clear. Those who partake of the eucharist are different from all others, further, in that they take the "spiritual food and drink along with eternal life" through Jesus, which is an echo of the figure of the manna, though in the phrase with which Paul referred to it rather than Jn.[52] The fishes have already disappeared, and in the final line the *Didaché* shows that "prophets" could and did celebrate differently. Whether this is a reference to celebration according to the soon to become standard tradition of Paul-Mk we cannot say.

Oesterley[53] has made it quite clear that the *Didaché* formula is itself an adaptation of Jewish liturgy, since unquestionable traces of identity still survive in spite of the number of editing hands through which the Jewish and Christian traditions have gone. When Jn 6 is considered with them, as it does not occur to Oesterley to do, parallels with the Jewish prayer increase. This evidence we cannot discuss here. The evidence which Oesterley presents, however, shows that the gathering together in the *Didaché* of the Church from the four winds, as a result of the bread broken and brought together upon the mountains, is an adaptation of a Messianic prayer that the twelve tribes be gathered together from the four corners of the earth when the "ensign" appears upon the mountains.

In terms of Jewish mystic thought, which seems to me to have been the starting point of Christian formulations of the sacrament, the twelve baskets, continuing the twelve tribes of the Jewish prayer, would make the Christian ceremony a rite of what Philo and later the Christians called the "true Israel." When the twelve become the seven, and the loaves are seven, in the Markan account of the four thousand the whole is made more directly into a celebration of the Logos in terms

---

[50]Oesterley, *The Jewish Background of the Christian Liturgy*, 81, quotes the Jewish evidence.

[51]*Didaché*: μετὰ τὸ ἐμπλησθῆναι; Jn: ὡς ἐνεπλήσθησαν.

[52]*Did.* x, 3: πνευματικὴν τροφὴν καὶ πότον; 1 Cor 10 3, 4: πνευματικὸν βρῶμα καὶ πνευματικὸν πόμα; Jn 6 55; ἀληθὴς βρῶσις καὶ ἀληθὴς πόσις. Paul seems not to have originated this phrase, at least not here. From his casual allusion to it he would appear to be quoting a detail ordinarily rehearsed along with the consecration of the elements, a ritual which itself may have been much like that in the *Didaché*, and which Paul may well himself have used earlier at Corinth.

[53]Op. cit., 131, 132, 188. In addition to what follows in the text Oesterley points out that in the Kiddush as in the *Didaché* the cup is blessed before the bread. See 1 Cor 10 16, 21.

of the mystic seven.[54] The seven is definitely the more sophisticated number, and it is interesting that it is found in Mk, along with the original twelve, rather than in Jn which knows only the more primitive five and twelve. Had the author of Jn had the Markan seven before him I am sure he would have preferred it. The exact history of the rite will never be reconstructed from our evidence. But the evidence together indicates that the eucharist in the early Church was actually celebrated in terms of the miraculous feeding, and that the value of the rite as thus celebrated was that in it one partook of Christ's body and blood, which brought "eternal life" and "gnosis." It is this celebration in a primitive form which the Johannine account reflects. Apparently its author had never heard of another form of celebration.

Already by the time of the composition of Mk, however, this story had ceased in many circles to be the official account of the institution of the eucharist. Mark has heard another and much better account of the institution, and so, while the multiplication of the loaves was still to him a sacred story, carefully preserved in two versions (presumably as told in two different communities), it was no longer his story of the institution.[55] For Paul, under stress of inner disquiet, as such things usually happen, had meanwhile "received from the Lord" the tremendous revelation of the institution at the Last Supper.[56] This story of the institution must rapidly have supplanted the other, and become the one rehearsed at the consecration of the elements. It was much better adapted to the purpose. Still, I suspect from Christian art that the fishes were long an actual part of the eucharistic food, and from this the Christ-fish symbol got its popularity. But that, I have said, is too long a story to rehearse here.

The point is that Jn presents us with the miraculous feeding as the story of the institution, while Paul and the Synoptics present the Last Supper. That the author of Jn knew but rejected or ignored the Pauline story, and created in its place a eucharistic meaning for the story of the

---

[54]See my *By Light, Light*, passim, for these ideas.

[55]A slight indication that Jn is here more primitively ritualistic than Mk is that Jn speaks of Jesus' preliminary blessing of the bread only as εὐχαριστήσας, while all the Synoptics have εὐλόγησεν. Both terms are used by the Synoptists in the story of the four thousand (cf. Mk 8 6), as they are, of course, at the Last Supper (Mk 14 22, 23).

[56]I have heard it argued that παρέλαβον means "I received" specifically in the sense of "received from tradition," and such is certainly a natural meaning of the word when used by itself. But παρέλαβον ἀπὸ τοῦ Κυρίου can mean only "I received from the Lord," not "I have received a tradition which originated from the Lord." Such translation is a consummate example of special pleading. It is obvious that the only way Paul could have received this story "from the Lord" was in a vision.

feeding as told by Mk is possible. But in view of the later unbroken loyalty of the Church to the Pauline account, this is a much less likely hypothesis (and this is all we can hope to show) than that Jn actually tells the original story of the institution, tells it because it is the only one he knows. At the time Jn was composed Paul may have already told his version in the letter to the Corinthians, along with his passing allusion to the earlier account.[57] But Paul's new story seems at once to have got such wide popularity that Jn would naturally be dated, if not earlier, at least not much later.

With this argument goes the generally admitted fact that Jn preserves the true (or original) date of the Last Supper in making it fall upon the evening before the day when the paschal lamb would have been killed and eaten, while the Synoptics all agree in making the Last Supper the Passover meal itself. The arguments for preferring Jn's date need not be rehearsed here.[58] Enslin[59] suggests that Jn changed the Synoptic date so that the death of Jesus would coincide with the killing of the paschal lambs, but this is highly artificial. For Jn did not change the date. Jn tells the right date because the author knew it and had no reason to change it. It was in the Paul-Mark tradition of the founding of the eucharist at the Last Supper that the date became changed, for it was in that tradition that the eucharist became the meal when the Christians ate not the manna from heaven but the "lamb that was slain." True, Jesus was "The Lamb of God which taketh away the sin of the world" to Jn (1 29), but this was not a figure from the Jewish paschal lamb: it was the lamb led to slaughter of Is 53 7, which in turn was the lamb of sacrifice of Ex 29 38-41. Nothing in Jn associates Jesus with the lamb of Passover.[60] It is Paul, in the very letter in which he tells of the Last Supper, who insists that Christ is our Passover, killed or sacrificed for us. In saying this Paul has the eucharist in mind as appears from the way he goes on to discuss the true unleavened bread (I Cor 5 7, 8). The date of the Supper was changed, that is, to equate the eucharist with passover. The author of Jn, who knew nothing of all this, left the original date. From this again we should presume that Jn is an early account as compared with Mk.

---

[57]See above.
[58]They will be found conveniently summarized in Bernard, I, pp. cvi-cviii.
[59]Op. cit., 445, 446.
[60]Bernard, II, 651, says that Jn 19 36 reflects the passover lamb of Nu 9 12, but it seems much closer to Ps 34 20 as B. Weiss suggested (*Johan.-Evang.*, in *Meyer's Kommentar*, 1893, 602). Barton's guess that all that was implied was a coincidence with, and hence a fulfillment of, an expression in the Torah seems the most likely suggestion: *JBL*, XLIX (1930), 16, n. 11.

Other details might be considered to indicate an early date for the Gospel, but they would be incidental, and the case must stand or fall with these.[61]

III. The Beginnings of Hellenistic Christianity

It is extremely difficult for our minds to leave a gap in history with not even a hypothesis to fill it. Lacking any specific information about how or when Christianity developed so as to make possible the writing of Jn, for example, scholars from earliest times have supposed that the Jesus of the Synoptics was the Jesus first preached, and that the Jesus of the Fourth Gospel was a product of the aged disciple or of a later generation. Everyone who does not accept the sermons of Jn as actual sermons of Jesus has presumed that early Christianity began with a Synoptic sort of message and only gradually became abstracted into such expression as is found in Jn. If Jn is by the foregoing arguments to be taken as primitive and early, we must accordingly set the Gospel in a new hypothesis of what happened in early Christian circles.

Such a hypothesis suggests itself as once from the New Testament writings. For the most obvious fact of early Christianity is the amazing divergence of points of view present in the NT itself. Mark describes the Jesus of wonderful deeds who was crucified and died. Q (if there ever was a single Q) presented Jesus as the teacher, with little concern for his deeds. Paul does not care about Jesus after the flesh at all, either in action or teaching, and knows only an incarnation of a divine potency (he calls it at least once the Spirit) whose victory over death on the cross and in the resurrection was his important contribution. With this other writers agree in principle, such as the authors of Heb and Jas, but each explains the matter in so distinctive a way that it is hard to believe that any one of them had read, or had read as a close guide to his thinking, the writings of any other. Apocalyptic and eschatology take the most varying roles in the different writers until they burst in the Book of Revelation. Some, like Mt and Jas, keep the Jewish legal

---

[61]Bernard, I, p. xciv, points out that Jn's μαθηταί rather than "apostles" seems early; that the way Jn has the disciples address Jesus (Rabbi, and the Lord), and the story of Jesus' baptism are both primitive may be disputed. Enslin, 440, makes exactly the opposite inferences from the story of the baptism. I can see nothing decisive in these either way. The same must be said of Torrey's emphasis upon the statement that there *is*, not *was*, the pool of Bethesda in Jerusalem: see Bacon, *Hellenists*, 125. W.F. Howard, 147, 148, notes that in Jn 1 28, 44; 2 18-20; 7 1-13; 10 40-42, show traces of drawing upon a tradition of Synoptic type, a historical tradition, that is, but one not found in the Synoptic Gospels. He is right also in seeing in Lk 22 27 a reflection of the Johannine foot washing rather than the reverse: cf. 1 Pet 5 5.

point of view (with important modifications, of course). The Johannine group only presents one more, distinctive, approach.

To take all these writings and arrange them in order according to a theory of the development of ideas among early Christians is fascinating, but (I am sure) futile. Most scholars have accepted Colossians and Philippians as Pauline, for example, and accordingly dated them earlier than Mk. Yet they have felt that Jn, which is in no respect more "advanced" than these two letters, must be late.

It is much more promising to look for the basic message of earliest Christianity in the common denominators among all these documents. From this point of view it at once appears that what they all unite in proclaiming is the conception of incarnation, crucifixion, and resurrection, along with the Messianic implication of these. Each of the NT writers uses this as a basis for rationalization, in which he feels amazingly free to construct for himself a theory for what we should call the person and work of Jesus. The most serious divergencies, those between the conservative Jewish group and the hellenizers, are presented to us in Acts and the letters of Paul largely in terms of Paul's problems. But meanwhile what sort of Christianity did the Ethiopian Eunuch take back to Ethiopia? What was the message of Philip or of Barnabas?

The impression the NT chiefly gives is that, stirred by the amazing story of Jesus crucified and risen, each person then, as each generation since has done, saw in this stupendous phenomenon the fulfillment of his hopes. To the eschatologists Jesus was the eschatological Messiah, bound to return to accomplish what his crucifixion had temporarily prevented. To the legists he taught the complete and perfect law. To the priestly minded he became the lamb that was slain, or the perfect and eternal High Priest. To one looking like Paul for a mystic appropriation of the heavenly Law as an escape from bodily compulsion and legalistic positivism, Jesus brought the Law of the Spirit which freed one from the Law of Sin and Death. To one like the author (or authors) of Jn and 1 Jn who wanted the Logos with its Life and Light so that one's personality could blend in the being of God, Jesus offered just that.

All of these quests are demonstrably pre-Christian. Each writer felt salvation as he discovered that Jesus was *It*, the objective of his own spiritual longings, such as he had felt before he was a Christian at all. And each writer confuses us in turn because he does not explain the Logos, or the Spirit-Law, or the Messiah, or the Son of Man, or whatever it is with which he is identifying Jesus. He does not tell what he means by spiritual rebirth, or by justification (to use the traditional word for δικαιοσύνη). Each man assumes that his terms, like his *It*, are familiar to his audience, and that all he needs to do is to announce that Jesus was, or brought to men, their hearts' desires. Not the nature of salvation, but the fact that Jesus saves, is the message of the writers. We must reconstruct with painful difficulty what they meant by that salvation in each case since they assume that the reader has known that long before.

The earliest presentations of the Christian message are precisely the ones with the most unified point of view. Mk and Q are much simpler than Mt and Lk because Mt and Lk try to combine the two earlier Christian messages into one. Paul is early. The Peter of Acts and of Paul's letters is early. The task of later Christianity was to combine all these points of view in the early documents into an inclusive presentation.

From all these considerations Jn seems to me to be a primitive Gospel. Its author had been looking for the Logos in Life and Light, and he found it in the risen Lord.[62] Whether he owed more to a Philonic sort of thinking or to eastern traditions need not concern us here. The point is that he could use an old hymn to Wisdom or Logos (the two are of course identical) for his Prologue, interrupting it with declarations by John the Baptist that Jesus was that Light, precisely because it was with a pre-Christian figure that he was identifying Jesus. He did not scorn Jesus after the flesh as Paul did. He tells a story of his life, and weaves into the story what snatches of Synoptic tradition he has heard or gathered in writing. The crucifixion and resurrection are by far the most important of these. But all is subordinate to the great message that the Life and Light of God was brought to men in the person of Jesus.

To such a conclusion he might early have come in one of the Hellenistic synagogues of Jerusalem itself, or in Samaria, after the

---

[62] At this point the evidence for the pre-Christian original of Jn's Logos should be reviewed, but that would need a volume, not a digression. I may say in passing that in the latest and best treatment of the subject, that of Bultmann in his new commentary already cited, especially his comments on the Prologue, the author speaks even more vaguely than in his earlier works (such as his "Die religionsgesch. Hintergrund des Prol. z. Johannes-Evang.," *Eucharisterion* dedicated to H. Gunkel, 1923, II, 3-26; i.e., *Forschung. zur Relig. u. Literat. des A. u. N. Test.*, XIX, ii) of a pre-Christian "Gnosticism" on which the Prologue was based. He has all along recognized that the immediate background of the Prologue must have been a Jewish form of that "Gnosticism," Hellenistic Judaism itself. Yet he not once stops to take Philo himself seriously: indeed he specifically says in the commentary (10, n. 1) that for Jn it is not necessary to do so. Like all the commentators on Jn I have seen he is still content to break Philo's mosaics up into pieces and use the isolated tesserae to match equally fragmentary bits in the pattern of Jn. The history of intellectual design can never be reconstructed by such a methodology.

Hellenistic Christians had been dispersed in the persecution first led by Paul, or in Antioch, or in Ephesus (if you will), or in Alexandria. The strongly Semitic tone of the work, which even those admit who deny an Aramaic original, and the special feeling for Palestinian topography, make me incline to put the origin in Palestine, or to make the author a Palestinian Jew in exile.[63] That seems to me relatively unimportant. What is important is whether or not the thesis of this essay is true: that Jn represents a primitive attempt to explain Jesus' person and work by seeing in him a fulfillment of pre-Christian dreams of the Logos-Life-Light of God made available to men.

---

[63]Since all we know of the Jews of the Diaspora suggests that they had no Semitic linguisitic tradition at all. It is in stressing the Jewish (Hellenistic Jewish) origin of Jn that I must differ from what seems to be the point of view of Gardner-Smith who appears (on p. 93, 94) to suppose that Jn was written in a place like Athens, Ephesus, or Alexandria, where "a higher education prevailed," that is through direct contact with pagan philosophy.

4

Professor Goodenough and the Fourth Gospel

Robert P. Casey, *Journal of Biblical Literature* 64 (1945): 535-542
Some years ago Professor Goodenough complained of the sluggishness of New Testament scholarship and declared that little advance need be expected in this field until critics turned their attention to the relations of early Christianity and Hellenistic Judaism (*JBL* 62 [1943] xi). In his recent provocative article ("John a Primitive Gospel," *JBL* 64 [1945] 145-182) he has evidently hoped to stimulate gospel criticism to a more lively pace and to illustrate his point of the importance of Hellenistic Judaism in the study of the Gospels.

Others will no doubt be moved to reply to Professor Goodenough's main thesis. The point of this note is to comment less on his conclusion than on the methods by which he reaches it and their implications for Johannine criticism.

As a preliminary several curious errors of fact must be noted: a. The statement that "Eusebius concludes from" Papias' mention of two Johns "that it was the second or 'Presbyter' John who wrote the Gospel," (p. 31 above) is a slip. Eusebius (*H.E.* 3, 39.5) concludes, from the mention of two Johns by Papias, that the Elder mentioned with Aristion wrote the Apocalypse; but like all other early Christian writers – except the Alogi – he had no doubt that John the son of Zebedee wrote the Fourth Gospel. b. The statement that "no certain acquaintance with the Gospels as a whole can be demonstrated until the latter part of the second century" (p. 32 above) should hardly be made with such confidence in view of the fragment of Johannine text published by C.H.

Roberts in 1935 and the Unknown Gospel with its evident dependence on John, both on papyri ascribed on paleographical grounds to the first half of the second century. Allowing a reasonable length of time for the circulation of John before its use in the Unknown Gospel it appears that the external evidence for John is not later than the early years of the second century. c. The remark that "nothing is said (in John) which goes beyond the eucharistic doctrine of Paul" (p. 45 above) is, to say the least, surprising. Paul is a believer in the Real Presence and in the Sacrifice of the Mass but he does not draw out the implications of the sacrament for the doctrine of immortality in the way John does.

Goodenough's main argument is that John need not have known the Synoptics and could have derived the elements which his Gospel has in common with them either from oral traditions or from lost documents with which the Synoptic writers were also acquainted. He has selected some examples of supposed dependence on Mk and has argued that the resemblances between Mk and Jn can be otherwise explained. It should be pointed out that: a. the argument for the literary dependence of Jn upon the Synoptics is cumulative; b. only if *all* the instances of Jn's supposed dependence rest upon oral traditions or lost documents is it possible to date Jn earlier than Mt Mk Lk; and c. as is well known, the evidence of Jn's dependence on Lk is more cogent than that for Mk, though I have no doubt myself that Jn was acquainted with Mk as well.

A word should be said about the magic of oral tradition and lost documents the charm of which has darkened the counsels of New Testament scholars for a generation.

An oral tradition which influences documents in an identical way, so that peculiar words and phrases and turns of style are reproduced, is already – in a sense – a text. It does not greatly matter whether it has been written down or not, if its verbal form has been fixed exactly and it is constantly repeated. A few such verbally fixed anecdotes might be assumed under the circumstances obtaining in early Christianity, although the variants in so well-known and important a story as that of the Last Supper should be a warning. The existence of so large a body as the background of so narrow a field of literature as the Gospels is wholly unprecedented. Neither the early growth of Buddhist or Mohammedan tradition, nor the anecdotes about Greek philosophers and the logia attributed to Jesus in papyrus texts, offer convincing parallels. To substitute the independent impact of oral traditions on our Gospels for the documentary hypothesis as an explanation of the close similarities between them, and to ignore the evidence of editorial procedure and evolution transforming Mk into Mt and Lk, and all three into Jn is the substitution of complexity for simplicity as the mark of truth.

The hypothesis of a multiplicity of lost documents interplaying with oral traditions is hardly more satisfactory. No one will deny that some early oral traditions and documents have not reached us in their original form or have been utterly lost. It should however be a critical axiom to ask when it is necessary to explain the known evidence by an internal analysis of its contents and when by the hypothesis of lost originals. Lost originals also have authors, and by assuming their existence we merely push the problem one stage farther back, where less rigor in critical method is required. The supposed fly-sheets on which so many of the *Formgeschichtler's* fragments are supposed to have been recorded are thought to have been used for liturgical purposes or as sermon illustrations but with the possible exceptions of The Lord's Prayer, Mt 28:19, and 1 Cor 11:23-26, there are no texts which can be properly described as liturgical and no early Christian preacher gives evidence of having anticipated the modern procedure of keeping note books and card-catalogues for topical homiletic illustrations. The addresses in Acts make no use of such illustrations, nor does II Clement (if it be a homily). Clement of Alexandria's *Quis dives salvetur* depends on the gospel text for its main illustrations and that is the fashion of the great preachers of the fourth century and after. There is no evidence that the apocryphal logia and secular Greek anecdotes achieved fixed literary form except when they were included in larger collections. We do not know the literary background of the logia. Some, if not all, are quotations from larger works, like the Unknown Gospel. The moving story of the woman taken in adultery is not an artless tradition but a miniature work of art, a conscious re-working of the theme of Lk 7:36 which in turn is a deliberate modification of Mk 14:3 ff. There is no certainty that the scribe who inserted it in Jn did not take it from a book now lost. In contrast to those pieces, it is quite puzzling that anyone should have written out the material found in Mk 8:1-38 and left it in the air.

Goodenough's treatment of the anointing of Jesus is an instructive example of what the appeal to lost sources accomplishes and what it overlooks. The materials of the story are the same in all four forms: Mk 14:3-9; Mt 26:6-13; Lk 7:36-50; Jn 12:1-8; only the details differ. Verbal similarities show that the four versions are related to each other either through literary dependence or through the influence of an outside source having a fixed literary form. Goodenough argues for the latter and writes, "To account for the similarities it is usually supposed that the author of Jn had both Mk and Lk before him, or at least had the story as told in those Gospels thoroughly in his mind, and that he put together details from each as he wished. Such a suggestion is based upon the presupposition that we are dealing primarily with documents,

– an idea which it is one of the real contributions of Form Criticism to have refuted. We now see that we are dealing primarily not with documents but with individual pericopes (I refuse to use the pedantic Greek plural), each of which had its own vicissitudes of transmission. That the author of Jn wrote this story with Mk and Lk before him, and took one phrase from one, another from the other, is of all reconstructions the most artificial. The phenomena of agreements and disagreements in the stories are those of oral transmission, not of documentary dependence at all" (page 35 above). The assumption of an oral transmission which cannot be reconstructed, however, explains the same phenomena as the assumption of a literary dependence which can be reconstructed. There is, furthermore, an evolution of thought and literary manner in the transmission of the tale which inheres in the editorial aims of Mt, Lk, and Jn; and this the hypothesis of oral transmission ignores.

The simplest form of Mk's and the historical situation it presents is most plausible. The drama in the Markan account derives from the tension between: a. the woman's generosity; b. the disciples' feeling that such valuable merchandise should have been contributed to their common poor fund; and c. the pathos of Jesus' approaching death which gave to this woman's gesture its special point and overruled the disciples' otherwise legitimate objection. All this moves easily and naturally in the historical sitting of Jesus' last days with his close friends. In Luke the point of the story is different. The meal is in a Pharisee's house. The drama arises from the fact that the woman is a sinner, yet is allowed access to the Lord. The objection is the same as that of the Pharisees in Mk that Jesus ate with publicans and sinners. Jesus justifies her action on the more general and theologically more advanced ground that devotion to him cancels her sinfulness. John, whose narrative displays stylistic characteristics of both the Markan and the Lukan stories, changes the scene to Lazarus' house. The drama lies in the hypocrisy of Judas Iscariot who raises the objection made by the disciples in Mark but unlike them for discreditable reasons. He was a thief, pilfered the common purse and Jesus with his supernatural clairvoyance, characteristic of the Johannine Christ, sees through his deceit and reproaches him with an allusion to his own burial – the occasion for which is to be Judas' betrayal. Here there is not merely difference but evolution in the development of the narrative. It is of course possible to argue that this evolution took place in oral tradition or in documents now lost before it was reflected in the Gospels we possess, but the supposition is wholly gratuitous and serves no critical end.

Another example of arbitrary criticism is found in Goodenough's statement that the verbal similarities between Mk and Jn in the story of Jesus' crossing the lake "are not so many that good oral transmission could not have produced them, but the immediate succession of the stories make an ordinary oral background for the two by far the least likely guess" (page 38 above). The only meaning which I can extract from this observation is that whenever an early Christian was prompted to tell the story of the feeding, he was by some internal compulsion led at the same time to add that of the walking over the sea. The likelihood of this is approximately the same as that an American who tells the story of George Washington and the cherry tree will naturally conclude with an account of the crossing of the Delaware. In Jn the connection between the two miracles is forced and their association is one of the least felicitous instances of Johannine compilation. It is entirely obscure why this infelicity – which in an author of a book may be excused on the ground that he has so much material to dispose of – should be regarded as a normal mental habit of early Christian storytellers or even preachers.

Goodenough derives the early eucharistic tradition from "Jewish mystic thought" (page 53 above). The eucharist began as a Messianic meal in which the Jews "partook of the Messiah in the form of fish, bread, and wine, in anticipation of his coming and of the great Messianic banquet of the future life" (page 51 above). Early Christians continued this practice and "found themselves partaking of Jesus Christ in the blessed elements, and the practice cried out for a definitely Christian justification, arising from an act or command of Jesus himself. Two stories thus arose. The first story would appear to be that given in Jn" (page 51 above). The other is Paul's (I Cor 11) with its variants in the Synoptics.

Goodenough does not seem to have considered this question: why did the Christians in this early meal find themselves "partaking of Jesus Christ in blessed elements"? What made the elements "blessed" and the communicants think they were "partaking"? In the evidence we possess there is development of thought, feeling, and practice in the texts: Mk 14:12 ff.; Mt 26:17 ff.; Acts 2:46; I Cor 11:23 ff.; Lk 22:7 ff.

The Markan accounts tells what happened at the Last Supper, Acts suggest that the meaning of it persisted and reasserted itself powerfully in the gatherings at Jerusalem. In I Cor reminiscence has been transformed into custom, the meal emerges as a sacrament, and the command to repeat has been added. The position of Luke in the series is not clear and his account is mixed but its elements are plain enough. The editorial procedure behind it can be seen, though it is not Luke at his best. Subsequently other meals at which Jesus was present in fact, or thought to have been, either in the flesh, as in the miraculous feedings, or after the Resurrection as in the story of Emmaus, attracted suggestions of sacramental significance. This implicit inclination to give to other meals a eucharistic meaning stems from the devotional life of early Christianity and achieves a subtle literary expression in the nuances of the stories of the feedings and of Emmaus. It is one thing to read a eucharistic significance between the lines of such accounts; it is quite a different matter to confuse the Markan account which reads like history with the stories of other meals which read like history transformed by piety and theological *Tendenz*. It is the story of the Last Supper which created the sacramental significance sensed in the other stories. Apart from such oddities as Goodenough's view that the early Christians communicated in fish as well as bread and wine, his theory offers no reason why Christians should have "found themselves partaking of Jesus Christ in blessed elements" and then invented the stories of the feedings and the Last Supper.

It cannot escape the critic who still believes that documents are not always wrong, that with Goodenough's method the whole earliest stage of Christianity disappears in a fog of vain conjecture. Where documents appear most plausible they must be most suspect. Where they appear primitive, this must be due to the refashioning of less plausible material. This is the real point of his article. The attempt to make Jn early and to disprove its literary dependence on the Synoptics is a means of disproving the dependence of the Pauline and Johannine phases of Christianity on the phase reflected in the Synoptics. The error, made already by Celsus and Porphyry, consists in being unable to see how so much could emerge from so little. The currents of Jewish apocalyptic and of Gentile mysticism crossed in the environment of early Christianity but the new religion emerged in the peculiar circumstances of Jesus' career, his association with his disciples, and the small beginnings in Jerusalem. It is a fundamental error to submerge these crucial facts in the larger movements of history. Tendencies of speculation, drifts of sentiment, and the embellishment of facts now lost are in Goodenough's mind the real Christian origins. He writes, "The impression the NT chiefly gives is that, stirred by the amazing story of Jesus crucified and risen, each person then, as each generation since has done, saw in this stupendous phenomenon the fulfillment of his hopes" (page 57 above). This is the language of religion but in the cold light of critical day the question arises, What made the story of Jesus crucified and risen "amazing" and "stupendous"? The answer given in the documents we possess is precisely the contrast between the Synoptic story, and the Pauline and Johannine insight into its meaning. Paul, whose sensitiveness at not having known Jesus in the flesh is apparent, nevertheless wrote to the Corinthians: "Whereas the Jews seek signs and the Greeks pursue wisdom, we for our part proclaim a crucified Messiah, an offence to the Jews and folly to the Gentiles, but to those who have been called, a Messiah who is God's power and God's wisdom."

5

A Reply

Erwin R. Goodenough, *Journal of Biblical Literature* 64 (1945): 543-544
The Editor, with Casey's hearty approval, has offered to let me reply to this critique of my article, but what I have to say will take little space. The three "errors of fact" need no comment, and all that really is left is the basic issue of methodology. The question is whether we are to stick exclusively to the old "documentary" procedure, or go the slight distance I do in form criticism.

Just what he means by the "documentary theory" Casey does not say, but his remarks imply that he thinks Mk, and presumably Q, sprang fully formed from their author's minds with no developments of consequence between the events themselves and their being recounted in one of these documents. The authors of Lk and Mt seem to have used Mk and Q as documents, plus a lot more material which likewise was without history between the events recorded and their inclusion in these new Gospels. Jn was similarly the product of documents plus a man making a new document, with similar access, apparently, to material which had existed *in vacuo* until he put it into his gospel. Casey admits the existence, to be sure, of oral traditions and of some lost documents. But these had authors he says, and so we are moving from the known documents to the unknown when we go back to them from the gospels and authors we already have. Casey would explain the known by the known and not get into the perplexity of this unknown background, this "fog of unverifiable conjecture." He finds it "simpler" to do this than to try to peer into the forever lost vicissitudes of oral tradition. To me that is the simplicity of solving an equation by ignoring one of its variables. That the authors of Lk and Mt had no knowledge of the events they tell except as they had them in Mk, had never heard of the feeding of the five thousand, for example, or the anointing of Jesus until they read the stories in Mk; or that, if they had heard such stories, they ignored what they had heard completely in editing Mk; this seems a very simple theory indeed.

I see, however, nothing in the issue to debate. The reader must conclude for himself whether by trying the impossible – the reconstruction of the tradition – he will supplement (not replace) the great achievements of documentary criticism, or will prefer to go on with Casey trying (with equal lack of proof) to explain the known by the known. Comparison of my reconstruction of the story of the anointing with Casey's is illuminating.

A few details are worth noting. In the paragraph where he quotes a sentence from me and then goes on to make whimsical parallels about oral traditions of George Washington he has not read me carefully. In the quotation itself I deny that oral tradition would account for the juxtaposition of the stories of the feeding and the crossing of the lake. In addition, at the bottom of the same page and over on the next (pages 39-40 above) I say that a written source is necessary, but is more likely to have been a document on which both Mk and Jn drew than a case of Jn's borrowing from Mk. I may be right or wrong here, but Casey is here rebutting something I myself specifically deny.

My section on the eucharist is, I admit, most unsatisfactory. Casey says I have not "considered this question: why did the Christians in this early meal find themselves 'partaking of Jesus Christ in the blessed elements.'? What made the elements 'blessed'," Casey asks, "and the communicants think they were 'partaking'?" This remark would have been quite justified if Casey had said I had not "answered" the question rather than not "considered" it. The answer is to be found in traces of Jewish sacramental and Messianic meals whose evidence I have long been considering, but said in this article I should have to present at greater length elsewhere. I can here only assure Casey that I am indeed "considering" it.

6

The Inspiration of New Testament Research

1952

In his last report as editor of JBL, Goodenough commented on what he saw as the sorry state of New Testament scholarship. His words there drew many responses; indeed, Robert Casey began his essay reprinted here (no. 4 above) with a reference to what Goodenough had written.

That report was printed in JBL 62 (1943) x-xi. For a more complete perspective, the other reports should also be reviewed. The first four are printed as reports of the Corresponding Secretary in JBL 55 (1936) xx, 56 (1937) xx, 57 (1938) xxi-xxiii, 58 (1939) xviii-xix. The others were presented as reports of the Editor and were printed in JBL 59 (1940) xviii, 60 (1941) xiv and 61 (1942) xiv-xv. Each is about the volume of JBL issued in the previous year. Together they reveal Goodenough's great concern for the viability of the journal and the health of the field. Behind his criticisms then is something professional and something personal. Both emphases appear in the following Presidential Address.

The professional or methodological comments are familiar by now: to understand the New Testament as it originated we must first grasp the world into which it came, and the religious aspirations of the gentiles and Jews who lived in that world. Those who do this properly will discover that the various positions taken within the New Testament are not usually the result of development within Christianity in its first decades,

71

but rather the reflection of and the response to pre-Christian religion and philosophy, especially as carried by hellenistic Judaism.

The personal position is just as clear. The address shows why Goodenough began to study the Bible, where that initial inspiration was lost, and how it might be rekindled again in a new, more global form. (See also Eccles 1985:117-18.)

Erwin R. Goodenough, *Journal of Biblical Literature* 71 (1952): 19[*]

In my final report as Editor of our *Journal* in 1942, a report printed in 1943, I made a brief statement from which I have had many comments: I shall take this opportunity to return to it and discuss it at greater length. I said at that time that one of the difficulties in editing the *Journal* was that not only in America, but the world over, research in the field of the New Testament had sunk to a nadir, so much so that even the conducting in the *Journal* of a regular section for reviews of works on the New Testament forced one often to discuss books which were really not worth much notice. This I did not elaborate, and need not do so now in the sense of decrying what is being done. I may assume that you will agree with me that the appendix to Schweitzer's *Quest of the Historical Jesus* which brought it up to date could mention few books of such creative importance as those he originally had before him. Schweitzer had recounted the works of giants whose thought profoundly affected the course of civilization: it can be simply said that New Testament scholarship has no such importance for our day. Sometimes we seem to me to be children playing at war on historic battlefields. I speak, of course, of historical criticism, what used to be called higher criticism. The field of lower criticism, the collecting of manuscripts and the approach to an ideal presentation of the Greek text, was never so systematically cultivated as now. Yet speaking as a higher critic I may seem supercilious (I do not remotely intend to seem so) when I say that I doubt if the course of civilization will be appreciably changed by the production of the absolutely ideal New Testament text, or indeed would be deeply affected by the discovery of the complete set of New Testament autographs. I should imagine that if we had Paul's letter to the Romans in its original form the problem of what he meant to say in it would be just about what it is now when we read it in Nestle's text. And the question of the relevance for modern man of whatever Paul may have said would certainly be exactly what

---

[*]The Presidential Address delivered at the annual meeting of the Society of Biblical Literature and Exegesis on December 28, 1951, at the Union Theological Seminary in New York City.

it is. It was a feeling that it made a profound difference to us what Paul and Jesus said that brought us oldsters to our teachers, and still more that brought them to their teachers. And this was the inspiration of the older, the creative, period in New Testament study, the hope that one might find out things in such study that really mattered, now and always, for mankind. Few young men in these days want to become students in the biblical field (and let the Old Testament scholars not hear me too complacently), for somehow there are few young men who feel that biblical scholarship has much that is creative to give them. I do not decry the young, they still have eager pressure to find creative truth, but it is not at our doors but at the doors of natural scientists, psychologists, sociologists, anthropologists and theologians that they are knocking. This, rather than my offhand reference to the nadir is what I want to discuss with you.

The young men are right: we have at the moment as a group no such vital and creative wares to offer as men in other fields. The pressure of contemporary problems is too great for it to matter much whether Q was in one piece, or was a series of disconnected leaves, pericopes, some of which Luke and Matthew had in common, while each had leaves unknown to the other; or whether there ever was a Q at all or not. Perhaps one of my students was right when he said on an examination that Q was Luke's German source. Of course I should be enormously proud to be able to announce a definitive solution of that problem: but I doubt if many people would change their way of living as a result of such an announcement, while what psychologists, sociologists, and theologians are saying is changing people's lives. Does this mean that we are, as a group, doomed to be superseded like the old herbalists? Frankly I think it does mean that if we propose to continue on the old lines of study, asking the questions, thinking in the framework, set in the nineteenth century. We cannot be alchemists endlessly repeating the same experiments. For a man's scholarship is vital only when it is part of his total vitality. The only excuse for biblical scholarship, like all scholarship, is that it promises to tell men, directly or indirectly, something important for their way of life.

The hope in all biblical study of the past was that by it man would go beyond speculation and ignorance into revelation, into the security of final and unquestioned knowledge of life's foundation, meaning and destiny. Before the eighteenth century, and often still today, biblical study was essentially the study of God's Word to men. This study was not, and still is not, what we now call "critical" study at all. It was and is study of a document, or series of documents, antecedently declared to be beyond human criticism, documents composed by the one omniscient Mind, given men, verbally, infinitesimally, indisputably, to be the guide and norm of all their thinking, the basis of their security. Study of such documents is essentially a matter of reverent comprehension. As a young man when I belonged to this group myself I was counselled, as many of you have been, that the best way to read the Bible was to read it when on my knees, and this, whether the actual physical knees or not, describes the attitude of such readers from Thomas Aquinas, Thomas à Kempis, Luther, Calvin, and Wesley to the devout fundamentalists, Catholic and Protestant, of our own day. Probably there are a number in this room who still read their Bibles in this way. I have no word of reproach, no slight innuendo, to apply to such biblical reading. That as you all know I no longer do so myself has not made me forget the values of such reading. I now imply no longer believe that the books of the Bible were any such direct product of omniscient composition, and with that most of you, perhaps like me somewhat to your sorrow, will agree.

In the eighteenth century the new critical spirit which was to produce the modern age of science turned itself to the Bible but only to reject the Bible, mock it, in that youthful exuberance which was the basic inspiration of the Enlightenment. Men of that time, Voltaire and Tom Paine, for example, read to us like cocky sophomores in what they say about Christianity and the Bible. They could do nothing else, I suppose. Critical study of the Bible was not born, and they faced a world in which it was militantly asserted that their new astronomy was discredited by the biblical statement that Joshua had stopped and then started the revolution of the earth, or of the sun round the earth. The new science was discarding all authorities, such as Galen and Ptolemy, discarding the very concept of an authority; certainly the new scientists could not be confined to the scientific knowledge of the biblical writers. The result was impatient, often shallow, revolt.

Few now want to continue that old fight, or feel that the value of the Bible is essentially negated, or even affected, by the fact that we look elsewhere for our knowledge of natural science. Here, however, is where our immediate ancestry as a scholarly group began. For in the late eighteenth century, much more through the nineteenth century, men took up the challenge of the historical criticism of the Bible. Believing in the divine origin of their Bibles, and at the same time in the new methods of historical criticism which Valla had so brilliantly demonstrated, they felt that when the irrelevancies of temporal contingencies had been removed the Bible would seem all the more valuable: only the divine metal would be left when the ore was purified. For the early scholars of Old and New Testament believed at the same time in the new science of history, if I may call it that, and in the old truth. They heartily believed that a true understanding of the

Old Testament would show God working through man to bring him out of ignorance to the light of truth: that if details showed the fallibility of the human instruments, the totality showed the infallibility of the divine plan of relevation. Biblical criticism was essentially inspired throughout the nineteenth and early twentieth centuries by the conviction that better critical scrutiny would bring deeper revelation of what lay behind the human writers in the divine Mind itself, deeper certainties. In New Testament study, especially, the motive was very clear. It was splendidly epitomized in the English title to Schweitzer's classic, *The Quest of the Historical Jesus.* For relaxation, conscious or unconscious, of the tension between the need for certainty and the belief in historical criticism seemed possible if one could appeal from a fallible record to an infallible, an authoritative, Person behind the record. Once one had found this object of quest, the historical Jesus, it was felt, one could recover the sense of certainty, find it through historical criticism itself. It was this desire which brought me into such studies, and I do not think I am simply projecting my own emotional problems when I say that this seems to have been the driving force from Reimarus to Wrede, to Schweitzer, Harnack, Bacon, Ropes, and now to Bultmann. To limit such a roll call is invidious. All I am saying is that magnificently loyal as these men have all been to their faith in, and the demands of, historical criticism, New Testament criticism has been for a century essentially a means rather than an end, and the end has been the quest of that historical Jesus, in whom men hoped to find the embodiment of their ideals, the basis of their certainty. It has not been the past for its own sake men have sought, or which pupils like us went to their masters to learn: it was that past in which we thought was the eternally present, the true social gospel or whatever was the problem of the day which most concerned us. This statement of motivation, like all statements of motivation, is drastically oversimplified; the motive as described would not account for interest in the Pauline problem, for example, or in apocalytpic. The basic idea I am presenting stands, however: that the drive behind the New Testament scholarship of the past was first a sense of its immediate and contemporary importance; secondly the hope that man would know better how to live in the present if he could understand the secret of early Christianity, because a man would have a base of certainty for his judgments and hopes; and thirdly that the new methods of philology and historical criticism would reveal this secret to him. In terms of these objectives of the generations of scholars just passed, New Testament scholarship has failed. I remember as a young instructor at Yale I once asked my senior, Benjamin Bacon, why he did not write us a life of Jesus. He said that that had been the goal of all his study, and that he intended to do so. But he never wrote it. I suspect that the reason he did not try to do so was that he was quite aware, as most of us here are aware, that a book on the life and teachings of Jesus would be so full of subjective judgments, or so studded with question marks, that it would not be worth the effort. It would be only a confession of failure in our quest for certainty. So we have now come to direct our thoughts and our students to smaller and smaller details of criticism, until we find that the students decide to major in some other field.

The position is on the whole clear. In view of the profound part Christianity still plays in the structure of our society, I see no reason to abandon hope that a better understanding of early Christianity will be of great contemporary importance. But if we are to seem to our generation to be challengingly creative we cannot go on simply with the old philological techniques, asking questions we know now we shall never answer, questions in which society has lost interest. We must begin afresh.

It seems to me first quite obvious that we must not look for the wrong things, for what is not there, in the early records. The problems of social justice in the modern sense, of international relations, labor relations, even of ecclesiastical organization, it is an anachronism to try to solve by New Testament proof texts. Much more direct is the light to be thrown on the whole question of the nature of religion and its place in human life. The fact beyond dispute is that in the teachings of early Christianity people of the ancient world came to see a new light. Their groping uncertainty ended in the crucified and risen Jesus; at first a small group, then the majority of the whole dying Roman civilization turned to the Cross, and this was the only substantial and immediate bequest of the ancient world to the medieval. There was a continuity in architecture and pictorial techniques in the basilica and the mosaics, but classical literature, law, and science had in the West all to be rediscovered by later scholars: only the religion of the last centuries of the Roman world became an important part of the early Middle Ages.

Now for a religion to have any appeal it must seem to answer the questions of the people who accept it. If we are to understand Christianity and its appeal, then, we must understand much more than Christianity: we must comprehend the problems of the ancient world, the sort of questions they were asking.

The study of Paul's letters is an excellent example. For to follow the arguments of Paul, we must understand the mentality of those for whom he wrote the letters quite as much as the mentality of Paul himself, which has been the almost exclusive concern of Pauline scholarship. The "Romans" for whom Paul wrote his greatest single letter were obviously a group of people who knew the LXX intimately, were quite ready to admit the inadequacy of paganism, but stubborn to defend the prerogatives of the Jewish people, and this latter Paul had elaborately to deal with. He had to deal with it in a way which did not challenge his readers' pride in the Jewish law, which had value, he assured them, "much every way"; but he had to lead them out into allegiance to a greater and higher law, the law of the Spirit which had been brought man in Jesus Christ. That is, Paul was writing to Jews in Rome, and asking them to go out from their tribal law to a more universal, unwritten law, the true law of God. Yet he can throughout assume that his readers will understand without definition the existence and nature of this higher unwritten law. The higher law he takes thus for granted is based upon a sharp distinction between flesh and spirit, the perishable and the eternal, the material and immaterial, a contrast essentially Orphic and Platonic. When the writer to the Hebrews assured his audience that only the things which could not be seen by the eyes of the flesh were eternal he assumed the same Platonic axioms. The great contribution of Paul, as of most early Christianity, was essentially this declaration that in the incarnation of God in Jesus Christ Christianity presented men with a bridge over which they could pass from the fleshly to the spiritual. That was not a new claim, we now go on to learn, but precisely the thing which men had been seeking in their idols, in their divine kings, their sacred enclosures, their initiations, their amulets, for by all of these means they had hoped to find the divine, the immaterial, in the only form they could imagine experiencing it, in the material itself. So the message of early Christianity was not a new philosophy of the immaterial versus the material, but the declaration that this old search for the spiritual in the material had been ended. For Christians declared that in Jesus Christ that immaterial reality which was alone real in pagan history, σάρξ ἐγένετο, had become flesh, material, available, and that through this miracle man had the bridge he sought, so that he could pass on through Christ from matter to spirit, from death to life. All of this philosophy is assumed in the writings of Paul. He simply denies that Judaism and paganism have met this need for the immaterial. He asserts that the incarnation of the Spirit-Law in the Letter of the Mosaic Code was ultimately as inadequate, as fallacious, as the claims of pagans to find it in their idols, for both were dead, the letter as dead as marble. Only in the incarnation of Christ, he boasts, as underscored by the Resurrection, was the incarnation a *living* embodiment, and hence powerful to save men. This new claim the Roman world finally accepted as true, and, in the ritual of the Church, or in the Christian Neoplatonism of the fourth to the

seventh century, became the basis of hope and certainty in the chaos of
a crashing civilization. Paul does not explain all this philosophy, I
repeat, he simply assumes it, and his letters are quite unintelligible
without knowing that this is what his readers were looking for, and
what his words about Christ meant to them.

Again he writes passionately about the fulfillment of this hope,
the personal experience of its realization, as being δικαιοσύνη, a new
regimentation of man within himself, whereby the mind can rule the
flesh. He never stops to say that this is what he means by δικαιοσύνη,
but assumes that this is what the word means to his readers. That is,
again he is assuming the Platonic-Pythagorean concept that the mind
is or should be a charioteer ruling the horses, or a king ruling the bodily
state, and that no man can have inner peace, harmony, what this
school called δικαιοσύνη, when such rulership was not effective. Paul
takes it for granted that the greater objective of the "Romans" for
whom he wrote was this δικαιοσύνη. All he is telling them is that the
higher law, to which the mind looks and by which it can alone rule the
passions, has been made available, not as the law incarnate in the
King, or the Torah, but as the Law of the Spirit incarnate in Christ
Jesus, so that now when we die with Christ we may live as new
creatures in the Law of the Spirit, without further guilt or
condemnation. Paul does not divine δικαιοσύνη; he only tells his
readers it is at last to be achieved in Christ. To not every man in the
ancient world would such δικαιοσύνη have seemed important. Most
men then as now were content with a "rice" religion, one that would
give them prosperity in this life, and security from catastrophe in
death, and they wanted that security with as little fuss as possible.
Paul was writing to a group of highly intelligent, and quite sensitive
people who not only knew and loved their LXX, but who had adopted
the finer distinctions of the more thoughtful pagans, so that they took
it for granted that true religion would mean release from this
"condemnation" of the fleshly by the spiritual within them, release
from their sense of futility in the struggle for a "purer," less fleshly,
life. Paul and Christianity, I repeat, contributed not this philosophy of
life, this sense of need for δικαιοσύνη, but its solution in the risen Jesus.
Paul did not have to send a Professor to Rome to hold a seminar for
those who first read his letter so that they could know what he meant
by δικαιοσύνη: they had known that word, and the desire for the
experience, long before Paul, on the road to Damascus, had found it in
the Christ of that vision. When we come then to reducing the letters to
their human value in terms of the men of the Roman Empire, we find
that we are approaching their universal, timeless, value. For the
δικαιοσύνη which is a state of "no condemnation," of the putting in

order of the whole gamut of man's motives, drives, and desires, begins to sound amazingly like the desire which we now call "adjustment," freedom from "inferiority complex." And we begin to see that if modern man is properly in quest of peace of mind, Christianity gave this to its early adherents in startling measure. We do not then need to begin to read castration complexes and "Oedipus" into the letter to the Romans, but we do see that Paul has in mind an eternal and unchanging element in human problems and aspirations, and can ask ourselves the very pertinent question of what in the old answers and techniques for solving those problems still has validity. I strongly suspect that a teacher of the New Testament who began thus considering the New Testament would lack neither pupils nor publishers.

I have been giving some examples of the sort of light to be thrown on the origin, and with it on the character, of Christianity by a method of approach not at all that of my teachers. The method is first that of intensive study of the thought-ways of the world into which Christianity came, the aspirations, vocabulary, and symbolism, of the pagans and Jews of the first centuries before and after Jesus, and then the fresh turning to early written and graphic Christian documents, as documents addressed to people with such vocabularies and symbolisms. If we study Christianity as the ancients saw it, that is as one religion among many, the one which finally won out because it offered the deepest gratifications, we shall, I am convinced, for the first time be in a position to isolate, and so go on to the second duty, to evaluate the unique contribution of Christianity.

For all our study is aimed, consciously or not, at evaluation. And our age will expect evaluation not only of the religion of the New Testament for the Roman world, though that must come *first*. It will then ask us what good the religion of the New Testament is for the mid-twentieth century. It will demand an answer not in Greco-Roman terms, but in its own vocabulary, will be interested in Christianity in so far as it seems to answer its own antecedent problems and fill its hopes, as Paul showed how Christ brought the δικαιοσύνη the Greeks and Romans wanted. The problem of the value for our generation of the teachings of Jesus, or of Paul, or of the Fourth Gospel, or of the creeds, is one which we historical critics must face if anyone is to do so. We must be able to see the New Testament in its historical setting, read it as it was read by those for whom it was written, with their background, aspirations, and problems clearly in mind. What the New Testament writers said to these people was their message, and it alone. We must then be able to see the universal elements in these ancient problems, and in the solutions the writers of the New Testament offered to them. We can then, and then only, be in a position to restate those ideas intelligibly for our generation. If, in the words of one of my most distinguished predecessors, we can neither "modernize Jesus," nor "archaize ourselves," the relevance and vitality of New Testament study seems at first questionable. It can be no more than antiquarianism until we learn thus to translate the message of the New Testament into modern terms. What is of value to us in the New Testament and what not, can be judged only after such a translation: for interpretation is only extended translation. Modern psychologists, sociologists, anthropologists, as well as popularizers of all sorts, are often only too eager to make these judgments for us. If interpretation is to have any validity, however, it must begin with such an understanding of historical civilization, texts, and symbols as only we historians can hope to supply.

For the study of no period or subject is worth doing if the end is merely factual knowledge. Not the theologians, I believe as an historian, but we historians ourselves, must so understand the past that we can bring its value into the present. Not by turning the clock back, or by stopping it, as authoritarians want to do, can we bring to our generation the values we have found in New Testament study. We can as little do so by denying the validity of the course of man's adventures through time which it is now the style to sneer at as "history." People who talk in this way speak not the general language of our day, but the language of escapists who would evade human responsibilities in the world of empirical reality. New Testament study has tremendous opportunity in this age, if we take the greatest single event in human history, and, by a historical study which uses the new techniques of our age in the way Strauss used those of his age, show in what its greatness consisted, and in what ways it can still consist. To do this we must know the documents of the New Testament, but know also the methods and findings of the history of religion, of psychology, and of many other modern studies. It is a large challenge, to say the least. But only as we try to meet it can we take exegesis from becoming in fact as antiquarian as is the old term itself by which we still call our Society. I trust my original statement may turn into a prophecy, and that the present state of New Testament study may indeed prove a nadir, one from which we rapidly rise to the heights plainly before us.

7

Religious Aspirations

1953
This essay is a schematic, unannotated statement of the religious situation of Late Antiquity; as such, it is valid for more than just the period 284-305, the reign of Diocletian. It is also Goodenough's attempt to demonstrate the relative importance or unimportance of Christianity in that period.

The paper was delivered at a symposium, "The Age of Diocletian," at the Metropolitan Museum of Art in New York City on December 14-16, 1951. The other speakers were Casper J. Kraemer, Jr., of New York University, Eberhard F. Bruck of Harvard University, William L. Westermann and Gilbert Highet of Columbia University, and Rhys Carpenter of Bryn Mawr College. (See also Eccles 1985:171-72.)

Erwin R. Goodenough, *The Age of Diocletian: A Symposium*, 1951 (New York, 1953), pages 37-48

The religious aspirations of the Age of Diocletian cannot be discussed until we agree upon at least a working understanding of the meaning of the term "religion." Today "religion" is usually associated with a formal organization – a church, a synagogue – or a stated formula of belief, along with certain traditional ways of worship recommended by these organizations and beliefs. Most people who accept these traditional institutions, as well as those who reject them, agree at least in restricting the word "religion" to mean acceptance of the institutions and their requirements; so that those who accept are called religious, and those who reject are supposed to reject religion itself.

Historically, psychologically, anthropologically, such a definition is quite useless, as, I believe, it is for understanding the religious impulses in our own civilization. The greatest religious geniuses in our own tradition, for example, began by rejecting in whole or in part the religious institutions about them. Also, men try to distinguish religion from magic and superstition. More liberal minds go so far as to say that the two are obverse and reverse of the same medal, but they fail to see that they themselves have kept religion as the design on the one face, a design which has no inherent relation to the magical design on the other. If one wants to define magic and superstition as the saying of such specific words, the performance of such definite acts or rites, the wearing of such charms or vestments, as will influence the deity, or the great if formless goddess Fortuna, then one must see that this definition describes the practices, the liturgies, of the great mass of followers of any of the so-called higher religions. I can see in many voodoo rites, charms, and amulets, attempts to control the powers or gods in a way I do not admire, but these are obviously the religion of those who use them. When one of the leading specialists in ancient religion says that to follow rules from "fear of offending gods or demons" is on a "superstitious level," he is of course describing the religious motivation of most that was done in the Age of Diocletian, but he comes perilously near to including as superstition any religion in which "the fear of the Lord is the beginning of wisdom."

In contrast to such definitions, it seems to me that man is always trying to get understanding and control of his confusing environment and his equally baffling inner conflicts, and that his various attempts at explanation and control which are not based upon empirical or scientific observation all ultimately fall under faith and religion. Accordingly, in discussing the religious aspirations of the Age of Diocletian, I shall regard as proper matter to be considered any of the ways men took to make themselves secure in the bewildering uncertainties of life and the grim certainty of death. I shall by no means limit the words "religion" and "religious" to the tenets or practices of any one form of cultus.

Both Professor Kraemer and Professor Bruck have spoken of the divine emperor, but they have done so from the point of view of the emperor, and discussed his claim to divinity as a political device. I want, in addition, to emphasize that it was an idiomatic expression of the dreams of the people. In all states of the ancient world the state organization was primarily what we would call a church, in the sense that its purpose was to bring divine order on earth and to offer collective worship. The secular state, which we take so much for granted, is a very modern invention. In the eastern Mediterranean, the original city-states and principalities had, under and after Alexander, all been absorbed into the great monarchies, in which the head of the state as church was the king. This was partially imposed upon the people by royal decree, but, even more, it was a good political device, because it allowed expression of a deep instinct in the people themselves, an instinctive desire to feel that the forces ruling them, whether just or unjust, were divine. God can do to us what we should never endure from men: He can make us ill, take our money, take the lives of our loved ones – even our little children – and it is all right so long as we feel it is His will. So when the state or ruler is divine, not only is the state stronger, but the people are happier. A democracy or a secular state is strong only in times of prosperity, or, even more, as long as the people feel that they are getting justice. There was little of either prosperity or sense of justice among the people whom the Romans conquered in the East. Hence, from the time of Pompey, the eastern subjects thrust divinity upon their Roman conquerors. They could not otherwise have endured them. The Romans naturally capitalized this idea of the divinity of Rome and the emperors and made it the cement of colonial loyalty. The conception of the divine emperor was, however, so foreign to Roman thinking that for many years it had to be disavowed before the Roman Senate.

All resistance to this idea disappeared by the time of Diocletian. Now, everyone admitted that a divine king, and only a divine king, could give true law; and as law came increasingly to be the product not of the Senate but of imperial decree, its sanction had to be the superhuman quality of the person who thus made as well as administered it. The idea was too basic to be displaced even by the victory of Christianity. True, as long as it was expressed in pagan terminology, which made the king himself a god, the Jews and the Christians refused to accept it, with the result that the strongest emperors turned out to be the severest persecutors. The persecutions were a religious war, that is, like most religious wars, a fight over terminology. In banding together to refuse recognition to the divine state and emperor, the Christians were considered by the rulers to be a great political menace, because they appeared to threaten the very foundations of society. The Christians changed, however, when they themselves became rulers, and in all but terminology continued the state religion without a break. The new Christian attitude began just as soon as a Christian, or one who allowed Christians to use their own terminology, became emperor. The great churchman Eusebius wrote an *Address to Constantine* which is as much an address to a divine ruler as are the orations of the pagan Dio Chrysostom. The new Christian distinction was that the king, as a man, could not be personally divine;

his office, however, was divine, and he had come into office by divine will and act. So "The powers that be [that is, rulers] are ordained of God" was the new way of saying the old truth. By it the religious function of the state, that is, the king, to produce right law and collective security continued. When the medievalists later argued whether the king got his power directly from God, or indirectly through the Church; when Shakespeare talked of "the divinity that doth hedge a king"; when Louis XIV and the Stuarts talked of divine right; they were all quite as near apotheosizing the king, in practice and attitude if not in terminology, as were the subjects of Diocletian.

I often feel that the greatest weakness of modern democracy is that it has renounced this dramatic and profound religious sanction for the state. When faced with such revivals of it as Hitler offered, or as Stalin now offers, the democracies seem at first uninspired, flaccid. Indeed, the greatest power we have to fear in the Russian state is the religious fanaticism with which it is regarded by the people. The amazing strength of the British, when administering a great empire, or now when struggling for decent survival, can largely be ascribed to what seems to us the quite incredible stabilizing power of their monarchy. An English doctor told me last summer that it was amazing how, when any crisis arises – a crisis not only of illness or childbirth in the Palace, but of trouble of any kind in the nation or empire – the people will assemble quietly, by the hundreds, sometimes by the thousands, before Buckingham Palace, and simply stand and look for hours toward it. They go away comforted and strengthened. The doctrine of divine nature and right, as doctrine, has been completely disavowed; the popular sense on which this doctrine is based still most actively survives. Do not misunderstand me; we in a democracy like America or Switzerland have other sources of strength. But we cannot ignore the appeal and power of political religion – a divine state and a divine ruler. The tremendous religious conflict of Diocletian's day, the shift to the new Christian terminology, only point up the fact that one of the most important religious drives of the Age of Diocletian expressed itself in this deification of the state as a way to collective security.

There were, however, other aspects of the religious life of the day. In the old days religion had been largely local: a deity or a group of deities were valid within a given region, perhaps at a single spot or shrine, but without power in other regions, where other gods dominated. This religious localism at once expressed the actual insularity of most people of antiquity, and helped to foster it. Civilization in larger units was possible only as these local religious units took their place in a larger religious conception.

The old localism of religion had largely been broken down by the collapse of the city-states and the expansion of the city of Rome. It is frequently pointed out that man turned from the local cults, as of Athena at Athens, to a syncretism, or a mingling, of gods and practices. This peculiar identification of values from various sources was a process especially active in the Age of Diocletian, and to it we shall return. The instinct for localism, however, was never by any means lost to paganism, and it persisted even into the Christian Age, as it still persists. The great mass of local holy places had such importance in late paganism that they were retained in large part by Christianity as the local shrines of saints, the place of some miraculous happening, explained now of course in Christian terms, though often the pagan original can plainly be seen beneath it. One needed a holy object of some sort to make one's field fertile. If later Christians destroyed most of the images of Priapus, or their like, which must have been almost everywhere in antiquity, their places were usually taken by a Christian shrine of some kind in the field. Almost every pagan city had an altar to the Tyche, the Fortuna, of that city, and local sacred grottos, groves, mounds, and mountains were to be found in all countries. These, with a mass of fetishes, were the common objects of religious veneration and security.

The fetishes have by no means been adequately studied. Bonner's magnificent new work, *Amulets*, may break the aloofness with which historians of religion have in general regarded such products of what they call magic and superstition, for Bonner has presented a great collection of them which can at last be studied. They do indeed show rampant syncretism. Symbols and divine figures and names from Syria, Greece, Rome, Egypt – even from Judaism – are mingled with a most confusing freedom. Bonner has demonstrated the particular value of some of these: one device on an amulet was especially good for sciatica, another for intestinal troubles, another for female difficulties, another for problems of the libido. I doubt if any amulet was used exclusively for the goal which the design primarily indicated. All were probably used with a sense that they brought general protection. We do not know the provenience of most of them, but we do know that many were found in graves, and I suspect that most of those now in existence were preserved by having been buried with the persons who had worn them in life. Obviously there is no point in burying a protection from sciatica or diarrhea with a corpse. To be included in graves the amulets presumably would have had some reference to the problems of life after death. They probably had reference to general security also when worn by a living person.

The whole meaning and function of such objects seems still to be inadequately presented. They appear to me to have been a protection from such evils as have been mentioned, or possibly from the evil eye; but also to have served a deeper purpose – what I may perhaps be allowed to call mysticism for the unmystical. The word mysticism may be taken to refer to a religious experience in which the devotee seeks to share in the nature of the divine, to assimilate it to and for himself rather than to pay respect to it at a distance. The amulets obviously often did just that for the wearer, even though he himself would not have been able to say so; and it is in that sense that I call these objects mysticism for the unmystical. One who wears a cross carries with him, as part of himself, some at least of the power of the cross. Similarly, one who wore a Triple Hecate had his powers both of resistance and aggression enhanced by having the Hecate as part of himself.

The worship of the one God of the universe, and the sense that it is this one God who is available to protect and help us personally in life and death, go quite beyond the horizon of the mass of men even today. In Protestant communities, where images, holy relics, sacred medals, the sign of the Cross, and even the idea of the real presence in the Eucharist, have been abolished, one is not prepared for the devotion shown to the specific embodiment of divine power which most people the world over use as their immediate approach to God, and beyond which it is hard to believe many of them ever go. In the world of Diocletian, such objects had practically never been challenged, and almost everyone seems to have had some direct representation, some object of power, on his person or in his house.

Historians of art like to treat the wall decorations still miraculously preserved in Pompeii, or the mosaic floors of Italy or North Africa, as purely decorative, and to discuss them only for their morphological importance, their place in the history of art forms. That they are decorative and have a morphological history is obvious; but that they are a beautiful presentation of religious motifs is just as obvious, and it is hard for me to believe that they lost their religious value as they became beautiful. They were the ancient concomitants of what are now called "holy pictures," and presumably, besides decorating the room, they brought divinity into the house in an intimate, palpable form, and gave protection to those within.

As a Protestant, I may be permitted to remark that the Protestant destruction of all this side of religion may have removed sources of corruption, but it has deeply impoverished religion for most of us. The pagan of Diocletian's Age called the images on his amulets by different names from those given often to the same images of later Christians, but many of the pagan amulets and figures continued under their new names, and some are in use today.

So far I have not spoken of any of the aspects of religion that most of you had thought would occupy all my attention. Religion in our minds is concerned not only with safety in this life, but with assurance of a future life of happiness. To our way of thinking, the pagan had in early times been oddly unconcerned about what happened to him after death. It is true that at least as early as Plato religion had opened up what I may call the other-worldly dimension, and in Orphism (a vague term) and probably even in the religion of Dionysus, man had found that the chief value of religion was its promise of a happy future in another world. We cannot trace exactly the growth of this idea, but as the Greeks became world citizens under the successors of Alexander, and then as the people of the East, after centuries of calamitous attrition, increasingly despaired of getting the rewards of virtue in this life, more and more their religions took the form of what we now call "mystery religions" – religions having rites by which a man could so be made to share in divine life that he took on the special prerogative of divinity, of immortality. With immortal happiness before him, he could endure the cruelty of this life.

The distinctive idea in all these mystery religions is that while the gods of the other religions were serene and happy, the gods of the mysteries suffered terrible pain. They had been torn to pieces by wild boars, or by enemy gods, or by women; and their consorts, their wives or divine mistresses, had each become the *mater dolorosa*. Largely by her loving devotion, the dead one had been restored to a life now completely heavenly. The walls or gates of Hades, the land of death, had been stormed, and, in Paul's phrase, "Death was swallowed up in victory."

There is no time for, or point in, trying to review the various local myths of Egypt, Syria, Asia Minor, Persia, and Greece which were made the basis of mystery religions by having been given this interpretation – by having had a god or goddess with some such adventure turned into a savior with whom one could be so identified that one could hope for immortality. Each myth, each god, produced a special organization, a little priesthood, with its own cult practices. The most important of these practices was what was called the "initiation" of the person adopting the religion, his induction into its secret teachings and passwords, and his taking the place of the god in some sort of pantomime. Just how this was done we are in almost complete ignorance, for each mystery religion was a secret society, and there were none to blab the secrets – at least to us. The mystic philosophy, the sacred myth, could be told, but the rites by which one got the benefit of the divine suffering were kept entirely secret. Early Christianity took over this pattern, and apparently still into the period of Diocletian the priests cleared the churches and let no one but those in full membership remain to see their central act of appropriating the divine suffering, that is, the consecration of the Eucharist, and its communion. Christians called themselves initiates into the true mystery.

Much as these organizations differed in the god and goddess they worshipped, in the form of myth they told about the divine suffering, each recognized the value of the other, and one who could afford to do so was initiated into several of them. The culmination, at least in some, came when the initiate put on the robe of the god, and so became the god. Phrases in Christian usage, such as "Put on the whole armor of Christ," or "For me to live is Christ," express in terms familiar to us what Apulius describes as his emotion when he put on the garment of Osiris. For those initiates death had indeed lost its sting.

Many people joined more than one of these organizations, because it was the very spirit of the age to feel that the specific god was never the universal, the true, God, and that all were striving in their various ways to each the same goal. Some were prompted by lower motivation, like a pupil of mine who returned from terrible service in the Pacific Islands with a medal of St. Christopher and a silver horseshoe on his identification bracelet: he said he wanted to be safe both ways. Many of those who joined several of the mysteries did so on this same level of religious life. The more intelligent, however, went into more genuine syncretism, if I may return to that word. Apulius prayed to Isis by a host of names from a wide variety of sources; Plutarch wrote his treatise on Isis and Osiris to show that the myths behind the mysteries of Dionysus, Osiris, and the Persian God all implied the same basic philosophy, had the same objective and the same object of worship. One of the commonest forms of address to God was to call him the "Many-named," by which they saved themselves the bother of listing all the names from various pantheons.

More important for the history of art, though each mystery kept its original rites and names and myths, there grew up a common language of artistic symbols which all mystic religions adopted and which is still largely the symbolic vocabulary of our religious devotion. The most obvious is the crown of victory which had swallowed up death. The crown could be shown as being offered to a man by the goddess Victory, or, in later Christianity, she might be called an angel; but that same figure with the crown, or the crown by itself, apparently meant, in many pagan religions, the mystic triumph over death. It still has this meaning when we carve it on our tombstones or public memorials for the war dead, or when we take wreaths to the funerals or graves of our loved ones. The wreath or its equivalent, the palm branch, could also be brought by a cupid, the symbol of God's love, when it was felt that it was the love of God that accomplished the victory. Another symbol, the cup of Dionysus, or his bunch of grapes, could be found on a late Egyptian mummy or among Christian symbols. Men would carve a vine with birds in it, originally the doves of Aphrodite, now become generally the representation of our love which abides in the vine. The shall of Aphrodite was made the background of the portraits of the deceased to show that they were born again in the new life of God, that they were immortal, as we still recognize the symbolism of a shell in a niche for a statue.

The vocabulary of symbols was large: the eagle; Pegasus the winged horse; the ladder; the lion; the Medusa head, now become the benevolent solar head; the fertile but fleeing rabbit; a domestic or harmless animal being torn by wolves or a lion; the rosette, elaborate or in the simple form of the square cross or the swastika; the fish or dolphin; the tree; the peacock; the duck; the rooster; the cornucopia; the mask; the snake; Orpheus taming his animals. These symbols were common to the various religions and could be found in all parts of the Roman Empire on the graves of those who presumably worshipped gods most diverse in names. The symbols became a *lingua franca* current in all religions, and told everywhere the story of a passionate hope for a future life. Probably in each land or religious circle a different myth was told as to why they were important, but behind the multitudinous explanations their essential value was identical. Most of these symbols survived into Christianity. Some, like the wreath, the dove, the shell, the ladder (magnificent on the front of the Abbey at Bath, England), are still current; some have become archaisms, like the fish; some seem to have lost all their symbolic force and to have become merely decorative or quite meaningless, like the rabbit (though the rabbit still lays the eggs, symbol of life, at Easter – itself the symbol of the conquering of death in the victory of Christ's resurrection).

What I want to convey to you, however, is that this elaborate vocabulary of symbols, if not the product of the late third century, was then in the zenith of its currency and expressed the very genius of the mystery religions. It is no coincidence that as Christianity felt itself to be the true mystery religion it took over this vocabulary for its catacombs, sarcophagi, and churches, to express its hopes of mystic immortality.

Still a higher type of syncretism found expression in the astralism of the late Empire. The sense of helplessness in this life had found from early times one escape in fatalism. The Greek tragedies wrestled with the problem, and Aeschylus came to his magnificent declaration of faith in a universal God who is just, and on the whole kindly, to men. But the Atomists, the Epicureans, and the Stoics alike reflected the popular feeling that the cards are all stacked when a man is born. Even Plato, although he allows a man freedom to choose his life pattern before he is born, considers him then sealed in this pattern by the Fates, so that in the course of life there is little a man can do about it. Such fatalism is one of man's constant attitudes in face of great danger or of unhappiness. Our soldiers in both World Wars took to it instantly with their legend of the numbers on bullets, while the English said: "If you're for it, you're for it." There is real therapy against terror in such fatalism.

Fatalism flourished everywhere in the days of declining Rome, and was elevated into a sort of religious science when it was identified with the newly-entered Oriental lore of the stars. Astralism was a belief which still survives in its Roman form as astrology. It is a belief that man is a part of the great cosmic cycle; that the stars, especially the planets, are ruling forces (or personalities) which control him, so that being born under a certain configuration of the stars imposes upon one an inevitable character and succession of events. This astral determinism had as its center the sun itself, which could be called by any convenient name, but which as it passed through the stations of the Zodiac seemed to furnish the moving power to everything else. This sun god, whom Greek-speaking people called Helios, was indeed equated with so many local deities that he came to have no specific reference, but was the one God whom all religions recognized as behind their particular saviors. So Helios in the Zodiac appears in almost every religious configuration of the period, and was the last god to die in antiquity; or rather, the last to disappear, for die he of course did not.

Sol invictus, the unconquerable Sun, was the god the Neoplatonists were most willing to accept, the god that Julian the Apostate wished to reestablish. It is most interesting that he had so become the symbol for God as such that in the excavations under St. Peter's, as elsewhere, Christ was found depicted as Helios. Helios was often a personal deity, but he was also often superimposed upon, or was considered as himself imposing, the rigid order of determinism. As the implacable and predetermined will and plan of God for each man, determinism survived in Christianity – predestination we usually call it – the term of Paul which was so central to Augustine and later to Protestants. If Christianity dropped the astral concomitants of that determinism as being too essentially mechanistic or polytheistic, the pagan form of that faith still survives in the unconquerable form of astrology.

One step beyond this led into the Neoplatonism, so popular in the day – or perhaps two steps, for there was an intermediate step in what we call Gnosticism. The origin of Gnosticism is quite obscure, as is, indeed, the very meaning of the word. Some define it as an aberration from Christianity, and hence say that it could not possibly have existed before Christianity. Others say that it was at bottom not Christian at all, that the Christian elements are tangential and superimposed, and that it was essentially pre-Christian in paganism. Still others think it arose in such a Hellenized Jewish milieu as that revealed to us by Philo. Essentially it was built upon a late Platonic notion, the one at the back of Philo's mind, and basic to the thinking of all Neoplatonists; so we may stop to say a few words about Neoplatonism before we go back to Gnosticism.

Neoplatonism was an attempt to put into monistic philosophical terms the otherworldliness of which we have been speaking. It used as its own the Orphic-Platonic notion that the life of man is an entombment of the soul, which has fallen from a better existence into his body, and that the goal of life is to rise above material embroilments into the true reality which is completely immaterial. Above the world of matter, Neoplatonists, especially Plotinus, taught, are three worlds: the first the world of Soul, the second of Mind, and third the One. This One or Monad is the one truly existing reality. It radiates out from itself as the sun emits rays which, as they leave the sun, become cooler, more remote, and are always essentially different from the sun in being derivative rather than themselves original and independent existences. On this analogy the first level of radiation is the universal Mind, the second the universal Soul, and then as the lowest level it forms itself into the material world; or, if dualism is allowed to creep in, the rays were thought to meet the great negation, unformed matter, enter into it, give it form, and produce the material world as we know it. In such a world, the business of man is, by contemplation, abstract thinking, prayer, and a life of strict discipline, to dematerialize himself as far as possible, until he can rise from his bodily interests and live so intensely in immaterial thought that he can ultimately discover even the One, the supreme Monad, and find his true self by losing it in the One, who is universal. Here the Age of Diocletian was reproducing that world-wide phenomenon which is called the Perennial Philosophy, in expounding which Aldous Huxley could quote quite interchangeably from the mystics of India, China, Neoplatonism, the Middle Ages, or the pietists of the Reformation. It is too difficult an approach to religion for any but the few in any age or country. It requires of the devotee a great deal of abstract thinking, and the power of so losing himself in the abstraction that, without seeming to become concrete in a personal deity, the abstraction itself becomes the all-absorbing, the me-absorbing, reality. It is a conception, however, of everlasting appeal to a certain type of mind, usually people of deepest spiritual potency, and so it has survived in any number of forms in Christian theology and mysticism.

In a paper of so brief compass the matter must be left without further exposition. I can only add that in working out this philosophy afresh the Age of Diocletian made a contribution to all later European life, East and West, beyond any appraisal.

Gnosticism may be defined as Neoplatonism for the minds which cannot take so abstract a path to the Ultimate. Themselves half way between mystery religions on the one hand, and the Neoplatonic hierarchy of abstractions on the other, the Gnostics had a hierarchy by which they could approach the unapproachable. This hierarchy, however, was not one of abstractions but of divine or semi-divine personalities. Instead of thinking that the One at the top had radiated abstractions, the Gnostics saw the procession from God as a series of begotten pairs of personalities, each begetting the pair beneath, until, in one way or another, the lowest one became the creator of the world. Man here, as in Neoplatonism, had to climb back up the ladder to the One, but man did so by knowing the secret passwords, appropriate in turn at each of the stations. These passwords he learned in initiations which probably much resembled the initiations into the mysteries.

The books these people wrote are practically all lost, and we have had to reconstruct our knowledge of the sects from what the Church Fathers said in their excoriations of them – not the most reliable source of information. That is still all we know about them, but, in a few years, study of the whole subject will be completely changed, for just recently eight or ten full volumes of their works have been discovered in Egyptian papyri. They still must be transcribed from the Coptic papyrus manuscripts, translated, and studied, but they will give us such an understanding of the field as was never before possible. All I can say myself is that the papyri are amazingly well preserved and beautifully legible, for I examined one volume of them myself last winter in Cairo. The church pretty well succeeded in destroying Gnosticism, but it had survivals, we may be very sure, in much of the heresy of the Middle Ages and in the cabala of Judaism.

Indeed all Judaism in this period was in one of its most creative moods. After the destruction of Jerusalem in 70 A.D., a few of the scholars of the day, ordinarily then called Pharisees, obtained permission from the Romans to settle in the coast town of Jamnia and found a school. Later they were allowed a Nasi, a chief to whom considerable legal power was conceded by the Romans, though how much it actually amounted to in practice seems to me quite uncertain. The little group at Jamnia began systematically to codify the laws of Jewish life and greatly to expand them by a system of casuistry essential in the development of all law – that is, raising the question of how a given law would be interpreted in this case or that. Sometimes the cases argued were trivial, and then one had casuistry in its ordinary sense of quibbling; but the rabbis were no more guilty of this than any modern law school, and the method was completely sound. In any case, about twenty-five years before Diocletian began to reign they had produced one of the most remarkable codes in legal literature, the Mishnah; the process of enrichment was in his reign at its very peak, as this code was further elaborated to make the Gemarra, the second chief body of material composing the Talmud. It was to be another century and a half before this second story of the Talmudic structure was completed.

How influential the work of these men was on their own generation is a matter of great doubt. In Babylonia this sort of Judaism became completely dominant, and indeed the standard version of the Talmud was not only finally written in Babylonia, but there for the first time, I believe, became the accepted guide of Jewish life. In this belief, you must understand, I am, as yet, almost alone. The few references to the Nasi and his delegates, the few occasions when a rabbi's decision was of importance for a community in the outposts of scattered Jewry, have been generalized in all Jewish histories into an unquestioned representation that all Jews everywhere in the period of Diocletian, as later in the Middle Ages, were orthodox Jews in the sense that the rabbis were their authoritative guide of life. Since the rabbinic literature was the only literature which later generations of Jews preserved from this period (except for a few scattered mystical works), there seemed no reason to question this conclusion. Rabbinic Judaism was thought to be what G.F. Moore called "normative Judaism," and what Wolfson calls "native Judaism"; and the passion of all Jews who have been what I call "propagating Jews" to conform to Jewish law was supposed to mean a passion to conform to the Talmud, even in those years before the Talmud was written, when it existed largely as the vision and intellectual property of the little group in Jamnia.

Recently a new approach has opened. Though the books written by the Jews in Rome, Alexandria, Carthage, and even in Galilee, were destroyed, archaeology is discovering that the remains of their synagogues and graves have extraordinary things to tell us. For here we find that, far from being an Aramaic-Hebrew-speaking people, they were, in the Age of Diocletian, preponderately or wholly, Greek-speaking in the East (including Palestine), Greek- and Latin-speaking in the West, and they could not have read a line of the Talmud if they had had it. They read their Bible, to which they were completely loyal, in Greek, either in the old Septuagint translation or in the later one by Aquila, with which the rabbis provided them. But the rabbis did not provide them with a Greek Mishnah; the services in the synagogues were conducted in Greek, and in the greater part of the Jewish Dispersion nothing suggests such rabbinic control as orthodox Judaism requires.

The Jewish graves and synagogues tell us much more than this. The Jews were Hellenized not only in language, but, to the complete bewilderment of those who hold to the standard interpretation of Jewish history, they adopted and used with complete freedom what I have described as the symbolic *lingua franca* of pagan mystic hope. Automatically, the list of symbols that I read to you as basic in this *lingua franca* was a list I had long since made up from a study of Jewish remains in this period. Victory crowns a naked young man in a Jewish cemetery in Rome; Helios drives his chariot in the mosaic floor of three synagogues in Palestine; the peacocks of immortality flank the flowing chalice in a synagogue near Tunis; the three nymphs attend the baby Moses in the synagogue at Dura; and, also at Dura, over the holy ark a mystic vine, with Orpheus and his animals in it, rises up to a great king on his throne, the symbol of God in the *lingua franca* and in Jewish Apocalyptic alike.

Debate on the meaning of this phenomenon can hardly be said to have begun. I doubt, when the dust settles, that scholars will feel they can come to any conclusion but that the Jews adopted the *lingua franca* because they believed Judaism also was essentially a mystery in the sense that it too promised man victory over death through its law, and especially through its great and god-given law-giver, Moses. This Judaism was probably much like cabala, in that, among other things, although cabalists have almost always obeyed the law in its essentials, the deeper significance of Judaism for cabalists was its revelation of a series of descending stages or worlds in the process of creation, with our material world at the bottom; and that the duty of man is to discover, and to come increasingly to live in, the higher worlds rather than this one. So in this period were being created the two great types standard in all later Judaism, the rabbinical Judaism of the Talmud and the mystical Judaism later called cabala.

It has always been supposed that the Jewish background of Christianity was rabbinic Judaism. But since Christianity used the Septuagint as its Bible, wrote all its earliest documents in Greek for pagans or Greek-speaking Jews, and suddenly began its art with that part of the *lingua franca* which Judaism had adopted, intimately associated with figures from the Old Testament as Jews presented them, it is much more profitable to look for the immediate Jewish background of Christianity in this Hellenized Judaism than in rabbinism.

Some of you had probably expected, from my title, that I would speak mostly about the extraordinary new religion which in the Age of Diocletian arose from the amphitheaters where it was being tortured, to be the dominant, I fear often the torturing, faith of the Empire. Instead of retelling that story, which I suspect is fairly well known to all of you, I shall close with a brief consideration of the question why, of all these forms of religion that I have been discussing, Christianity should have been the victor, indeed, except for Judaism, the sole survivor.

First, I remind you that Christianity is to be understood only if we think of it as the omnium-gatherum of all the different religious values, including those of Judaism, which we have been discussing. There were new Christian amulets, but the favorite ones seem to have been such slight alterations of pagan-Jewish amulets as were made when the Christians took the old cavalier-god killing with his spear the representative of evil, just put a cross line on the spear, and called the figure by one of several names for saints. The divine state was still the divine state, though people were to argue for a millennium and a half how the king got his divine powers. The old idols were destroyed, though some of them, like the figure of Isis holding Osiris, could still be used by cutting off the old name and writing "Mary" or "Mother of God" in its place. The religious values of the local deities were carried on in the local saints, so that every church was dedicated not only to God, but to a particular saint. The pagan ritual of sacrifice of animals disappeared entirely, but the Lamb that was slain was daily available in the sacrifice of the Mass, and in Communion.

The Church Fathers took the best of Neoplatonism and constructed out of it an extraordinary system of theology. There were points of difference, such as that the final mystical achievement for the Neoplatonists was the absorption of the person in the One, while the beatific vision still kept the integrity of the Blessed individual. All of this continuity seems to me epitomized in the fact that the symbolic *lingua franca*, first of pagan religions, then of Judaism, was – and to a large extent still is – also the symbolic language of Christian devotion.

To become the exclusive religion of the Empire, Christianity had, however, to do more than reaffirm the values of the religions it displaced. As to what this "more" was, we shall never agree. To the orthodox Christian – Catholic or Protestant – the great addition was that while the other religions taught myth, Christianity, in teaching the incarnation, was teaching historical fact and metaphysical truth. No one is in position to dispute the reality of the incarnation; if we accept it, however, we can do so only on faith. Still we can all agree that the Christians were deeply convinced that the incarnation was indeed an historical fact, and they see in that conviction a power whose absence was the greatest lack in even such lofty pagan formulations as those of Porphyry and Julian.

With the conviction went a church organization which not only kept men in line, but was always at hand to administer the consolations of the sacraments and to offer a most gratifying liturgical cultus. Soon to express itself in the glories of Romanesque and Byzantine architecture, Christianity did indeed take unto itself – and go beyond – all else that was the religious genius of the Age of Diocletian. I have given it relatively little space because I wanted you to see the age as a whole for what it was, that is, one of the greatest creative periods in religious history.

8

The Bosporus Inscriptions
to the Most High God

1957

This essay is not about early Christianity first of all, but rather about the relations between Greek-speaking Jews and Gentiles outside the Holy Land. It is included for three reasons. For most scholars, understanding those Jewish-Gentile relations is important first of all because of what that will reveal about the expansion of early Christianity among those Jews and Gentiles. In addition, recent archaeological discoveries at two sites in western Asia Minor (modern Turkey) have raised the "relationships" question again in important new ways. Finally, a new understanding of Saint Paul is emerging, one which Goodenough would have warmly welcomed.

The new archaeological evidence comes in the main from Sardis and Aphrodisias. The excavation of the Sardis synagogue has revealed a Diaspora Jewish community of political power and social status, architectural and iconographic creativity, and a genuine self-confidence over against its Gentile neighbors. Goodenough knew of the initial Sardis discoveries, and they excited him greatly. He managed to insert a reference to them, with illustrations, toward the end of the last volume of the Symbols *to come from his hand, see* Symbols *12:191-95. In particular Sardis provided a precise response to the "two insuperable difficulties" which had been raised by Schürer (JQR, page 225 below): the most important Sardis inscription, squarely in the center of the floor of the main hall, mentioned a "teacher of wisdom" named Samoe, who was also a* priest. *And the main furnishing of the building, the lectern which was the focus of worship, was embellished at each end with a huge* eagle *in high relief. (Generally on Sardis: Hanfmann 1983.)*

The Jewish inscriptions of Aphrodisias (Reynolds/Tannenbaum 1987) have opened up the old question of the presence of the God-fearers, or Gentile "sympathizers," in Diaspora Jewish communities. First and foremost, this is an issue for the history of earliest Christianity, beginning with the Book of Acts *in the New Testament itself (Kraabel 1981, 1985, 1986, Feldman 1985, Gager 1986, van der Horst 1989).*

The new understanding of Paul focusses on the social context for Paul's statements about Judaism, the Law and the Gentiles. It attempts to dispel the historical distortions which arose when Paul was seen through the eyes of the Protestant reformers. Watson calls this new view "delutheranizing Paul" (Watson 1987:18), the "Lutheran" view being represented in recent times pre-eminently by Rudolf Bultmann and Ernst Käsemann. The result is also a more accurate picture of the Jews and the Gentiles with whom Paul was concerned.

In a 1947 letter about the years spent on Jewish Symbols in the Greco-Roman Period, *Goodenough wrote, "with the completion of this work [the* Symbols] *I shall at last be ready to begin the work I have all my life [been] preparing to do, namely to write an equally extensive study of the origin of Christianity in view of all the new material I shall have presented on its Jewish and symbolic background" (Eccles 1985:85). His point is obvious: the Christians and Jews of the Greco-Roman world can only be understood mutually. Misinterpreting one side inevitably blurs our picture of the other. When Paul is seen as a timeless theological figure, that conveys a biased and inadequate picture of the Jewish communities out of which he came and with which he remained involved. In the last sentence of this essay, Goodenough insists: "We must inevitably come to recognize that hellenized Judaism was still a true Judaism." Without that recognition, there will also be gaps and limitations in any historical reconstruction of the early Christian communities with which these "hellenized" Jews interacted.*

. . . .

The fifteen illustrations to this article were printed more satisfactorily in volumes 3, 7 or 8 of the Symbols, and are not reproduced here. The numbers of the illustrations are listed below, with the volume and illustration number in the Symbols to which they correspond.

1 = 8:107	6 = 3:475	11 = 3:598
2 = 3:531	7 = 3:522	12 = 8:122
3 = 8:108	8 = 8:111	13 = 8:121
4 = 8:110	9 = 3:465	14 = 3:993
5 = 8:109	10 = 3:569	15 = 7:2

Erwin R. Goodenough, *Jewish Quarterly Review* **47 (1956-7): 221-244**

The famous study of Emil Schürer on the Θεὸς "Υψιστος inscriptions in the Bosporus[1] made one of those solid contributions whose findings have not been challenged for nearly sixty years. Two of the inscriptions,[2] from Panticapaeum, record that Jews manumitted a slave or slaves by committing them to their God at their προσευχή, or synagogue building. The only requirement was that the slaves thereafter be regular attendants at the synagogue, and the group, the συναγωγή, a Jewish counterpart of θίασος, were to keep watch that they did so. The slaves were presumably pagans, since Jewish slaves would have been freed in the Jewish way. Their standing with the Jews of the synagogue after they were freed is not hinted.[3] The two inscriptions seem about contemporary, and one is dated at 81 CE.

Schürer demonstrated that the method of manumission was taken directly from pagan usage, where slaves were freed by consigning them to some deity at a temple. The inscriptions say directly that "Jews" were the actors in this transaction, so that their existence in the region is definitely established. Clearly, also, the Jews were so much influenced by gentile ways that this, and presumably other, legal procedures were adapted to the synagogue.

A third inscription, from Gorgippia in the Bosporus,[4] dated 41 CE, gave more trouble. It is also a document of manumission, dedicated to

---

[1]"Die Juden im bosporanischen Reiche und die Genossenschaften der σεβόμενοι θεὸν ὕψιστον ebendaselbst," *Sitzungsberichte der Königlich Preussischen Akademie der Wissenschaften zu Berlin,* 1897, Part I, 200-225.

[2]They are to be found also in J.B. Frey, *Corpus Inscriptionum Iudaicarum,* I, nos. 683 f. (hereafter *CIJ*).

[3]Schürer and others thought the freedmen became "God-fearers," but some have read the Greek as a prohibition against their even entering the synagogue. For a guide to this debate, as well as bibliography of the process of manumission, see Frey's note to his inscription 683.

[4]Schürer, *op. cit.,* 204.

the "Most High God, Almighty and Blessed," and frees a slave in the same way with reference to the synagogue, but here the phrase is added that the act is done ὑπὸ Δία, Γῆν, Ἥλιον, "under Zeus, Ge, Helios." Schürer shows that the opening address of this inscription is even more Jewish than the others, for while God is called Almighty a great many times in the Septuagint, apocrypha, the New Testament, and early Christian literature, the term has never once been found in a pagan setting. Actually "Almighty" appears as an epithet of Hermes on one inscription,[5] but Schürer's judgment is still sound that it should ordinarily be taken to indicate Judaism. To address God as "Blessed" likewise recalls Judaism, since God is rarely mentioned in Jewish writings without "Blessed be he" being added.[6] The inscription, then, must be taken as an address to the Jewish God. But Zeus, Ge, and Helios cancelled all this for Schürer and his successors. "Anyone who could use this formula, even only as a formula and quite carelessly, was no Jew."

Subsequently discovered papyrological evidence, however, quite changes the picture. We now know that in documents of manumission of slaves the formula "Zeus, Ge, Helios" was so established that it seems legally to have been quite *de rigueur*. Granfell and Hunt printed the names in Greek as a single word, and translated: "She is set at liberty under..."[7] That is, they did not translate the names at all because a literal translation would for modern age be a mistranslation, as, I am convinced, it was for Schürer. Clearly this phrase was expected in, and probably legitimized, such documents in what may be called the Greek common law of the regions under the Diadochs. It carried no implication of the person's belief,[8] but was introduced into this Jewish document to make the manumission legal in pagan eyes, and involved no threat to the monotheism of the Jew who used it. If it does imply a bit of elasticity in the Jews of the region, it goes no further than does a modern Jew who takes his oath in court upon a Bible containing the

---

[5]G. Kaibel, *Epigrammata Graeca*, 1878, no. 815. From Crete.
[6]See the two Greek inscriptions found in a temple of Pan in Edfu, Egypt: "The blessing of God (ϑεοῦ εὐλογία). Theodotus the Jew, son of Dorian, was saved from the sea," Frey, *CIJ*, II, no. 1537; "Ptolemaios the Jew, son of Dionysius, blesses God (εὐλογεῖ τὸν ϑεόν)," ibid., no. 1538.
[7]B.P. Greenfell, and A.S. Hunt, *The Oxyrhynchus Papyri* I, 1898, nos. 48 f.; IV, 1904, no. 722. In the last inscription they do translate the phrase: "under sanction of Zeus, Earth, and Sun." F. Preisigke, *Sammelbuch griechischer Urkunden aus Aegypten*, 1, 1915, no. 5616.
[8]Frey recognized this also, though on other grounds: see his *CIJ*, I, notes to no. 690.

New Testament. Actually the Judaism of this inscription is strong and unbroken.[9]

From this inscription we learn that Jews in the region called their God the Most High. Similarly an inscription from Athribis, Egypt, tells how a prefect of the guard, along with the Jews of the place, dedicated a synagogue (προσευχή) in the Most High God.[10] The Most High appears also in four votive inscriptions[11] and two inscriptions of curses[12] from the synagogue at Delos. Josephus quotes a decree of Augustus in which John Hyrcanus is called "Chief Priest of God Most High."[13] Schürer was convinced that the term came from paganism.[14] We need not repeat the elaborate documentation by which he demonstrated that in paganism it began as "Most High Zeus," then was used sometimes absolutely, the "Most High," but more often as the "Most High God," all in pagan environments. Its use seems a part of the tendency towards monotheism that characterized later antiquity. Jews, however, did not have to adopt the phrase from paganism. As עֶלְיוֹן or עֵלִי it was often used in their Bible, and was translated in the LXX as ὕψιστος.

From these inscriptions Schürer went on to a group of twenty-one others[15] which commemorate the setting up of little groups of "newly received brethren" (εἰσποιητοὶ ἀδελφοί) who were worshiping God Most High. The group was a σύνοδος, or συναγωγή[16] its members

---

[9]S. Lieberman and A.D. Nock have both recognized that this phrase was within the scope of legitimate Jewish elasticity at the time: see Lieberman, *Hellenism in Jewish Palestine*, 1950, 214. But note that the use of the formula on such inscriptions is not an oath. It is a declaration that the slave is freed "under the subjection, control, dependence" of the three divinities: see Liddell-Scott-Jones, s.v. ὑπό, C, II. Philo allows Jews to swear by many personal and cosmic entities, including the sun, but never by such pagan divinities as Zeus, Ge, Helios: see my *Jewish Jurisprudence*, 43 f.; Lieberman, *Greek in Jewish Palestine*, 1942, 124 f., 138. There seems a real distinction between calling on a god in oath to witness an act or statement, which no Jew that I know ever allowed, and repeating an accepted formula that an act was done "under such and such names" to legitimize the legal act in gentile eyes. For a Jew had not emancipated his slave in gentile society at all if he did not validate the transaction in gentile terms.

[10]Schürer, *op. cit.*, 216; *CIJ*, II, no. 1445.

[11]*CIJ*, I, nos. 727-730.

[12]*Ibid.*, nos. 725 *a, b*.

[13]*Antt.*, XVI, 163 (vi, 2).

[14]*Op. cit.*, 208-216.

[15]Best published by B. Latyschev, *Inscriptiones Antiquae Orae Septentrionalis Ponti Euxini*, Petrograd, 1890, II, *Inscriptiones Regni Bosporani*, nos. 437-458.

[16]*CIJ*, p. lxx, n. 3, says that at Rome "synagogue" is always the congregation, *proseuche* the building. But since he has only one reference to the building from Rome, such a generalization is dangerous. On the Bosporus inscriptions,

ϑιασῶται, so that the group must also have been called a ϑίασος. They were enrolled under one or more presbyters, and their names followed, as well as the names of various officials, including a "priest," a "father of the group" (πατὴρ συνόδου),[17] an "officer for physical exercise" (γυμνασιάρχης) and a "supervisor of the youth" (νεανισκάρχης). The groups were apparently quite small, since at most only forty names were listed for each, and several of the inscriptions were set up at about the same time in a single place.

In these inscriptions, Jewish as they appear, Schürer found two insuperable difficulties to calling them such. The first is that they had a "priest," which to him implied sacrifices. The second is that five of the stones, perhaps more if the stones were complete, had eagles at the top, and these, he thought, could never have been acceptable to Jews. A third objection might be raised, the fact that we have at the beginning of the stones the phrase "to (or for) good luck" (ἀγαϑῇ τύχῃ). To speak of this last at once, the phrase seems quite without reference to the goddess Tyche. It was widely used as a sort of talismanic formula on documents, and Liddell-Scott-Jones furnish a great number of parallels, all of which they properly spell with the small letter. The phrase does not appear on Jewish tombstones, or any of our other inscriptions, but "luck" appears frequently in the writings of Philo as a causative factor in human events. It seems not at all to imply polytheism in the ordinary sense of the term or to go beyond the good luck most earnest Christians and Jews customarily wish their sons as they go off to war. Indeed Schürer felt the reference to luck so unimportant that he did not mention it at all, and we can safely disregard it as a bar to the Judaism of the inscriptions. The two objections he did raise, however, must be examined.

First that these thiasoi or synagogoi used "priests" among their officials seemed to Schürer to mark them as non-Jewish, because to him ἱερεύς meant one who offered sacrifices, a function so far as we know never performed in the synagogues. Dr. D.D. Fearer of Yale hopes shortly to publish in the *Yale Classical Studies* a paper in which he shows that the meaning of the term was by no means thus limited even among the Greeks. Still more directly important for our question is the evidence of inscriptions published since Schürer wrote. For we now know

---

the distinction is usually kept, and probably would be when the two conceptions appear together, but it is by no means generally observed: see e.g., CIJ, I, 720, 722 f.

[17]The title πατὴρ συναγωγῆς appears clearly seven times in *CIJ*, I: see nos. 88, 93, 319, 509 f., 537, 694, and in other inscriptions, as 645 f., it is a probable restoration.

that at Rome two Jews on their tombstone are called "priest,"[18] two "chief priest,"[19] and one "priestess."[20] A synagogue inscription in Greek from Jerusalem before its fall shows that the synagogue was built by Theodotus, Priest and Archisynagogus, son and grandson of an Archisynagogus. It may be that the priesthood of Theodotus' father and grandfather was implied since he himself was a priest, but it is not so stated. Presumably it was an office he held like that of archisynagogus. The synagogue of Dura was built, according to an inscription, in 244/5 CE during the eldership of Samuel the "priest."[21] There is plenty of evidence, accordingly, to show that the term "priest" was a living one in Jewish synagogues in those early years.

The Dead Sea *Manual of Discipline*, if we may take it as genuine, has of course freshly emphasized the importance of the priest in that Jewish Sect. There the "priests and Levites" have special blessings and curses to pronounce.[22] These two have to lead the others in what appears to be a procession into the "Covenant,"[23] though it is priests and elders who lead in another passage.[24] The priests have authoritative judgment in matters of property,[25] and special penalties are prescribed for their misdemeanors;[26] they are especially to be "weighed according to their spirit" whatever this form of judgment may prove to mean.[27] Who were these priests? They are commonly called in the *Manual* the sons of Zadok or of Aaron,[28] and this has been taken literally by commentators, so far as I can learn. But the admitted sons of Zadok were a small and select group, while those called by this title were indeed common in the little sects. Any cell of the group, if I may use the term, had to have ten members and a priest,[29] while the "Council of the Community," whatever its jurisdiction, consisted of

---

[18]*CIJ*, I, nos. 346 f.
[19]*Ibid.*, no. 405, cf. no. 355. Frey dismisses the difficulty by changing ἱερουσιάρχη[ς] into γερουσιάρχη[ς], but the photograph of no. 405 which he publishes makes this quite impossible.
[20]*Ibid.*, no. 315: ἱέρισα.
[21]*Ibid.*, II, 828, *a*, *b*; see J. Obermann in the Yale preliminary report of Excavations in Dura Europos, VI, 390.
[22]William H. Brownlee, *The Dead Sea Manual of Discipline*, 1951, I, 19-11, 18 (*BASOR*).
[23]*Ibid.*, II, 20.
[24]*Ibid.*, VI, 8.
[25]*Ibid.*, VI, 19; IX, 7.
[26]*Ibid.*, VII, 3.
[27]*Ibid.*, IX, 14.
[28]*Ibid.*, V, 6, 9, 21.
[29]*Ibid.*, VI, 3.

twelve laymen and three priests.[30] That the Sect could get such a steady supply of literal sons of Zadok is quite possible, of course. But "the men of the Community shall be set apart as a house of holiness for Aaron,"[31] and the Council itself seems to have become a most holy abode or institution for Aaron, with eternal knowledge to enact laws and to offer up an agreeable odor,[32] the Council that is of the laymen and the priests. The sacrificial term "odor" is clearly not a reference to the sacrifices in the Temple, and the priests as lawmakers are the lawmakers of the code of the *Manual* itself. An entirely new light is thrown on the priesthood when it appears that their special function was to bless the bread and wine at the communal meals. We are getting very close indeed to the transition from the priestly function of the sons of Zadok in the Temple to the function of future Christian priests. When all this is put together, it seems to me quite possible that the priesthood of Zadok in the Sect was a title or office, not a sign of literal descent from Zadok, and that it is precisely here that we have the beginnings of the transition to the Christian priesthood. I strongly suspect that it was because only the priest could consecrate the bread and wine for these people that every cell of ten men had to have a priest. Be that as it may, even without the evidence of the *Discipline* there is ample precedence for the office of priest in Jewish communities outside the Temple,[33] and the presence of such an official or such a title in the Bosporus communities is far from estranging them from Judaism.

A final objection seemed to Schürer also insuperable, that eagles were carved on five of the twenty-one stones, and, from the fragmentary condition of the stones, might well have stood on others. But even if they originally appeared on only this one quarter of the stones, it is clear that the groups countenanced them freely. Since no other such figures are on the stones except the eagles, one would at once conclude in any other religion that the eagle has special symbolic importance in the group. It will be well to examine the five stones as reproduced by Stephani years ago.[34] In fig. 1 the eagle is so drawn that it looks like an owl, but the half-spread position of the wings shows that it is the eagle used throughout the Near East, as the other stones indicate. The

---

[30]*Ibid.*, VIII, 1.
[31]*Ibid.*, IX, 6.
[32]*Ibid.*, VIII, 6-9.
[33]See also similar passages in the Genizah Fragments (ed. R.H. Charles, Apocrypha and Pseudoepigrapha, II, 799-834), I, 5; VI, 1; VII, 6; VIII, 11; X, 7-9; XI, 1 f.; XV, 1-6; XVII, 1 f. It is worth recalling that the title of the Hasmonean priest-kings was "chief priest of the Most High God."
[34]L. Stephani, Commission impériale archéologique, Compte-rendu, 1870-71, 231, 232, 253, 255, 258.

round decoration within the gable is what I call a "round object," and was a favorite symbol in Jewish use. Fig. 3 shows at the top the same eagle, but with head turned. What was on either side of it would be dangerous to say, but, in view of the garland held by the eagles below, it is worth suggesting that the upper corners may have contained garlands also, since there is room for nothing but the end of a garland in those lost parts of the gable. The eagles below look back over their shoulders to hold the garland. A garland was simply an untied wreath, and had exactly the same symbolism. The anthemion at the top of the gable would at a glance seem to be only decoration, but will appear an integral part of the design. In fig. 5 the eagles face a central wreath, to which they bring palm branches. Palm branches are another alternative for the wreath: both mean victory, of course, but in religious art they can mean, as they still do, the crown or victory of achieving life, in Paul's terms, or of the vision of God in Philo's mystical language. In fig. 4 what the eagles face between them is entirely lost. Fig. 8 gives us simply a pair of eagles in the usual form.

In Schürer's opinion these eagles showed that "the cult of the θεὸς ὕψιστος , in spite of all Jewish influences, still continued attached to Zeus."[35] He took comfort in the nine stones out of the twenty-one so complete that such ornament could not possibly have appeared on them, and also in the appearance of pairs of eagles. Zeus had a single eagle, he argued, and when one could put two or three together they had obviously become ornamental, and hence, while a definite reminiscence of Zeus, were so far removed from the actual eagle of Zeus that the God being worshiped was still closer to Yahweh than to Zeus. Even so, he thought, Jews could not have carved them there.

Without going into the highly complicated problem of the meaning of the eagle in the ancient Near East,[36] we can at once dissipate the notion that Jews of this period so much disliked the eagle that its appearance on the inscriptions makes it impossible to ascribe the stones to Jews. The eagle actually has been identified many times as a device on the synagogues of Palestine. From the synagogue of Capernaum alone six stones show eagles, or traces of them, for they were often savagely hacked away by later Jewish reformers. On only one piece could recognizable eagles from Capernaum be photographed but that is very important, fig. 6,[37] since here is carved a pair of eagles holding a

[35]*Op. cit.,* 220.
[36]This subject, the eagle on the Temple of Herod, and the eagle in Jewish and Christian tradition, is to be discussed in a chapter on the eagle in Vol. VIII of my *Jewish Symbols in the Greco-Roman Period.*
[37]See my *Jewish Symbols in the Greco-Roman Period,* III, fig. 475.

garland between them exactly as on the inscription. It is also to be noticed that the anthemion was at the left beside them, something I can hardly regard as a matter of chance. On another, fig. 9,[38] the eagles are chipped away, but the archaeologists who inspected the stone assure us that the stone originally had a pair of eagles beneath the wreath holding its tie strings in their beaks. Fig. 7[39] shows an eagle with garlands and wreaths from a lintel on the door of the synagogue at el-Jish, and fig. 2[40] the undoubted remains of an eagle in what we now recognize as its stereotype position from the synagogue at Umm el-Kanatir. Fig. 11[41] shows a drawing of the design on what was taken to be the lintel stone of a synagogue at Khirbet Dubil: here again are the eagle and the wreath. But if one is looking for unorthodoxy in eagles, fig. 14,[42] a mosaic in the synagogue at Yafa, shows an eagle over a female head. In fig. 10,[43] also a lintel from Yafa, two eagles, each holding a wreath, flank a central wreath. Lest we go too far with this material, and conclude that the eagle in these positions was a distinctive mark of Judaism, let me show you fig. 12,[44] the lintel from a temple of the Sun God at Hatra, where identical eagles, bearing little wreaths, confront the central figure of the rayed sun god. The Jewish pattern we now see is a deliberate adoption, and the wreath has taken the place of the pagan god to make it conform to Jewish notions. The God, now that he has become Yahweh, still has eagles as his attributes, as did the sun god of Hatra, fig. 13.[45]

The eagle was also a funerary device for Jews in Palestine. Three occurrences of them have recently been found at Sheikh Ibreiq, or Beth Shéarim. One, Avigad wrote me, is so lightly incised in the wall that it cannot be photographed, though it is certainly there. Another he has just published. It shows an eagle in the familiar half-spread form, dominating an animal frieze which, as he says, strongly recalls the carving of the synagogue at Capernaum.[46] But of the third he sent me a photograph, from a sarcophagus end, fig. 15. Avigad wrote that he had

---

[38]Ibid., fig. 465.
[39]Ibid., fig. 522.
[40]Ibid., fig. 531.
[41]Ibid., fig. 598.
[42]Ibid., fig. 993.
[43]Ibid., fig. 569.
[44]From Harold Ingholt, *Parthian Sculptures from Hatra*, 1954, plate VI, 3 (Memoirs of the Connecticut Academy of Arts and Sciences, XII).
[45]From *ibid.*, plate VI, 2. I do not bring in as evidence the eagle on the coin of Herod I, because his use of eagles has been so much misinterpreted by the misunderstanding of his putting the eagle on the Temple. I shall discuss this at length in my study of the eagle in Vol. VIII of my *Symbols*.
[46]*Archaeology*, VIII (1955), 240. It is from the Mausoleum of Catacomb no. 11.

found the sarcophagus there last summer, and said: "On either of the two long sides are carved two lions flanking a bull's head. On one of the short sides is carved a bull's head, on the other an eagle whose photograph I send you. Two similar eagles are carved on the front side of the lid, and on either of the latter's sides is carved a bull's head."

It is natural to assume that for pagans the eagle was at once the god and the agent or attribute of god, who brought men god's mercy and salvation, and, in other representations, carried the souls of men back to god. All of this can be elaborately illustrated. How deeply such an eagle could be taken into Judaism appears in the book, *The Rest of the Words of Baruch*, a slightly Christianized version of a Jewish original, where, after the eagle does many wonderful things, including restoring a man to life, the people exclaim: "Is not this the God who was manifest to our fathers in the wilderness through the instrumentality of Moses, and who has made himself into the form of an eagle, and appeared to us by means of this great eagle?"[47] But we are not concerned with the eagle directly, only with Schürer's argument that the eagles on the stones in Bosporus were the eagles of the Greek Zeus, and that the stones must accordingly be classed as pagan. Quite the contrary, the use of the eagles on these inscriptions, and the way the eagles are used, show that they are the eagles of the solar deities of the East, and that they were used to show the mercy and power of θεὸς ὕψιστος in a way completely acceptable to Jews.

What, then, were these little communities? Were they made up of Jews or gentiles?

After having said all this about the harmony of everything with Judaism I still hesitate to conclude definitely that the groups were made up of native Jews. They may well have been converts. That they are called "God-worshipers" by no means leads me to this opinion, for certainly no Jew would feel himself belittled by so honorable a title. But Schürer has shown that the inscriptions seem to set up distinct little groups of "newly received brethren," five groups in the same city within a short while, and this looks like a rapidly growing community. There was no reason why new generations of Jews should not join their parents' groups, so that the new thiasoi seem to reflect converts, rather than that large immigrations of Jews were coming to this little city in the third century. I have no proof that the groups were not made up strictly of new Jewish arrivals. But I should take the inscriptions to witness the appeal of Judaism at the time to gentiles who became fully Jewish in their point of view. The new converts may or may not have been circumcised. One always must recall Philo's remark that

---

[47]James R. Harris, *The Rest of the Words of Baruch*, VII, 18.

uncircumcised gentiles who accepted the worship of the Jewish God were often a far nobler progeny of Abraham than some of the circumcised.[48] Such may have been the members of these thiasoi. But the movement itself to worship the Most High God in thiasoi and to symbolize their worship by eagles, seems to be a product of hellenized Jews. For if the people named in these inscriptions were not native Jews, there is nothing in the inscriptions alien to what we know of the practices of loyal Jews of the period. We must inevitably come to recognize that hellenized Judaism was still a true Judaism.

---

[48]See my *Introduction to Philo Judaeus*, 1940, 53, 173, 207; *By Light, Light*, 1935, 115. *QE* II, 2: "For the proselyte is one not who has circumcised his foreskin, but one who has circumcised the pleasures and desires and other passions of his soul...The attitude of mind (διάνοια) of the proselyte is alienation from polytheistic opinion, and attraction to the honor to the One and Father of all things." Cf. Philo's remarks on nobility, in *Virt.*, 187-227.

9

An Early Christian Bread Stamp

1964

In this little essay, printed after his retirement from Yale, Goodenough continues to grapple with the relationships between Judaism and Christianity. In this case he is working not with texts but with symbols, familiar territory for him, where there is less demand for logic and doctrinal precision, and where the artisan may be creative and even paradoxical. The artifact published here is a striking example. It bears a cross on both faces, but the central *image on one face is a* bucranium, *on the other a* menorah.

The Germanos inscription from Avdat (see note 17) was later published by A. Negev (1978). In this article Negev notes that two of the inscriptions from the church of St. Theodore show "a palm branch with seven leaves" (page 104): no. 16, the Germanos inscription, and no. 14. Such a design, he asserts, "is most unusual, and had it not been found in a church it would certainly have been considered as a menorah" (page 105). It is true that the symbol on inscription no. 14 (see Negev's photograph 16, plate 11) resembles a palm branch. But the Germanos inscription (Negev's photograph 18, plate 12) surely bears a menorah, flanked by crosses. A glance at Goodenough's figure 7 shows Goodenough, not Negev or Avi Yonah, to be correct.

Erwin R. Goodenough, *Harvard Theological Review* **57 (1964): 133-137**

The interesting little object which I publish here for the first time is a stamp, presumably for bread, at the Royal Ontario Museum in the

University of Toronto. Mrs. Neda Leipan, Assistant Curator of the Museum, not only sent me the photographs, figs. I and 2, with permission to publish, but lent me the object itself to study at home! I am indeed grateful. She tells me that it is marked as having come from Egypt, but that she has no further information about it. Made of limestone, it is 7.6 cm. high, and the two faces are 9 cm. in diameter.

Nearly half of one face, fig. 2, has been broken off, but the other half shows letters encircling a central device. Of this inscription we can read only +ευ........ιθωνευο.. There is space for about eight letters in the first break, and for a single letter at the end. Mrs. Leipan takes the third letter to be a sigma, but since we have only the lower part of the arc, the whole might have been an epsilon, omicron, theta, or omega. The fragmentary up-stroke at the other end of this break might have been part of an iota or eta. With the cross at the beginning I can conclude only that the object was made by a Christian. The central device is a bull's head or bucranium, incised as a whole, not merely in outline. Its form is quite recognizable, though most of the right half has been broken off. There are incisions above the bull's head that may have been letters. The first would seem to have been an iota, since the flat top precludes its being a horn of the animal. After it come part of an arc, and then a vertical line. I make no guess about these letters, and indeed leave to epigraphists to reconstruct the inscriptions on this face.

I must do the same about the inscriptions on the other face, fig. I. The dominating motif here is a menorah standing on now two, probably originally three, legs after the most common form of Jewish representation. This side must be Christian too, however, for just under the right arms of the menorah stands an unmistakable Christian cross, with what I take to be two other objects. The Greek letters ΙΙΡΟ stand above the menorah, and ΒΟ beneath it at the left. At first glance it would seem that the V on the right of the menorah's stem should be read as a letter with the ΒΟ. But what Greek letter would it be? It is unlikely that it is an upsilon, for two upsilons are on the other face, both with the lower stroke. If it is an upsilon, we should have to read the poetic genitive of Aeschylus and Sophocles, πρὸ βοῦ, a highly dangerous reading. For reasons to be given directly, I doubt that it is a letter at all, and read only προ βο, about whose meaning I make no suggestion. I have struggled too often with "magical" abbreviations which as inscriptions mean nothing at all not to feel that this probably belongs in the same class.

We are left with the symbols themselves, accordingly, without help from the inscriptions. The bucranium appears very rarely on Christian monuments, so rarely that it is not even mentioned in the Cabrol-Leclercq *Dictionnaire.* Jews used it on tombs, however, though not often.[1] I shall not repeat the material on the bull I have already published,[2] but simply say that it had clearly become a symbol of immortality in various pagan religious circles, and that it had quite explicitly come to symbolize the Messiah in Jewish literature, especially in the Book of Enoch and in the Testaments of the Twelve Patriarchs, two Jewish books much used and adapted by Christians.[3] Since symbols stamped on bread to be eaten usually have value as sacramentals, we may presume that the bucranium had such value here.

The same would be concluded about the menorah, cross, and two other symbols on the other face. The latter two seem to mark the design as being definitely one taken from Judaism. They are the V already mentioned and a deeply cut bar with round ends. These seem to me to be badly degenerated Jewish ritual objects of the sort very common on Jewish lamps, tombstones, and the like.[4] By the fifth and sixth centuries they were so carelessly represented that I often had to call them "indeterminate objects."[5] For example, fig. 3 has forms under the menorah quite similar to our bar; the object is a bronze stamp, presumably also for bread.[6] I should guess that the "bar" on our stamp was in origin a Jewish lulab.

The V seems similarly to have originated from the Jewish shofar. A conventionalized shofar appears with a lulab on a stone from the synagogue of Priene in Asia Minor, marked as such by the hole at each end, but otherwise simply an angled band, fig. 4.[7] At least twice, however, the shofar appears on Jewish objects as a plain V, that is, fig. 5 from a Palestinian tombstone,[8] and fig. 6, a capital at Jericho.[9] So I take it as the most likely assumption that the V of our stamp is to be construed not as a letter, but as a shofar. That the menorah should have had a shofar and lulab beside its stem is quite to be expected, granting the borrowing of the menorah by Christians in this way in the first place.

---

[1]See my *Symbols*, III, figs. 17, 45, 548.
[2]*Ibid.*, VII, 3-28.
[3]*Ibid.*, VII, 24-27.
[4]*Ibid.*, III, figs. 335-337, 571f., 574-576, 769, etc.
[5]*Ibid.*, figs. 577, 580, 582.
[6]From *ibid.*, fig. 1012; cf. figs. 891, 1016, 1018; II, 217.
[7]*Ibid.*, III, fig. 878. In II, 77 I say that I think Sukenik wrong in calling this a shofar; but I have regretted saying this for several years.
[8]Courtesy of the Palestine Archeological Museum. I refer, of course, to the stone on the left. See my Symbols, I, 88; III, fig. 99.
[9]The photograph was kindly given me by my friend I. Ben Dor. I do not know of its ever having been published.

Figure 1

Figure 2

Figure 3

Figure 4

Figure 5

Figure 6

Figure 7

Figure 8

Some years ago I said that Christians of our period had no use for the menorah as a symbol, since it was so completely identified with Judaism, though I did recognize that the early Fathers had allegorized it as representing Christ, the Light of the World.[10] Such new explanation seemed a fine example of a new religion's adapting the value of a symbol which it was taking over from an older religion, for we saw that the menorah's value for Jews was to symbolize God as the divine light of the cosmos.[11] Our new stamp, however, forces us to review the evidence again, and in point of fact several other examples survive where perhaps Christians used the menorah with the cross. It was actually integrated with the cross in some inscriptions, as in the

mentioned in my *Symbols*,[12] and several such combinations

appeared in Moab.[13] The same design appears on the lintel of a Christian church in the Jaulan.[14] With these go the famous lamp from Carthage,[15] on which Christ enthroned holds the cross but has the menorah, reversed, at his feet. This may only spell out the symbol at

Moab, , though here, as Avi Yonah thinks, the identification may

be with the palm branch of victory. Both seem to me more probably to be menorahs, however, and to say, like the Christian Fathers, that Christ is the Light of the World. The same idea could be expressed when the Copts put a "round object" upon a cross, itself an Egyptian ankh of life.[16]

Or, a recent discovery in Israel, the Christians could put the menorah between crosses on an inscription in a sixth-century church at Avdat, fig. 7.[17] The inscription tells us nothing but that the blessed

---

[10]*Symbols*, IV, 94, n. 144.

[11]*Ibid.*, II, 136f.; IV, 71-98.

[12]*Ibid.*, II, 102; see n. 15 there.

[13]Reginetta Canova, *Iscrizioni e monumenti protocristiani del paese di Moab*, Vatican, 1954, plate III at p. cxxvi, kindly sent me by Avi Yonah. The work is not accessible to me.

[14]*Symbols*, III, fig. 587; cf. I, 222.

[15]*Ibid.*, III, fig. 957; cf. II, 102.

[16]*Ibid.*, VII, 196, and figs. 222f.

[17]Courtesy of the Department of Antiquities, Israel, and of Dr. M. Avi Yonah. It is published in a booklet for tourists prepared by Dr. Mosche Pearlman, but he will soon publish it critically with the other Avdat inscriptions. This was in the church of St. Theodore.

Germanos, son of Alexander, died at a certain date,[18] unmarried, at the age of seventeen. The cross at the beginning of the inscription indicates his religion sufficiently, but the cross at the end is followed by a menorah and another cross. Avi Yonah wrote me that he again considers this menorah a palm branch, but so far as I know he is alone in this case. The solid base for a menorah is less usual than a tripod, but is abundantly established,[19] and we have a number in which the base is a triangle, as at Avdat.[20] The menorah is easy to distinguish from the palm branch with its short spikes running up the stem, and I know no case in which the branch was drawn with the side spikes rising to make a horizontal row at the top.

A Palestinian lamp, fig. 8,[21] has on its spout a semicircular arch, under which an amphora stands between a pair of free-standing columns.[22] A pair of menorahs, one with seven and the other with nine branches, flank the arch. But below the menorahs, at the center of each side of the lamp, is another arch with a square cross under it. Avi Yonah wrote me that he could not believe these two to be crosses, since only a Christian could have put such crosses on a lamp, and a Christian would not have thus subordinated the cross to the Jewish symbols. He said that therefore what appear to be crosses must be understood as human figures with outstretched arms, though only two crossed lines are represented. Our new stamp shows that Christians did subordinate the cross to the menorah on occasion, and the crosses on the lamp can be taken only as crosses.

What sort of Christians would have done all this? We at once would say "Jewish Christians," as did Reifenberg when he first published the lamp. But now with evidence so widely scattered, Palestine, Moab, Egypt, and North Africa, we must admit that if it indicates Jewish Christians, such Christianity was more widespread and persistent than we had ever supposed. For most of this material, including the new stamp, seems to be of the sixth century or later. I do not think that so large a conclusion is justified, yet the fact of the evidence remains, and seems to me to show unmistakably that at least some Christians, probably many, carried over strictly Jewish symbols into their new faith, just as so many symbols (for example, the eagle, cupid, peacock, dolphin, and Victory) persisted on into both Judaism

---

[18]By our reckoning, Avi Yonah writes me, A.D. 551.

[19]One recalls at once the menorah on the Arch of Titus: *Symbols,* IV, fig. 1; see also III, figs. 592, 646, 663, 707, 716, 719, 768, 805, 958, 983, 1021, 1026.

[20]*Ibid.,* figs. 761, 763, 771, 945.

[21]From *Symbols,* III, fig. 288; cf. I, 153f.

[22]On two free-standing columns in Jewish art see *ibid.,* X, 106.

and Christianity from paganism. Presumably the old Jewish value was given new Christian explanations,[23] and I should guess that the menorah, in art as with the Fathers, was now thought to represent Christ as light so vividly that even the cross could be subordinated to it. For one thing cannot now be denied: we now know that Christians actually did on occasion subordinate the cross to the menorah.

10

The Perspective of Acts
Studies in Luke-Acts.

1966
This essay marks the beginning of that final analysis of early Christianity which Goodenough had long anticipated. A position on Acts had to be staked out early in any such study, and this summarizes Goodenough's. The footnotes reveal that his re-entry into current New Testament scholarship had only begun, but his presuppositions are perfectly clear, note for example the last sentence.

The place of Acts in Goodenough's understanding of early Christianity is discussed more fully in the introduction to the final essay in this volume. (See also Eccles 1985:122-23.)

Erwin R. Goodenough, *Studies in Luke-Acts. Essays Presented in Honor of Paul Schubert.*[*] Ed. L.E. Keck and J.L. Martyn. Nashville: Abingdon, 1966. Pages 51-59

Many years ago Kirsopp Lake said to a class that if Acts is not a basically sound historical document we know nothing of the origin of Christianity. The loss of Acts would indeed be a crippling blow, but it is just as devastating to use Acts as literally sound history. We know, or have some evidence, of much in early Christianity that Acts would never have led us to suspect. A historian who writes without a thesis is a chronicler, not a historian at all. "This is written that" lies behind all ancient history, whether Greek or Jewish. I believe we shall not

---

[*]With all the best wishes to my honored colleague of many years at Yale.

know how to use Acts until we have some inkling of the author's purpose in writing.

The book presents many acute problems. For example, the Gospel of Luke, presumably written by the same man, paints an amazingly different picture of the importance of Jesus from that in Acts. Luke's Gospel gives us our most vivid picture of Jesus the "rabbi," as Bultmann called him, the teacher of new law and parables. In Acts not a trace of this Jesus appears. Peter says at Pentecost that the Jews had crucified Jesus although he had been attested before them by his miracles (Acts 2:22), but not a single passage connects the Jesus of whom he says, "God has made him both Lord and Christ" (Acts 2:36) with the great teacher of parables and ethics in the Gospel. To say the least, here is a new approach. It seems that, like Paul, the author of Acts will know Christ after the flesh no more.

Again, what has become of the Eucharist? Luke tells the story of the institution at the Last Supper, and while he presumably had the Marcan account before him, he is in some details closer to the wording of Paul for that event than to Mark (Luke 22:17-19; Mark 14:22-24; I Cor. 11:23-25). Paul not only tells of the institution but shows that the sacrament had the deepest significance in his life. "The cup of blessing which we bless, is it not a participation in the blood of Christ? The bread which we break, is it not a participation in the body of Christ?" (I Cor. 10:16.) The sixth chapter of the Gospel of John, which I think also reflects early Christian thinking as does Paul, is like Paul in showing great concern for the necessity and power of the Eucharist. I agree entirely with Catholic tradition which makes the early church deeply eucharistic. But Acts gives not a single instance of its celebration, or of any sacramental idea connected with bread and wine. The allusions to common meals, "breaking of bread," in Acts 2:42, 46 make no suggestion of sacramental value, and indeed such value seems definitely impossible in the account of the trouble with the "Hellenists." For at that time the "Twelve" said that their business was to pray and preach, not to act as waiters at table (Acts 6:1-2). A man who felt himself a priest administering a sacrament could hardly have referred to the sacrament with such contempt. The "breaking of bread" on the first day of the week at Troas may have been a celebration, but Luke's casual allusion to it gives no hint of anything but a weekly communal meal (Acts 20:7). Bread, Luke tells us (Acts 27:33-36), was blessed and eaten aboard the ship that was wrecked on the way to Rome, but here it is specifically said that the company ate to get strength to swim ashore from the ship before it broke up completely. I can suppose only that Acts deliberately omits reference to current celebration, although to judge from Paul, John, the synoptic accounts of the institution, and the developments in the early second century, they must have played an important part in the life of the early church. I can further suppose only that Luke omitted reference to the Eucharist because for some reason he did not like the way it had developed.

The persons qualified to celebrate had by the end of the first century begun clearly to distinguish themselves as what later came to be the priesthood from those not so qualified, but this distinction, or its beginning, does not appear in Acts. Matthias was simply "counted in" as one of the Twelve (Acts 1:26). The apostles did, indeed, "pray and lay their hands upon" the Hellenists chosen to "wait at tables"; but that this gave the new waiters more than a general blessing is not suggested. The incident is told much like Peter's and John's laying on of hands which gave the Spirit to all Samaritan converts without distinction (Acts 8:14-16). It may have been an ordination, and I rather suspect it was; but in that case the text deliberately belittles it. Acts tells how Paul established "elders" whenever he got a nucleus of converts at a single place (Acts 14:23), and he went to Jerusalem to confer with the "apostles and elders" there (Acts 15:2, 4, 23), but Acts gives no suggestion that they had special sacramental function. I see no reason to deny the Catholic claim that these officials reflect the beginning of a sacramental priesthood; I only say that the text would give no hint of such an interpretation to a non-Christian contemporary reading Acts for the first time. Actually I cannot believe that such a priesthood was not taking form during those years, just as the blessing of bread and wine was reserved for special officials in the Qumran groups.[1] With these groups it was "priests," *kohens,* who could bless the bread and wine, men who would seem to be definitely identified as "sons of Zadok." That this meant literally members of the high priestly families I have long doubted, without any but an a priori incredulity that one in ten of covenanters at Qumran had such an elite ancestry. Jewish inscriptions seem to suggest that a priest was rather an official than always the son of a priest.[2] Similarly "elder" was a title in the synagogues, whose meaning there is quite varied. In one bilingual inscription "presbyter," elder, is used to correspond to the Hebrew *kohen,* priest,[3] but the word is used in the feminine form for women in four Jewish inscriptions.[4] The Letter of Aristeas speaks of "priests and elders of the Jewish

---

[1]*Manual of Discipline,* 6:1-8; see my *Jewish Symbols,* VI, 135 f.
[2]*Jewish Symbols,* I, 179 f.
[3]J.-B. Frey, *Corpus Inscriptionum Iudaicarum* (Vatican 1952), Vol. II nos. 828 f.
[4]*Ibid.,* I (1936) nos. 581, 590, 597, from Venosa, Italy; no. 692 from Thrace.

community,[5] a completely undefined usage. We are reminded of the apostles and elders already mentioned in Acts. All we can say of the elders of Acts is that they may have been priests in the new Christian sense, but that there is no evidence that the author of Acts recognized them as such. The apostles had the great gift of conferring the Spirit upon people by laying their hands upon them, as Simon Magus saw with envy, but nothing suggests that this, done properly to all converts, conveyed or implied a special priestly office.

Baptism presents a similar problem. Acts lays great emphasis upon baptism in the Name, followed by the reception of the Spirit for all Christians. But except that it was given now in the "Name of Jesus" the rite itself seems to be the one formerly preached and administered by John the Baptist. He too preached a baptism of "repentance for the forgiveness of sins" (Mark 1:4), exactly what Acts describes as a "blotting out" of sins (2:38; 3:19). A person thus "freed" (Acts 13:38-39) would be ready for the great judgment at the founding of the new kingdom. This is exactly the sort of forgiveness Jews have always prayed for, especially in the great rituals of the high holy days. Paul opens an entirely new conception of baptism when he says that the rite removes one's sinful "nature," that one is baptized into Christ's death in order to walk in a newness of life, now dead to sin and alive to God in Christ Jesus, become a new creature in Christ Jesus. This is the Fourth Gospel expressed in terms of a new "birth" of water and the Spirit, a figure that created the great sacramental conception of baptismal regeneration. Even if the figure of birth in the Fourth Gospel is "later" (which, as is well known, I do not think likely),[6] still the new sacramental idea is expressed so clearly by Paul himself in his letters that he must have been preaching it long before Acts was written, since he is the famous hero of Acts. That is, theological and sacramental thinking about baptism was fully alive at the stage of Christianity Acts describes, but Acts does not describe such thinking. Here is another deeply important part of the Christianity of Paul which the author of Acts strips away.

Such misrepresentation of Paul's theology goes, as Vielhauer has pointed out,[7] properly with Acts' rejection of the sacramental, hierarchical, and mystical developments of the early church. Vielhauer sees the author as reacting from this to return to a Jewish Christianity. To me, Acts seems to be a piece of deliberate propaganda

[5]Aristeas, 310; cf. the "elders and priests" in Matt. 16:21; 27:12, 20, 41; 28:11 f.; Mark 8:31; 15:1.
[6]"John a Primitive Gospel," essay 3 above.
[7]Philipp Vielhauer, "On the Paulinism of Acts," *Studies in Luke-Acts.*

designed to assure Theophilus that Paul also had preached this faith in a call to men everywhere to repent, be baptized, believe that Jesus had risen from the dead, and await the great Return.

For this the author not only minimized or denied Paul's real gospel, but anchored him in Judaism by making him a trained rabbi. In Philippians (3:2-7) Paul indignantly answers some "dogs" who had demanded that the new Christians be circumcised, apparently on the ground that Christianity was the fulfillment of Judaism, and that they spoke with a Jewish authority Paul could not offer. For Paul goes onto make the most of his right to speak as a valid Jew. He lists his qualifications: born of the tribe of Benjamin, circumcised on the eighth day, he had followed Pharisaic interpretation of the law with blameless zeal. This is apparently the best Paul can do for himself. But Acts (22:3; 23:6) has him claim to have been a Pharisee, son of a Pharisee (that is, presumably both were formal and full members of the Pharisaic party) and a pupil of Gamaliel. No one is in a position to say that Paul had or had not been a pupil of Gamaliel, but I cannot believe that he would not have claimed such authority against the "dogs" if he had had such a distinction. And although Gamaliel was a famous liberal in rabbinic circles, he certainly taught his pupils the law in Hebrew, while Paul's fluent Septuagint allusions suggest someone steeped from childhood in the Septuagint as John Bunyan was in the King James Version. But Acts has Paul say not simply that he had studied with Gamaliel, but that he had been brought up at Gamaliel's feet. The statements in Acts can very well be only a part of what seems increasingly to be the author's creation of a largely fictional Paul. Paul may have been a pupil of Gamaliel, but we cannot, as is usually done, take Paul's "rabbinical training" as a known fact in terms of which we must interpret his letters. The test will be not the straining out of occasional gnats of rabbinical parallels, but similarity or contrast between the basic *Denkweise* of Paul and that of the Tannaim. Even in so cursory a review as I am giving here, it is still in point to recall that talmudists have uniformally hated Paul's attitude toward the law, and have seen nothing in common between themselves and Paul whatever.

Paul the Roman citizen seems to me in all probability still another part of Luke's fiction. Paul gives no suggestion of Roman citizenship in his letters, but in Acts he claims not only to be a citizen, but to have been one by birth (22:25-29), which would mean that Paul's father had been not only a Pharisee, but a Roman citizen as well. If this were true, the father may himself have inherited the citizenship, but if he was given it personally before Paul was born, he must have got it under Augustus or Tiberius. The situation is possible but so unlikely as to be incredible. For such a distinguished honor in the relatively provincial city of Tarsus, which Acts makes Paul's birthplace, was possible in those years only for a few of the great benefactors of the new regime. Caesar and Pompey had granted citizenship somewhat freely to such people and to soldiers in their armies, but Augustus and Tiberius stopped doing so almost entirely.[8] It is of course possible that Paul's grandfather was a soldier in Caesar's legions, but it is hard to believe. In Paul's own day even an officer of the Roman army with a rank roughly corresponding to our colonel, the tribune who commanded the regiment at Jerusalem and who had Paul arrested, said to Paul that he had had to pay a great sum of money for his citizenship (Acts 22:28). If Paul had been born a citizen, then it would mean that he whom Acts itself calls a tentmaker by trade was from one of the greatest families in the East.

Silas, Acts says, was also a Roman citizen. But he and Paul, according to Acts endured being beaten with rods at Philippi and being put into prison by Roman magistrates. Only the next morning did he terrify the magistrates by sending word that they had done this to uncondemned Roman citizens. The magistrates hurried down to apologize and led Paul and Silas publicly and in honor out of the city. (Acts 16:19-29). Silas is first heard of at Jerusalem as one high in the confidence of the Christian "apostles and elders" there. Paul told the Corinthians that the Jews had given him their thirty-nine lashes five times, and that he had been beaten with rods (apparently at Roman hands) three times (II Cor. 11:23-25). According to Acts it was to stop such a beating at Jerusalem that Paul told the centurian that he was a Roman citizen (22:24-25). I believe Paul's own words that he had been beaten three times with rods by the Romans; but from that we are probably to deduce that he failed to stop the torture by announcing he was a citizen because in point of fact, he was not. That Silas was also a Roman citizen, and that he and Paul had submitted to the Roman beating at Philippi and then demanded an apology the next day, seems a bit of quite unlikely historionics.

We can therefore discuss the problem of Paul's Roman citizenship from only two points of view: first, its inherent probability in terms of what we know of Roman citizenship at the time; and second, in terms of the general reliability of the source, in this case Acts, which alone reports it. It seems to me that we have little reason to accept Paul's citizenship on either count. But we must face the consequences of this fairly, since Paul's arrest by the Romans in Jerusalem and his being sent on to Rome – that is, nearly the whole last quarter of Acts – can then

---

[8]See Kornemann, "Civitas," Pauly-Wissowa, *Real-Encyclopädie der klassischen Altertumswissenschaft*, Suppl. Bd. I, 300-317, esp. 313-15.

have no claim to historicity inasmuch as it all hangs upon Paul's claim of citizenship and his appeal to Caesar. One detail in that section does sound genuine, namely that he was accused of having taught everywhere against the law and the temple (Acts 21:21, 28). It is the only passage in Acts which recognizes such an aspect in Paul's teaching, but the author implies that such an accusation was pure slander. Yet it is at the core of Paul's letters that keeping the law, even circumcision, is not only misleading but quite wrong for one who has died to the old law and been saved in the new law of the Spirit in Christ Jesus. The text shows, at least, that the author knew very well what Paul was actually teaching.

Just as the author of the Fourth Gospel seems deliberately to have invented a whole new body of teaching for Jesus, and written a romance in which Jesus teaches it, so the author of Acts seems to have invented a Paul who was the great Roman-Pharisee pupil of Gamaliel, one who taught that Christianity fulfilled the scheme of salvation in Jewish history. We have no way of testing the stories of the earlier days of Peter's preaching and the first community, but this early part of Acts sounds to me quite as credible as the nonsacramental Jewish Christianity, of which Acts makes Paul the great exemplar, sounds incredible. Why, then, and when would such a romance have been written?

Vielhauer says he will not discuss the date of Acts in his small study, but he implies that it was quite late. On the contrary, its ending – if, as I think, we have the original ending – would in itself imply that it was written while Paul was still preaching in Rome, although this would require that the Gospels were written still earlier, in the late forties or fifties. To this I see no objection, even if in thinking so I stand rather alone. In neither the Gospels nor Acts do the narratives suggest that the authors are talking of a lost temple and civilization at Jerusalem. Even the warning in Luke that armies will surround Jerusalem and destroy it need not at all have been a *post eventum* reference (19:43-44), any more than are the many vivid portrayals now current of man's destruction by the atom bomb. The possibility of such besieging and destruction of Jerusalem must have stood out sharply in the minds of great numbers of people in that city under the Romans. Siege and destruction were everywhere understood to be the price of revolt.

Dating these books has usually been based upon an assumption that Christianity advanced from stage to stage as a block, that is, that it began with ardent hopes of eschatology (a fact which cannot be challenged) and then turned in solid phalanx to theology and sacraments only as the early hopes of Christ's immediate return proved false. Vielhauer is excellent in showing how eschatology in Paul already by the forties and fifties was becoming integrated with theology, and how in Paul's later thinking it lost its central position altogether, that is, presumably by A.D. 60 or 65. Similarly eschatology was integrated with sacramental mysticism in the Fourth Gospel and in the Letter to the Hebrews. Hebrews, indeed, calls the earlier doctrine only elementary milk for children, and lists in excellent outline the essential features of the Christianity of Acts: repentance and faith (for forgiveness), baptism, laying on of hands (for giving the Spirit), the resurrection, and the judgment (5:12-6:2). The author of the letter wants something more mature in Christianity, he says, and so gives us the great High Priest. He is clearly speaking to early churchmen, or people with their point of view, men who still live on the elementary milk, as does Luke. The difficulty is that simplicity of ideas does not indicate with finality an early date. Many Christians must have clung to the early eschatological hope long after others had practically, at least, abandoned it. Indeed, many persons of our own time still hold to it; I myself was brought up in ardent and daily expectation of the Return. But such hopes do not endure with most people: five years, ten years, twenty years – at each milestone those who could live in this tension would be fewer, and men who had deeper values to offer in Christianity would increasingly come into favor. Luke is also retreating from the more ardent expectation, but his solution, as Vielhauer has pointed out, is that of Jewish Christianity. For he sees Christianity not as a new covenant, which superseded the old by offering a mystic and sacramental union with the body of Christ, but as the fulfillment of the old covenant itself.

My own guess, accordingly, is that the author wrote Acts in the early sixties to assure Theophilus that, even though he might have heard disturbing rumors of Paul's teaching, Paul was actually a very great man who preached and lived for what he, like the author of the Letter to the Hebrews, considered the childish milk of the gospel (I Cor. 3:1-2).

Such a fiction could, indeed, have been written at almost any time, but I should guess that Acts is a very early production, written before Paul had died and while the issue was still an acute one.

One wonders if it was someone thinking like the author of Acts whom Paul had in mind when he wrote to the Galatians: "Even if we, or an angel from heaven, should preach to you a gospel contrary to that which we preached to you, let him be accursed" (Gal. 1:8). For no one in the Galatian or Corinthian churches would have recognized in the pages of Acts the Paul they had heard preach or had read in his letters.

11

Paul and the Hellenization of Christianity

1968

The background for this essay is given in its first footnote and in more detail in the Preface to this volume. (See also Eccles 1985:123-28, 173.)

I don't recall ever discussing with Goodenough why the bulk of this essay should be devoted to Romans. Beginning with Acts is logical enough, see the essay just previous. But it is not equally self-evident that all of the rest of the study ought to be devoted to just one Pauline letter. After all, Goodenough could have addressed himself to some or all of Paul had he wished, either by proceeding thematically or by taking up selected passages from several letters.

But I suspect that Goodenough selected Romans for several reasons, conscious or unconscious. It has traditionally been seen as the heart of Paul's message and a kind of "dogmatics in outline." It has also been the beginning of movements of renewal within the Church, witness Augustine, Luther, Barth. Finally, going through Romans chapter by chapter allowed Goodenough to experience the Pauline "gospel" in comprehensive form a final time.

Paul was an author Goodenough returned to again and again in his research and writing. Why did Paul the Christian fascinate him, when most of Goodenough's thinking was devoted to Judaism and not to Christianity? Two parallels in their careers may supply part of the answer. Both men –

Goodenough and the Apostle Paul – insisted on viewing Judaism and Christianity simultaneously. Of all the Christian texts available, only Paul's letters come from the time when the separation between the Jews and the followers of Jesus was not yet final, and perhaps could have been reversed. As a Christian missionary Paul was in the middle of those debates, and his letters inevitably reflect the conflict. By the time of the gospels and the other later New Testament writings the decision has been made, but Paul came from a social location and from a decade or two in which the parting of the ways had just begun. Goodenough too could not accept that retaining Christianity meant letting go of Judaism. In his work he moved constantly from the one to the other, and had there been time he would have interpreted both, the one by the other.

But Paul was also moving in a particular direction. A snapshot would show him linked to both religious traditions and would depict them indeed as perhaps more than one but surely not yet two, separate and distinct. But a videotape of Paul would reveal him in motion, leaving old positions behind, abandoning them just as his opponents had claimed he was doing. With Paul the movement *was from the old to the new, no matter how much it seemed to him to be otherwise, no matter how much his writings appeared to retain some of each in tension or in paradox. I suspect that this circumstance of being in motion or "in between" also attracted Goodenough to Paul. After all, that movement was the subject of Goodenough's research as he originally conceived it. Paul was the figure who exemplified that progression, more than any other. And through his entire teaching career Goodenough was in motion too, out of traditional Christianity to whatever the next stage for him might be. (The young William F. Buckley unwittingly attests to this in the opening chapter of* God and Man at Yale *[Buckley 1951:8-9]. The Goodenough Buckley knew of in the late 1940's was clearly in motion religiously, something Buckley was not prepared to appreciate when he wrote in 1951.)*

....

What direction would Goodenough's work have taken if he had had another two decades to write?

His use of Jewish literary sources over those years would have benefitted significantly from the aid and influence of Jacob Neusner and his students. The two men had come to know each other well in a relatively short time. Goodenough's estimate of Neusner's contributions, actual and potential, is reflected in a sentence from the Preface to volume 12 of the Symbols, *dated October, 1963: "A new obligation has arisen from the critical aid that a recent acquaintance, a brilliant young scholar, has given during the last two years, Jacob Neusner."*

Goodenough would have been delighted with recent archaeological discoveries. When he and I first met, it was to discuss my working with him on what would become the essay below. But almost before I knew it he had plans, photographs and reconstructions of the Sardis synagogue spread out before me and was commenting on them with obvious pleasure and excitement. He knew enough about Sardis and its marvelous synagogue to believe it would corroborate his views of Diaspora Judaism and of the development of Christianity. He was able to add a bit about Sardis to Symbols *12 just before publication, see pages 191-95.*

He surely would have been all over a number of important Greek inscriptions unknown or at least unappreciated in his lifetime. The 80 new texts from Sardis would have been first on his list; here are some others:

> *Louis Robert's study of Greek funerary curses (Robert 1978) calls attention again to such inscriptions as IG III^2 13209, 13210 = SIG 1239 (from Athens) and SIG 1240 (from Chalcis in Euboea), in which curses resembling those in Deut 28:22, 28 are used to protect the graves of well-to-do sophists of the second century. (See also Horsley 1983, No. 96 and Kraabel 1981:121 note 26.)*

> *New inscriptions from the Greek island of Delos show that the* Samaritan *Diaspora had reached the Greek world and adopted many of its conventions far earlier than had been directly attested previously (Bruneau 1982, Kraabel 1984 and White 1987). If this tiny sister-tradition of Judaism was so well represented on Delos as early as the third century* BCE, *as one of these inscriptions suggests, how much more extensive and "Hellenized" might the Jewish Diaspora have been at that time!*

> *The century's single most important Greek inscription, as far as the history of Judaism is concerned, is the* theosebeis *text discovered at Aphrodisias in Caria in 1976 and recently published*

(Reynolds/Tannenbaum 1987). It has already prompted a great deal of comment and discussion, some appearing even before the inscription itself (Kraabel 1981:121 note 26, 1985, 1986, Meeks 1983:39, Feldman 1985, Gager 1986).

Goodenough's major concern, however, would have been for New Testament studies and the "hellenization of Christianity." Recent comments by Dieter Georgi suggest that Goodenough would have had an increasing influence upon New Testament scholars like himself. Goodenough was just coming to know and appreciate Georgi's writings during our work on his last paper. In the second edition of his book on 2 Corinthians, Georgi confesses himself "strongly influenced" by Goodenough's "monumental work" on Diaspora Judaism, criticizes the neglect of that work by other scholars, and asserts that "the basic theses of Goodenough appear to be vindicated more and more" by recent discoveries. He cites the Nag Hammadi Gnostic texts and especially the excavations of ancient synagogues in this connection (Georgi 1986:368-71).

Goodenough also would have been pleased with the approaches to Paul and to Acts represented in three recent monographs. I single them out here for two reasons: they are or soon will be typical of most writing being done on these topics, and in them the issues are particularly accessible. They are well organized and clearly written, and their extensive documentation offers ready access to the work of other scholars. (See also Kraabel 1989.)

In The Jews in Luke-Acts, *Jack Sanders (1987) demonstrates two things: 1) how completely Luke-Acts is "theology in historical guise" (to use a term of Jacob Neusner's) and not straightforward narrative at all. While this will come as no surprise for the gospel, since that conclusion is one of the sure results of* Redactionsgeschichte, *it will cause great difficulty for many readers of Luke's second volume. Acts has no "parallels," as the gospel has, to reveal its* Tendenz. *And Acts is also the only account we possess of the careers of the first generation of Christian leaders. For nearly two millennia it has been* the *story of how the earliest church developed and grew, and in particular how it related to outsiders, both Jew and Gentile. In later centuries the Church often used the pattern of examples set by "the Apostles" in Acts as it worked out its own relationships to non-Christians, and particularly to Jews. Sanders then draws on the work of many other researchers to show 2) how fundamentally anti-Jewish Luke was in his theology, and how that view of Jews is carried particularly in the many stories about them in Acts.*

Goodenough many times cited Kirsopp Lake's statement about the historical value of Acts, and his own demurrer. He repeats it in the first paragraph both of the previous essay and that reprinted below. He would have accepted readily Sanders' first point, and quickly drawn the conclusions of the second for his own work.

Räisänen (1983) and Watson (1987) also represent directions in the study of Paul which Goodenough would have welcomed, even though they would have required his reconsideration of a number of the points he makes in the essay below. They argue that Paul must not be removed from his first century context and made into timeless dogmatics as in particular the heirs of Luther were wont to do. First of all, they say, Acts must be set to one side; particularly with regard to Paul's understanding of the Law and his relations to non-Christian Jews, the Lukan image cannot be credited. Here they echo some of the concerns of Sanders already noted.

According to Räisänen in Paul and the Law, *because Paul's letters are occasional pieces, the product of passion and intuition rather than of detached and logical thought, they can be inconsistent and self-contradictory, secondary rationalizations of positions Paul found himself driven to adopt. And they must be interpreted as such.*

In Watson's view in Paul, Judaism and the Gentiles, *Paul's own experience with the Gentile mission brings him to see Christianity as a sect, of itself, rather than as a movement of renewal remaining within Judaism. This puts Paul on a collision-course not only with non-Christian Jews, but especially with those Jewish-Christians (and their converts) who did not wish to become detached from the ancestral community. It also requires Paul to depict the Law in a negative, polemical fashion, an image which has hampered the establishment of proper relationships between Christians and Jews to this day. Watson believes that the social setting of Paul's work was missed during the many centuries when the Church saw him as its premier and earliest theologian, and that Paul's original intent has been lost and his position (particularly with regard to non-Christian Jews) distorted as a result.*

Goodenough never had the chance to grapple with issues of Christian origins as fully as he had always desired and intended to do. In a longer active career he would have had a great deal forcefully to say about "the hellenization of Christianity" and about "the relations between Christians and Jews." His broad familiarity with the thought and the imagery of Greek-speaking Judaism would have made him a formidable contestant in these debates. The republishing of much of his work, initiated by Jacob Neusner, will allow our greatest native-born historian of religions to influence a new generation of readers, perhaps in ways he and his editors could never have predicted.

Erwin R. Goodenough with A.T. Kraabel,* *Religions in Antiquity. Essays in Memory of Erwin Ramsdell Goodenough,* Ed. J. Neusner. Leiden: Brill, 1968. Pages 23-68.

I. The "Paul" of the Book of Acts

Understanding of Paul and his message has from the beginning been thrown into confusion by many factors. The Book of Acts gives a beautifully written, straight account of Paul and his preaching, the various journeys, the first trial with its autobiographical speeches –

---

*[Dr. Goodenough had long intended that his last major work would be a multi-volumed study of "the hellenization of Christianity"; in the winter of 1964-65, when he learned that he had only a short time to live, he determined to carry the project through, as far as he could. As his research assistant, I was responsible for investigating and summarizing the work done by New Testament scholars on the texts and issues with which he was concerned.

When it became clear that there was not time to complete a book, Dr. Goodenough deliberately began to rework his notes and preliminary material into a long article on Paul; he reasoned that in an essay on this seminal and very early Christian writer he could clarify the methodology and indicate many of the conclusions of the larger work.

At the time of his death, March 20, 1965, Dr. Goodenough had written or dictated the material which is contained in the body of this article; as he requested, I have rewritten and edited it, and supplied such footnotes or parts of footnotes as are enclosed in brackets. I have attempted to carry out his wishes and instructions to the best of my ability, but it should be made clear that he had read little of the rewriting and none of my footnotes at the time of his death.

Three of my teachers have assisted me in this work: Krister Stendahl first brought me into contact with Dr. Goodenough and, at the latter's request, assumed final responsibility for this article and its publication; Helmut Köster and Dieter Georgi advised me in the preparation of the manuscript. A grant from the Bollingen Foundation provided financial support both while I worked with Dr. Goodenough and while I completed the article after his death. With gratitude I acknowledge all this assistance. – A.T.K.

Dr. Goodenough's books which are often cited in the notes are abbreviated as follows:

Light – By Light, Light: The Mystic Gospel of Hellenistic Judaism, New Haven, Yale University Press, 1935.

Introduction – An Introduction to Philo Judaeus, 2nd ed., Oxford, Basil Blackwell, 1962; New York, Barnes and Noble, 1963.

Symbols – Jewish Symbols in the Greco-Roman Period, New York, Pantheon Books, vol. 1-3, 1953; vol. 4, 1954; vol. 5-6, 1956; vol. 7-8, 1958; vol. 9-11, 1964; vol. 12, 1965. (Bollingen Series XXXVII).

Psychology – The Psychology of Religious Experiences, New York, Basic Books, 1965.

In the footnotes, "G." is the abbreviation for Erwin R. Goodenough.]

and these seem completely plausible.[1] His message as Acts presents it –
about Christ and salvation and about the coming Great Event – is quite
identical with the ideas attributed to Peter and James in the same
book.[2] In practically all the older lives of Paul, and in many present-
day popular accounts, the authors approached Paul primarily through
Acts. The youth of the Church are commonly trained to outline the
missionary journeys on maps. Kirsopp Lake said to a graduate class
years ago that if Acts is not an historically reliable account of the
beginnings of Christianity, we know nothing of that beginning, and so
he and Foakes Jackson compiled their great work called *The Beginnings
of Christianity*, which was almost exclusively a study of Acts.[3]

At the same time it is widely recognized that Paul's own letters
reveal a man presenting a scheme of salvation which calls not just for
belief that Christ was the son of God who rose from the dead and was
soon to return, but a belief *in* Christ, a death of the self and a union
with the savior which Acts never suggests.[4] To take a specific example:

---

[1][In his article "The Perspective of Acts" reprinted above, G. argues 1) that Acts
presents a "largely fictional Paul," 119 above, with an over-simplified and
thoroughly Jewish-Christian theology; and 2) that, for the most part, it is
deceptively and deliberately silent about the true nature of the Church's
developing theology and organization. On the basis of the way Acts ends, G.
concludes that "it was written while Paul was still preaching in Rome," 121
above.]

[2][M. Dibelius delineates some of these similarities in *From Tradition to Gospel*,
1935, 16ff. In his *Studies in the Acts of the Apostles*, 1956 (hereafter abbreviated
Studies), 165ff, 184, he points out that the repetition of the same themes in the
speeches of different men is due in part to Luke's didactic purpose, cf. H.
Conzelmann, *Die Apostelgeschichte (HNT)*, 1963, 8: "wollen die Reden nicht
die individuelle Art des Redners verführen, sondern die substantielle Einheit
der urchristlichen, dh normativen Predigt."]

[3][*The Beginnings of Christianity*, I (five volumes, 1920-33, hereafter abbreviated
Beginnings) turned out to be just what G. calls it here. However, in a letter
dated April 5, 1965, H.J. Cadbury, who collaborated with Lake on the final two
volumes, says that the work on Acts was originally planned as the beginning of
a much larger study; this is indicated in the prefaces to volume 1, page vii, and
volume 2, page v-vi, and by the method of numbering the volumes i.e., the five
books on Acts together form only part I of *Beginnings*.]

[4][G.'s understanding of Paul in the epistles is elaborated below, 140 ff. in the
major section of this article – but not only there. He often found occasion to
refer to Paul at length in his studies of Judaism in the Roman Imperial period,
e.g. in *Light* and in *Symbols;* so also, when he turned his attention to the
modern world and its religions, e.g. in *Toward a Mature Faith*, 1955, and in
Psychology (see the indices to these volumes). Thus, long before he began this
article, G. had approached Paul from a number of sides and published some
preliminary conclusions; for this reason many of G.'s earlier writings have been
brought in to amplify and illuminate the present article.]

there has recently been much dispute about the validity of Paul's speech at Athens[5] as Acts reports it, with the final judgment that there is nothing in it that Paul could not have said. But this does not establish the validity of the speech, since Paul writes in his letters much that would indeed have instructed the Athenian pundits, but which does not appear in the sermon.[6]

The point is that it is sheer perversity to go from Acts to Paul's letters, from a second-hand account to a man's own exposition of his thought. We must work the other way: first look for Paul in his own writings, and then go to the narrative in Acts; be fully prepared (if necessary) to find discrepancies, and to let the first-hand sources have complete right of way in case of disagreements. We can thus judge the value of the secondary work as a historical source, and read with greater or less credulousness the incidents and speeches for which there is no comparable report from Paul himself.

In a study of the hellenization of Christianity as effected in Paul's work, we are under no obligation to make so complete an analysis of Acts as the preceding paragraphs would suggest. But it is so common to read the letters with Acts in mind that we must at the outset raise a few points to show why Acts seems to be a tendentious document written to exaggerate Paul's Jewish conservatism and the unity of the early Christian preaching.[7]

---

[5][Cf. B. Gärtner, *The Areopagus Speech and Natural Revelation*, 1955, 249. G. had read Gärtner carefully and critically; many parts of the book he considered excellent, but he also felt that it defined "Greek philosophy" much too narrowly along Stoic lines, cf. his comment in footnote 39 below and in *Symbols* 12: 187 note 1. Gärtner would also minimize the distinctions G. makes between the "Paul" of Acts and the Paul of the Pauline letters; see Gärtner's concluding chapter, "The Areopagus Speech and Paul," 248-52.]

[6][Conzelmann, *op. cit.* 103, lists the Pauline theologoumena missing in this speech: the "wrath of God" (cf. Rom. 1), the contrast between faith and law, the *theologia crucis*, the dialectical relationship between "present" and "future," and the idea of an imminent Parousia. In *Studies*, 58, Dibelius calls it "a hellenistic speech with a Christian ending" (17:31); for the non-Pauline elements, see 57-64.]

[7][Most scholars would agree that Acts has a Tendenz which becomes clear in what the author chooses to stress or play down, to include or omit. In "Le plan des Actes des Apôtres," *NTS* 1 (1954-55), 44-51, Ph. Menoud finds the pattern of Acts in the missionary command of the risen Lord, Acts 1 : 8. This command is fulfilled "theologically speaking" by the time of the Jerusalem Council, Acts 15, when both Jews and non-Jews have heard the gospel, and the council's action assures that the Church will include both groups. "Geographically speaking" the command is fulfilled when Paul reaches the center of the Roman Empire, Rome, from which the gospel will penetrate "to the ends of the earth." According to Menoud, Paul is emphasized in the latter part of Acts because of

Begin with Paul's early life, before his conversion; the most famous passages are Gal. 1:13-5 and Phil. 3:4-6.[8] The first passage says that he "advanced in Judaism beyond many of my own age among my people, so extremely zealous was I for the traditions of my fathers (or, my father, αἱ πατρικαί μου παραδόσεις)." [9] This continued as he persecuted the Church, but he was suddenly changed when God, who had elected him, "was pleased to reveal his Son within me (ἐν ἐμοί)," vs. 16. The RSV makes this conform to Acts by rendering "reveal to me," precisely the sort of reading Paul *through* Acts which I am deploring.[10] The RSV

---

this mission, i.e., because he is the one designated and qualified to carry it out, not because Luke is writing tendentious biography.

B.S. Easten, in *Early Christianity: The Purpose of Acts and Other Papers*, 1954, holds that Acts portrays Christianity in Jewish terms because Luke's purpose is to show Christianity as "nothing more nor less than Judaism" and thus entitled to recognition as a religio licita, 43. This attempt failed: Luke "could not persuade the Roman government because he could not convince his fellow Christians. Paul had done his work too well" 114f. Conzelmann's understanding differs widely from Easton's e.g., his summary, *op. cit.* 10.]

[8]In 2 Cor. 11:22, Paul simply asserts that he was a Hebrew, an Israelite, a descendant of Abraham. We must not look for shades of meaning in this pleonasm, but note that he seems to be dragging in every word he can think of to establish his Jewish character.

[9][G.'s good friend, M. Enslin, takes this text as clear evidence of Paul's orthodox and unhellenized background, "Paul – What Manner of Jew" in *In the Time of Harvest: Essays in Honor of Abba Hillel Silver*, 1963, 158f. G.'s vigorous notations in his offprint of this essay reflect the divergences in their views, cf. also the article of Enslin discussed in note 17 below.]

[10][G.'s remarks here would probably extend to the NEB's elaborate translation "to me and through me" and to F. Blass and A. Debrunner, *A Greek Grammar of the New Testament*, 1961, which says that *en* here "appears...to stand for the customary dative proper" and suggests the translation "to me" or "in my case" because "'in me' i.e., 'in my spirit' would be unnatural" (para. 220:1). W. Bauer, *A Greek-English Lexicon of the New Testament*, 1957, takes the same position (s.v. *en* IV:4,a). However, in all but one of the "parallels" which these authorities offer from Paul, the object of the preposition is plural (Rom. 1:19, 10:20; 2 Cor. 4:3, 8:1); an examination will show that the "local" translation "among" for these plurals, and the "local" translation "in" with a singular object (as in Gal. 1:16), are just as plausible as "to" or "for." But, further, are these "parallels" with plural objects really germane to Gal. 1:16? The translation for which G. is arguing here is neatly excluded when plural objects of propositions are alleged to be similar to the singular *emoi* in the Galatians text. (The one example cited with a singular object is 1 Cor. 14:11, ὁ λαλῶν ἐν ἐμοὶ βάρβαρος; Blass-Debrunner seems correct in saying that *en* is used here to prevent taking *emoi* as the indirect object of the participle. The difficulty of the reading is obvious, cf. such manuscripts as p. 46 and Codex Bezae, which omit *en.*) G.P. Wetter suggests a translation in line with G.'s; he asks, "Wäre hier von einer visionären Erfahrung in erster Linie die Rede, wie könnte Paulus von einer Offenbarung *in* ihm

translation presupposes the vision on the road to Damascus (Acts, chs. 9, 22 and 26), a story I think Paul himself had never heard;[11] I prefer to follow Paul,[12] both on historical principles and because this inward mystical experience, implied by his "revealed (with)in me," will prove to be the heart of Paul's message.[13] The zealous early years can

---

reden?" ("Die Damaskusvision und das paulinische Evangelium," in *Festgabe für A. Jülicher*, 1927, 82).]

[11][Lake suggests, Beginnings 5:190, that Paul knew of this story in a version or versions told by his detractors and is deliberately opposing them in, e.g., Gal. 1:1, where the phrase "an apostle not from men or through a man" cannot be reconciled with the figure of Ananias in the Acts account, 9:10ff. See also Conzelmann's summary, *op. cit.* 59; and, for a defense of the historicity of the Damascus vision, J. Munck, *Paul and the Salvation of Mankind*, 1959, 11-35, where an attempt is made to reconcile the accounts in Acts with those of Paul.]

[12][Wetter, art. cit., draws the following conclusions regarding the Damascus vision: 1) Paul's letters reveal that he was conscious of having received direct commands from the Lord, who often spoke directly to him and sometimes appeared to him. In this way Paul's life and mission were guided; this is the source of his sense of election and of apostolic authority, and the reason for his stubborn attacks on opponents – in matters about which the will of the Lord has been clearly revealed, there can be no compromise. 2) But Paul does not mention a "Damascus vision" in the texts where it would greatly strengthen his argument e.g., where he feels compelled to refer to, or "boast of," his own ecstatic experiences, as in 2 Cor. 12. Had it been possible, surely he would have brought in this vision in such cases. The event thus did not happen to Paul as Luke tells it, but Paul was known to be the kind of man who could and did experience such things, i.e., the kind of man about whom such a story could easily have been told.

G.'s own understanding is similar to Wetter's. In "John a Primitive Gospel," page 54 above, he argues strongly that Paul's "tremendous revelation of the institution at the Last Supper" must have come in a vision. In Symbols 5:53 note 106, he quotes A.D. Nock's assertion that "certainly Paul's account of the Last Supper was what he had been taught by early disciples;" G.'s reply: "Since Paul denied that he had received anything from them, and says directly that he received this 'from the lord,' the certainty of Nock is strange to say the least." Nock's statement is now available in *Early Gentile Christianity and its Hellenistic Background*, 1964, 125.]

[13][G. constantly used the terms "mystery" and "mystic," e.g., in *Light*, which is subtitled "The Mystic Gospel of Hellenistic Judaism"; he realized, however, that they were often misunderstood, see his comments below, page 59. One attempt at clarification was his article "Literal Mystery in Hellenistic Judaism" in *Quantulacumque: Studies Presented to Kirsopp Lake*, 1937, 227-41. There he indicates that "mystery" may refer to the Greek mysteries or to the mystery religions, which offer *lusis* in their initiation rites. However, for Plato and later Greeks, philosophy also offers *lusis*, and on a higher level; "this λύσις consists in philosophy's teaching that reality lies not in things perceived by the senses, but in the invisible things perceived by the soul," 230. Further, Plato commonly used terms from the vocabulary of the mysteries and "the question of whether these terms in Plato were intended literally or figuratively turns on the

be taken as no more than they say, namely that Paul was a completely observant Jew until convicted by a great revelation of Christ within himself.[14]

The passage in Philippians builds up a ponderous pleonasm for Paul's Jewishness: circumcised on the eighth day, of the people of Israel, of the tribe of Benjamin, a Hebrew born of Hebrews,[15] in his attitude to the law a Pharisee, a persecutor of the Church and blameless before the Law (Phil.: 4-6). This passage adds nothing to the other except the allusion to the Pharisees. Much as it would have added to his argument to say that he was himself a Pharisee, he does *not* say it – only that he followed the Pharisees (as did most of the Jews, apparently), rather than e.g., the Sadducees or Essenes, in his understanding of the Law.

In contrast, the Paul of Acts states, "According to the strictest party of our religion I lived as a Pharisee" (Acts 26:5); "Brethren, I am a Pharisee, a son of Pharisees" (23:6); and even "I am a Jew born at Tarsus

---

existence not of an initiation rite, but of a belief that the process of learning the higher truths was a real purgation and means of salvation," 229. Thus G. could call philosophy a "mystery" without requiring it to have mystery rites, rites of initiation. He then called hellenistic Judaism a "mystery" in the same sense, but argued at the same time that there may have been rites of some sort in the Jewish cult (for his evidence, chiefly from Philo, see *Light*, 259-64). When a heavy, altar-like table was found to be a focus of worship in the huge ancient synagogue at Sardis in Asia Minor, G. considered it strong evidence for his position, see *Symbols* 12:195. – For a description of the mystic who influenced G.'s own youth, his "Uncle Charlie," see *Toward a Mature Faith*, 1955, 15 ff.]

[14][On the basis of Paul's involvement in the death of Stephen, Acts 7:58f, Enslin suggests that Paul may have been much more conservative and orthodox than the average Palestinian Jew. As an equally plausible alternative to the view "so easily noised about today, that all Jews of the Diaspora must of necessity have been far less Jewish than their fellows in Judea," he suggests that these Hellenists (Acts 6:9), may be "'diaspora Jews' who had settled in Zion for the precise purpose of getting free from the contaminating danger of the larger world. In a word...we are free to wonder if these synagogues of 'hellenistic Jews' were not of the most ultraorthodoxy, composed of those who had at last been enabled to return to Zion, and that their reason for disputing with Stephen was due to a feeling of outrage that some of their own members had become infected with a sorry heresy," art. cit. 157. G.'s reaction to this hypothesis (and Enslin insists that it is only an hypothesis) might well have been that, were it true to the evidence *in Acts*, it would be but another example of how the author has "Judaized" Paul.]

[15]The NEB suggests that this could mean "a Hebrew-speaking Jew of a Hebrew-speaking family." I can see this only as another attempt at "Judaizing' Paul.

in Cilicia, but brought up in this city at the feet of Gamaliel,[16] educated according to the strict manner of the law of our fathers" (22:3). These passages state that, while his opponents might be Jews, Paul was all of that, and in addition had received the highest rabbinic training, that under the great Gamaliel himself, and had even been a member of the closely guarded ranks of the Pharisaic party, where his ancestors had preceded him. Such references to his background could have been used to great advantage in the letters, as Paul defends himself and answers his Jewish detractors; but he says nothing which corresponds to these texts from Acts. An argument from silence may be weak when used to support an unwelcome judgment, but the natural inference is that Paul would have said the more if he could have done so, and that Acts is expanding Paul's remarks for him. In that case, we should suppose that Acts was interested to pull Paul closer to Judaism than he actually was. Thus far we have grounds only for suspicion that such may be the general purpose of Acts, but unless these grounds of suspicion are removed, we have no right to assume that Paul had been a member of the Pharisaic party and a pupil of Gamaliel merely on the basis of the statements of Acts.[17]

There is much other evidence in Acts for questioning the Lukan version of Paul. Paul himself says that he did not return to Jerusalem after his conversion until he had spent three years in Arabia, and even then he stayed privately with Peter and consulted no other Jerusalem Christians except James. Then he went to Syria and Cilicia where he began a preaching campaign on his own (Gal. 1:18-24). But Acts 9:26-30 says on the contrary that when he left Damascus he came to Jerusalem,[18] where Barnabas brought him to the apostles, and told

---

[16][In "Paul and Gamaliel," *Jour. of Rel.* 7 (1927), 360-75, Enslin has summarized what can be determined about this account of Paul's training in Jerusalem by Gamaliel, *if* the Pauline letters are used as sources and Acts discounted. His verdict is that Paul's "rabbinic exegesis" is what anyone who attended synagogue services regularly might acquire, but that "there is not the slightest trace...of any technical halakic training," 370, such as might be expected from a student of Gamaliel. Further, "there is no trace of any connection with Jerusalem prior to his conversion," 372. Enslin is not arguing here for a "hellenized" view of Paul (see notes 10 and 15 above); rather he is questioning the reliability of the Lukan picture of Paul, much as G. himself is doing.]

[17][Lake considers it highly unlikely that a "pupil of Gamaliel" could have produced "so gross a caricature" of the Jewish law as does Paul, *Beginnings* 4: 278f.]

[18][„Nach dem Plan der Act kann sich Paulus noch nicht an die Heiden wenden, denn die Heidenmission ist noch nicht sanktioniert; andererseites soll er nicht untätig bleiben: die Wirkung seiner Bekehrung muss demonstriert werden." Luke's solution is to have Paul preach in the synagogue of Damascus (Acts

them of his conversion. According to Acts, Paul did considerable preaching in Jerusalem until the Hellenists wanted to kill him; then he was taken away to Tarsus (which is in Cilicia).[19] The interesting main points here are that he was for an unspecified time preaching along with the apostles in Jerusalem, and that it was the Hellenists who wanted to kill him. He was apparently fully acceptable to the "Hebrews" in the Jerusalem congregation, but the Hellenists rejected him.[20] The author is indeed laying it on thick, that Paul's gospel, far from being hellenistic, especially turned the "Hellenists" to murderous fury.

The accounts of the great conference in Jerusalem, which Paul says occurred fourteen years later (Gal. 2:1), show discrepancies in exactly the same direction. Possibly the two accounts refer to different incidents, but I agree with the overwhelming majority of scholars who hold that they report the same Jerusalem meeting. Acts 15:1ff. says that some Judean brethren (who had come to Antioch when Paul and Barnabas were preaching) had insisted that without circumcision a Christian could not be saved. Paul and Barnabas opposed this, until the group sent them with some others to Jerusalem to have the point out with the "apostles and elders" there. A group of believers from the Pharisaic party upheld the requirement of circumcision (15:5ff.), but Peter, Barnabas and Paul successfully opposed them, and required only that the converts accept the "Noachite law," i.e., that they "abstain from idolatry, from unchastity, from things strangled, and from blood"

9:19ff.) and then go to Jerusalem, Conzelmann, op. cit. 59. The differences between these accounts in Galatians and Acts are discussed by Lake in *Beginnings* 5:192-94.]

[19][Acts 9:30 and Gal. 1:21 may be in agreement at this point, one giving the name of the city, the other the name of the larger district in which the city is located.]

[20][Acts 6:1ff. describes an argument in which the Jerusalem congregation is divided into "Hebrews" and "Hellenist." G. assumes that the "Hellenists" are the hellenized Christians of Jerusalem, i.e., the group whose position is close to that of Paul, and that 9:29f. is an attempt to conceal Paul's "Hellenism" by having this group attack him. Cadbury argues that the "Hellenists" are gentiles, *Beginnings* 5:59-74, but most scholars consider them Jews whose native language is Greek rather than Aramaic. Conzelmann states: "Sie müssen mit der Gesetzeshaltung des Judentums in Konflikt gekommen sein, dh sie dürften die Linie Jesu klarer als die Zwölf fortgeführt haben;" they were driven out of Jerusalem (8:1) after the martyrdom of the "Hellenist" Stephen, op. cit., 43, cf. 52. Nock agrees (St. Paul, 1937, 61ff.), but Munck holds that while the "Hellenists" and the "Hebrews" differed in language and perhaps in place of birth, "we know nothing of any dogmatic or ethical differences between the two groups," op. cit., 221, cf. 219. Enslin suggests that the "Hellenists" may in fact be ultra-orthodox, see note 15 above.]

(15:28f.).[21] To this Paul and Barnabas agreed, and they separated to go on different missions. But Paul had no sooner come to Derbe and Lystra when he at once circumcised Timothy so as not to offend the Jews of that region (16:1-3). Paul opposes circumcision at Antioch, then his view prevails in Jerusalem, then he circumcises a gentile as soon as he reaches Asia Minor – a story of incredible contradictions.

Paul's own account of the Jerusalem council (Gal. 2:1-10) is that he had a revelation that he should go to Jerusalem; accordingly he went to talk his gospel over privately with the leaders there, taking along Titus and Barnabas.[22] Titus, a Greek, was uncircumcised and, in spite of protest, remained so; the only thing asked, as the leaders gave Paul and his party the right hand of fellowship, was that they remember

---

[21][Problems connected with this "apostolic decree" have been widely discussed. Conzelmann, *op. cit.*, 84f., concludes that 1) originally the decree embodied a "concession by the gentile Christians" to facilitate social intercourse with Jewish Christians. But 2) Luke's understanding is „heilsgeschichtlich": "das Dekret stellt die Kontinuität zwischen Israel und der gesetzesfreien Kirche dar." Finally 3) the Western text shortens the decree and turns it into timeless moral commands adding the Golden Rule. See also Lake, *Beginnings* 5:204ff.]

[22][Lake's solution of the discrepancies between Acts and Galatians posits a certain amount of confusion or differences of emphasis among the participants and in the later written accounts: 1) Galatians 2 brings out the *theological* questions: Is circumcision necessary for Christians? How does the Law apply to gentile Christians? 2) The actual decree was intended to "facilitate the *social intercourse* of Jewish and gentile Christians by establishing rules of conduct for gentiles which would remove the possibility of offense in Jewish circles," *Beginnings* 5:209f., (emphasis supplied). But since Christians were soon rejected by Jewish society, "social intercourse" was soon no longer a problem; by the time Luke wrote, although he knew the content of the decree itself, "he did not quite know what the exact controversy was," *loc. cit.*

In *Studies* 94-7, Dibelius shows that the council speeches in Acts 15 presuppose things known not to the men of the council, but only to the reader of Acts. Peter's speech, vs. 7-9, refers to the story of the conversion of Cornelius not as it occurred in more common tradition but as it had been reworked and amplified by Luke in Acts 10:1ff., cf. *Studies* 108ff. The important speeches of Paul and Barnabas are barely mentioned, vs. 12, "because God's acts in the mission to the Gentiles have already been related, not in this gathering of the apostles, but in the Book of Acts." James' speech, vs. 13ff, is surprisingly out of character and also refers to the *Lucan* version of the Cornelius story. Dibelius' conclusion, 99-101, is that Luke has composed the story of the Jerusalem Council to fit the plan of his book. "We thus have only one account of the meeting...that of Paul in Gal. 2. We are not justified in correcting it according to the account in Acts."

Conzelmann, *op. cit.* 89, suggests that Paul's co-workers (including Titus? Gal. 2:3) must be circumcised so that they may enter the synagogues where (according to Luke's presuppositions) Paul's work always begins. See also the preceding note.]

the poor (presumably the poor in Jerusalem). That is, not a single trace of legalism intruded into the settlement.

The differences are indeed considerable. The Acts account, even without the Timothy incident, contradicts Paul's repeated insistence that the legal approach in any form cancelled the approach through grace and faith. James in Acts does not explicitly say that it was necessary to be circumcised to be a Christian, but such is the clear implication.[23] The incident of Timothy's circumcision comes in after the narrative about the council is closed, as though the author of Acts is saying, "...but Paul was not really so rabid about circumcision as he is reported to be."[24]

Since Paul himself says that even a commandment like "Thou shalt not covet" destroys one when it is presented as law (Rom. 7:7ff.), I cannot believe that he would have meekly accepted the law of kosher meat as Acts 15:28f. implies; indeed this rule was one he openly flouted in his missions (e.g., Gal. 2:11-21). Paul, as we shall see, just did not like what Philo called "specific laws."

On less secure grounds, Paul's Roman citizenship (Acts 22:25ff.) also seems dubious.[25] At one time, under Ptolemy and Caesar, citizenship was given rather freely in the East to those who would help in the army, either in service or by contribution. It is conceivable that Paul's great-grandfather had had such an honor, and that is why I consider it a possibility. But it is by no means a probability, for in that case Paul would have come from a great and probably rich family, and of this there is no indication whatever. The only argument for the truth of the tradition is the name Paul; this is the sort of *gentilicum*[26] one would have taken over on being made citizen (usually by adoption). The story

---

[23][On the basis of investigations by, e.g., Dibelius, Menoud and Conzelmann, many scholars would hold that the pictures of James and Paul have both been softened to suit the purposes of the writer of Acts.]

[24][Nock, *op. cit.*, suggests an explanation for the contradiction: "Timothy was the son of a Jewish mother, and on Rabbinic theory obliged to be circumcised, and Paul emphatically held that except in matters of tablefellowship...a convert should abide by the status which was his by birth...So he might fairly hold that Timothy was by birth in the category of circumcision," 108. Nock also points out that a strong emphasis on circumcision might well have resulted in a lower status for uncircumcised Christians; for Paul, however, "you were 'in Christ' or you were not 'in Christ': there was no half-way house, and there were no second-best Christians," 103, cf. 109, 149.]

[25][On the question of Paul's citizenship, see G.'s "The Perspective of Acts," 119-121 above. Lake and Cadbury appear to accept Paul's citizenship at face value; see *Beginnings* 4:283ff.; Cadbury's note "Roman Law and the Trial of Paul," *Beginnings* 5:297-338; and his 1955 book, *The Book of Acts in History*, 65-82.]

[26][See Cadbury, *The Book of Acts in History*, 76.]

of Paul's various travels and his trip to Rome are so brilliantly told that it seems utterly perverse to doubt their veracity, but if Paul was not a Roman citizen, there could have been no "appeal to Caesar" (Acts 25:9-12) and we must regard that part of Acts as romance or propaganda, wonderfully disguised as history.[27]

My chief objection to using Acts *alongside* Paul's letters as a source for his ideas is that the essential preaching of Paul in Acts is a Jewish-Christian message practically identical with that of Peter and James, one which asked of converts only that they believe in the resurrection of Jesus and the coming resurrection of men. Paul could use such language himself, as when he said, "If you confess with your lips that Jesus is Lord, and believe in your heart that God raised him from the dead, you will be saved" (Rom 10:9) – and this after the long explanation in that letter than much more indeed was involved. While much can be found in Paul's letters that resembles his speeches in Acts (e.g., 1 Thessalonians as a whole is very similar in tone), what appears in *most* of the letters to be the *essential* Paul is not there.[28]

I am not concerned with Acts as such, but only to recover that essential Paul, and to see what his manner of thinking was. For this I consider it extremely dangerous to use Acts as a primary source, implicitly or explicitly[29] When we have the Paul of the letters more clearly in mind (we shall never have him clearly so, since his writings are often far from clear), then perhaps we may evaluate the historical reliability of Acts. In this article, however, our problem is to ascertain what Paul contributed to the hellenizing of Christianity, once we have seen what Paul was trying to teach.

---

[27][Conzelmann, *op. cit.*, points out that, when the specific references to Paul are omitted, the account of the sea journey in Acts 27 becomes a unified narrative and is "in höherem Grade literarisch als irgend ein anderer Teil des Buches," 146; he quotes similar texts from Lucian and Achilles Tatius, 151-54. His conclusion is that the chapter is neither an eyewitness account nor an elaboration thereof, but a literary composition with clear parallels in the pagan literature of the time. E. Haenschen has recently tested Conzelmann's arguments and evidence in his article "Acta 27" in *Zeit und Geschichte: Dankesgabe an R. Bultmann*, 1964, 235-54.]

[28][In "The Perspective of Acts," G.'s criticism of the "Lucan" Paul is more severe, witness the final paragraph, page 122 above.]

[29][G.'s doubts about the objectivity of the writer of Acts have the support of many New Testament scholars, cf. the summary opinion of Conzelmann, *op. cit.*, 9f.]

II. The Letter to the Romans

Method or plan is the first problem in trying to reconstruct the "essential Paul." None of Paul's letters conveys exactly the impression of any other, especially in details, and some seem quite different in kind. Perhaps this diversity stems from Paul's wish to speak to each church on its own terms (cf. 1 Cor. 9:19-22). In 1 Thessalonians, for example, he says that the Thessalonians "became imitators of the churches of God in Christ Jesus which are in Judea" (2:14); I strongly suspect that the Thessalonian church was made up largely of Jews and their church "imitated" the churches in Judea. Accordingly, when Paul writes to this particular church, he uses the word "faith" as the Judean church might define it, i.e., much more along the lines of Acts than of Galatians or Romans. In 1 Thess. 3:5-10 he is anxious to know about their faith, and that they "stand fast in the Lord," which seems to be what he means here by "faith;" he even hopes to supply what is lacking in their faith if he can come to them. He appears to mean: "Hold the faith" in Christ until those events occur which are related soon after in what we might call Paul's "little apocalypse," (3:13, 4:13-5:11, 23). As he uses it in this letter, faith is acknowledging that a body of statements of external facts is true – facts such as that Christ is Lord, that he rose from the dead, and that he will return for the final judgment. When Paul defines faith differently in other letters, it is due in part to his concern to "speak the language" of the particular congregation to which he writes.

In view of these apparent fluctuations, is it legitimate to attempt to extract from a single letter what we take to be the essential message of Paul? I believe it is, since in this letter, Romans, he is provoked by no outside vagaries or problems; he is expounding the message of Christ, the theme of which is salvation. He does this quietly and as systematically as I think his mind ever could work. He becomes deeply emotional in places, but the gospel was a very deeply emotional message and he a deeply emotional person. Nevertheless, his intent in this letter is clear; he is simply telling to the Romans the gospel of Christ as he understands it.

Our approach in this essay is thus akin to that of the text critic, who strives to establish a single critical text, the text which seems to him the most accurate, then he considers the variants as variants from this. We must have a ποῦ στῶ and Romans seems quite the safest one.[30]

---

[30][G.'s view of Romans as a general summary of Pauline thought is supported by T.W. Manson's article, "St. Paul's Letter to the Romans – and Others," now reprinted in *Studies in the Gospels and Epistles*, 1962, 225-41. Manson

Romans, Ch. 1

The letter opens with Paul's greeting to "God's beloved in Rome" (cf. vs. 7). He states his qualifications as an apostle, one set apart for the gospel of God (vs. 1). In verses 3 and 4 he makes the puzzling statement that the Son was "descended from David according to the flesh, and designated son of God in power according to the spirit of holiness by his resurrection from the dead." Many have felt that this text manifests an adoptionist conception of the divinity of Christ, one that would contradict other passages in Paul's letters. I think the passage too brief to allow taking a stand, thus I pass it by completely.[31]

Paul's commission was to bring about "the obedience of faith for the sake of his name among all the gentiles" (vs. 5). It should be noted that the word "obedience" implies a legalistic conception of faith or, at least, includes in "faith" some kind of acquiescence;[32] this is echoed in chapter eight, where Paul speaks of the law of the spirit in Christ Jesus. One thing we may say surely: this is not an obedience to the law of Moses; of that there is no hint whatever.

---

concludes: "We should think of our document primarily as the summing up of the positions reached by Paul and his friends at the end of the long controversy whose beginnings appear in I Corinthians and...in Philippians iii. Having got this statement worked out to his own satisfaction, Paul then decided to send a copy of it to his friends in Ephesus...At the same time he conceived the idea of sending a copy to Rome with a statement of his future plans...Looked at in this way Romans...becomes a manifesto setting forth his deepest convictions on central issues, a manifesto calling for the widest publicity, which the Apostle did his best – not without success – to give it," 241. Munck summarizes the Manson article and agrees with its conclusions, *op. cit.*, 197-200.]

[31][Many scholars explain this "contradiction" by identifying vs. 3f. as Christological tradition of the pre-Pauline community; see G. Bornkamm, Studien zu Antike und Urchristentum, 1959, 199, note 25. G. points out that Philo ascribes a "similar double birth" to Moses, see *Symbols* 9:118f, where the passage (QE ii, 46) is printed.]

[32][The relation between obedience and faith in 1:5 is explained by A. Schlatter as follows: "Der Glaubende untergibt sich dem gnädigen Willen Gottes und stellt sich unter Christus. Weil er bewusst und wollend in die Stellung eintritt, die Gott ihm bereitet hat, erhält das Glauben den Charakter der Gerhorsamsbetätigung. Darum sah Paulus für das, was das Gesetz über die Stätte des göttlichen Gebots und seine Einwohnung im Menschen sagte, im Glauben die Erfüllung," Der Glaube im Neuen Testament,[5] 1963, 363. (G. commended an earlier edition of Schlatter's book for its definition of the idea of *pistis* in Philo, *Light*, 400 note 212.) Cf. R. Bultman: "Paul understands faith primarily as obedience; he understands the act of faith as an act of obedience...Thus, he can combine the two in the expression ὑπακοὴ πίστεως ('the obedience which faith is,' Rom. 1:5)," *Theology of the New Testament*, 1:314 (1951).]

Paul begins his great exposition of the gospel in verse 16. He first speaks of the gospel as the power, δύναμις, of God for salvation to everyone who has faith; the sentence states that the gospel brings salvation, but words are otherwise unclear. We are not in a position to bring Philo[33] at once into the picture as a criterion of interpretation, but

---

[33][G. will often refer to Philo because this older contemporary of Paul is the major figure in the hellenistic Judaism which G. sees behind the hellenization of Christianity. He once states his argument as follows ("New Light on Hellenistic Judaism," *Journal of Bible and Religion* 5 [1937] 21f.): "First, there is the fact that Christianity grew out of Judaism, and never lost the sense of its Jewish roots...Second, it is equally well recognized that Christianity was steadily hellenized, even though we disagree on the extent of this hellenization...Third, it is equally evident that at every stage in the development of their religion Christians felt themselves bitterly opposed to paganism, especially to the Mystery Religions toward which in many ideas they seemed steadily tending...There is a fourth fact...which is the most perplexing of all, the crux of the problem of the origin of hellenistic Christianity...namely, that Christianity, in the process of hellenization, never disintegrated into a thousand sects...Only after this process of the hellenization of Christianity was completed did the great controversies arise which ended in a number of separate Christian Churches...Why, if Christians were in *any* sense borrowing pagan notions, taking them directly from the pagans about them, were there not as many hellenistic Christianities as there were Christians under pagan influence?...Why hellenization, but at the same time a solid front against *acute* hellenization?"

G. finds the answer in the Judaism behind early Christianity, a Judaism exemplified by Philo and manifesting three important characteristics: 1) It is already heavily hellenized, has already drawn much from mystery religions and the religious philosophies of the time. 2) It is Jewish, and so escapes Christian attacks on "paganism". 3) It is a unity in the sense that it possesses a normative text, the Old Testament, and a standard method of interpretation (see below); drawing on this common tradition, not on "paganism" directly, early Christianity resists fragmentation while it becomes steadily more hellenized.

This hellenistic Judaism has two important similarities to early Christianity: "First (in both)...the Old Testament is made into a mystic document, in which literal adventures of Abraham and Sarah, for example, have much less significance than their typological meaning...Second (in both)...salvation is made available to men by the great struggles of the Patriarchs whose lives are our patterns as they fought down the cloying power of matter and received the crown of victory, union with supra-material reality."

Philo furnishes the clearest evidence for this kind of hellenistic Judaism, but he is himself no innovator; he stands within a well-developed tradition. G. explicates this most thoroughly in his book *Light*, the thesis of which he once defined as follows: "Philo is directly in line with this tradition (i.e. the combination of religious philosophy and mystery religion which presents the "true philosophy" as the "true mystery"), and the Old Testament was for him a guide to the true philosophy by which man was though saved by association with the immaterial," art. cit. (note 14 above), 235 with footnote 31.

we do recall that he regarded the extension of God's power as a series of powers, which collectively was the Logos;[34] thus, to say that the gospel is "the Logos of God which works salvation" is by no means a poor guess at what this passage means, for in this gospel "the righteousness of God is revealed" (vs. 17). Here we first meet the term δικαιοσύνη, righteousness, a word whose importance greatly increases as we go on.[35] We shall see that righteousness is a fixed and absolutely stabilized organization of all one's parts, and that the righteousness of God means his absolutely stable reliability, his unchanging character. Here it is hard to see how a mere conception of this righteousness, a mere revelation of it, would bring salvation.

It is revealed "out of faith into faith" (vs. 17) and commentators have long failed to agree as to what this might mean.[36] I would suggest

---

If G. was to prove his hypothesis, he had to show that hellenistic Judaism as he defined it was wide-spread in the ancient world. Some of his strongest evidence here is in the Jewish art remains assembled and published in the monumental *Symbols*; in this series (especially volumes 7-8, "Pagan Symbols in Judaism"), many of the references to early Christian writings and art are intended to show how the Greco-Roman world influenced Christianity *not directly*, but via hellenistic Judaism. At the beginning of *Symbols* 12, G. states explicitly that this hellenistic Jewish background to the New Testament has been his major scholarly preoccupation, beginning with his doctoral dissertation, (*The Theology of Justin Martyr*, 1923); his "approach to hellenized Judaism has been from two directions, as dictated by the data," i.e., from Philo and from Jewish art, 3. He also lists here six kinds of sources for determining "what impact Greek religion and thought had upon Jews of the ancient world," 184. The first three are covered in *Symbols*: 1) the literary evidence, chiefly from Philo; 2) the archaeological remains; 3) "the biblical paintings of Dura". The others are 4) the rabbinical writings and 5) the Septuagint as these manifest Greek influences, and 6) "the new mystic-gnostic material...from the early rabbis" as studied e.g., by Gershom Scholem.]

[34][On the "Logos-Stream" and its powers, see *Light*, chapter one, "The God of the Mystery," and, more briefly, *Introduction*, 100-10.]

[35][On *dikaiosune* in Paul, see the recent discussion carried on between E. Käsemann, "Gottesgerechtigkeit bei Paulus," (reprinted in his *Exegetische Versuche und Besinnungen* II, 1964, 181-93) and R. Bultmann, *ΔΙΚΑΙΟΣΥΝΗ ΘΕΟΥ*, *JBL* 83 (1964), 12-6. The second article is a critique of the first; when the first was reprinted, Käsemann included new footnotes in reply to Bultmann's criticisms. For the distinctive stamp put on *dikaiosune* by the translators of the Septuagint, and its relation to the use of the word by Paul, see C.H. Dodd, *The Bible and the Greeks*, 1935,42-59.]

[36][W. Bauer says that this phrase "merely expresses in a rhetorical way the thought that πίστις, is the beginning and the end," *op. cit.* s.v. πίστις 2,d,a. However, his explanation neither suits the verb *apokaluptai* (as it is used in vs. 17f.), nor explains the repetition of *ek pisteos*, i.e., of only half the "rhetorical" phrase in the Old Testament text which ends vs. 17. G.'s interpretation suggests

that it harmonizes with what follows if we recognize that "righteousness" and "faith" have meanings very similar; faith is really "fidelity, stability", so that Paul is saying that out of the faithfulness, fidelity, righteousness of God we ourselves come into faith.[37] This explanation gives an active meaning to the sentence, something very much needed if it is to be regarded as the theme of the letter to follow.

"For the wrath of God has been revealed..." (vs. 18). Here Paul continues to speak along exactly the same lines. There should have been no need for this revelation of wrath, since God had fully revealed himself in nature. He has not been shifting and changing through the varieties of revelation; he is the same faithful, reliable, identical God in whom we may come to the reliability and steadfastness of *pistis* (faith) and *dikaiosune* ourselves. Paul parallels Philo when he says that the nature of God has been revealed in the created world, that his eternal power and deity could have clearly been perceived in the things have been made.[38]) We are thus "without excuse" (vs. 20); we

---

that this vexing phrase in a brief but crucial verse deserves more attention than Bauer would allow.]

[37][This interelation of *dikaiosune, normos* (law) and *pistis* is brought out clearly in G.'s essay "Law in the Subjective Realm," printed as an appendix to *Light*, 370-413. The relation of *dikaiosune* and *nomos* becomes clear in this sentence: "That blessed state which a man achieves when he turns from sin to a life in harmony with God's Spirit or Law is the state of *dikaiosu‰onh*, specifically explained as the voluntary following of the Laws of Nature. To say that a man has acted unjustly, has broken the higher Law, or has committed impiety, these are but three ways of saying the same thing, according to Philo and Paul alike," 398. *Pistis* is "in brief that ultimate trust and dependence upon God that marked the achievement of the life completely oriented in God," 400. God is not simply the God of the Old Testament here, but the God whose law is in a sense co-terminous with the laws of nature, as indicated by the first quotation. G. goes on to point out the differences between *pistis* defined by Philo and that defined by Paul, but then concludes: "In any case it is clear that to Philo as to Paul the association of *dikaiosune* and *pistis* was very close," 401.]

[38]The Old Testament would say, "The heavens declare the glory of God," etc., but to say that the invisible nature of God has been made known in its *dunamis* and *theiotes* (1:20) is to use the hellenistic approach. [For Philo see the discussion of Moses' vision of the "back" of God, Ex. 33:17-23, in *Light*, 213f. and the references to Philo given there. For Plutarch, see *de Iside* 71-75. B. Gärtner concludes that 1:20-23 has little in common with hellenistic philosophical thought; he understands these verses on the basis of Old Testament – Jewish tradition, although he acknowledges that "what really makes Rom. 1:20 ...so difficult to interpret is the number of terms familiar to us from Greek philosophy"! (*op. cit.* 82, cf. 133-44). G. wrote the following note in his copy of Gärtner's book: "In the paragraphs on Greek philosophy and hellenistic Judaism, Gärtner considers only Stoicism. His argument is that Paul's thinking

have not come into the faith of God, because we have blinded ourselves to the revelation already given. Men wanted something more immediate, could not take anything so abstract; they exchanged the great God for "images that resembled mortal men or birds or animals or reptiles" (vs. 23).[39]

Romans, Ch. 2

The result of men's failure to recognize God as revealed in nature is that God has abandoned them to the lusts of the flesh, given them up entirely and will condemn them in the last day of judgment; he will render to every man according to his works (vs. 6), to the Jew first and also to the Greek, whether of reward or of punishment (vs. 9f.). Men were to be obedient to the power and glory of God as revealed in nature, but Paul does not say that this revelation in nature is a revelation of God's *law;* he calls it the revelation of God *himself* and his grace, and it amounts (as we shall see) to a law that is higher.

If verses 14ff. *nomos* (law) clearly has two meanings, so that I would paraphrase: When the gentiles do by nature what the *Jewish* law requires, they are a law to themselves, even though they do not have the Jewish law. For what the *universal* law requires is written on their hearts, "while their conscience also bears witness and their conflicting thoughts accuse or perhaps excuse them..." (vs. 15).[40]

---

in Rom. 1 must *either* follow Old Testament-Jewish tradition *or* Stoicism, and while he finds traces of the latter, he says this is only a small addition to the former." See also footnote 6 above. On the other hand, M. Pohlenz finds that 1:19f. has perhaps its closest parallels in Philo e.g. "die platonische Scheidung der ὁρατά und νοητά, die für Philon den Eckpfeiler seiner Welterklärung bildet, und vollends die Worte τὸ γνωστὸν τοῦ θεοῦ die doch voraussetzen, dass Gott in seinem innersten Wesen unfassbar bleibt," "Paulus und die Stoa," *ZNW* 42 (1949), 71. Pohlenz' section on Philo and Paul, 69-82, buttresses G.'s interpretation of Paul at a number of places, in spite of the fact that Pohlenz would see much more Stoicism in Philo than does G. The Pohlenz article has been reprinted in *Das Paulusbild in der Neueren Deutschen Forschung*, ed. K.H. Rengstorf, 1964, 522-64.]

[39]This could easily have come from a hellenistic Jewish treatise in Egypt; certainly God in the form of birds, animals and reptiles is a way of speaking which would be unusual elsewhere. [In *Symbols* 9:6 G. suggests that "Paul might have drawn from either Philo or Gamaliel" for 1:22f.; he refers to Philo, *Decal.* 66-81, and to *Introduction*, 83ff.]

[40][Gärtner again stresses the "Old Testament-Jewish" evidence, citing Test. Judah 20 and the *Qumran Manual of Discipline*, 1QS 3: 18-4: 26 as parallels to Rom. 2:14-16; see his excursus, *op. cit.*, 83-5. However, in "Gesetz und Natür: Röm. 2:14-16" in *Studien zu Antike und Urchristentum*, 1959, 93-118, G. Bornkamm points out four elements of 2:14f. which are clearly hellenistic: "1. das durchaus unbiblische, spezifisch griechische Begriffspaar'ὑσις/νόμος, 2. die ebenfalls dezidiert unjüdische, aber umsomehr griechische Wendung

Clearly a gentile never had the *Jewish* law, the Mosaic code, "written in his heart", but a few righteous gentiles have known the *natural* law, the real law, the law of the spirit, and have obeyed it. Such people become a "law to themselves", because they are guided by the true law; even though they have never heard of the Jewish law, they can be fully acceptable to God.

In addition to this natural law available to all men, the Jews have had the Jewish law, which is a wonderful revelation but which they have not kept (vs. 12f., 17ff.).

The summary in verse 29 makes the contrast clear: the real law is in the spirit, not in the written code, ἐν πνεύματι, οὐ γράμματι. The gentile who has neither the *gramma* nor fleshly circumcision (vs. 25ff.) but still fulfills *the law* will condemn the Jew who for all his *gramma* and circumcision still breaks the law. Clearly there are two laws, the law of the spirit and the law of the letter, i.e. the law written down, the law in nouns and verbs. Of these the law of the spirit is the only true law.[41]

Philo also makes a great point of this contrast between the written law and the universal law (what Paul here and later calls the spirit-law or the law of the spirit); I explicated his understanding of it at great length in my book *By Light, Light* (1935). Philo was a loyal Jew; he kept the law, he did not abandon it as Paul did.[42] But he was

---

ἑαυτοῖς, εἰσιν νόμος 3. das unverkennbar griechische Motiv des ἄγρᾳος νόμος in 2:15 und 4. der wieder nur aus griechische Voraussetzungen verständliche Verweis auf die συνείδησις der Heiden (v. 15)," 101f. This idea of personal self-examination in 2:15 (quoted here by G.) has its nearest parallels in Philo and Seneca, 113. Bornkamm concludes, "dass Paulus in Röm. 2:14f. nicht nur Einzelheiten des Vokabulars, sondern ein in sich zusammengehörendes Gedankenfüge aus der Tradition der heidnischen theologia naturalis positiv aufnimmt, ihm aber durch die Beziehung auf Gottesgesetz und Gericht eine neue, völlig ungriechische Deutung und Ausrichtung gibt," 117.]

[41]Cf. Gal. 2:18: "If I build up again these things which I tore down, then I prove myself a transgressor." Paul is very cryptic here – How would he have been a transgressor, a lawbreaker in establishing the law? The next verse suggests the answer: "Through (the) law I died to (the) law." Translators may twice insert the "the" which I parenthesize, but διὰ νόμου νόμῳ ἀπέθανον is purposely vague and is most reasonably understood to refer to the paradox that, by rising to the new law in Christ, Paul destroyed or died to (what are a few mixtures of figure?) the old law of Mosaic precept. To bring back the old laws, or to have any hope in them, denies the whole meaning of the higher law. [See pages 136-38 above on the Jerusalem Council, Acts 15.]

[42][Philo found it necessary to attack fellow Jews who looked for the "higher meaning" of the law but neglected the "letter" of it; G. suggests Paul himself as an example of this kind of "reform" Judaism which Philo repudiates, see

presented with a great difficulty in that he was looking for a law higher than anything which could be put in writing.[43] The approach to this higher law, he says, is a matter of allegorizing, of really coming to understand what is implied by the text of the Torah; only those who are in a special, spiritual frame of mind can come through to this understanding.

The spirit-law, according to Philo, is revealed also in the great patriarchs, from Enos to Moses, who lived righteous, i.e. *law-abiding* lives before the existence of any written code. They offered the Jews access to the higher law, since the spirit-law was also revealed in the Torah, in the stories about these patriarchs.[44] Their victory was so great, their power of salvation for other men so mighty, because they had revealed the higher law directly and before there was any written code. This is the very heart of Philo's message. He describes these men as νόμοι ἔμψυχοι, incarnations of the law.

I discussed the *nomoi empsuchoi* at considerable length, with parallels from contemporary hellenistic writers, and showed that the phrase does not mean an incarnation of a written code; both for the Greeks and for the hellenized Jews it rather means the incarnation of the higher general law, what the Stoics call the law of nature, a law which by its very nature could not have been a code.[45] In theistic circles this law became the way, the will, the nature of God himself; the word "nature" came to mean "God" and the law of nature, the law of God. This is the law which was revealed to everyone and which could

---

Introduction 79f. In *Symbols* 12:9ff. he discusses the agreements and disagreements between Philonic and rabbinic views of the law.]

[43][In *Symbols* 12:13f. G. briefly describes the four levels of "law" in Philo: 1) "At the top is the nomos-logos, the metaphysical law (with the true Being above it, of course). God used this as the formal principle in creating the universe, as Plato described the Creator doing in the Timaeus." 2) Next come the "incarnations of the nomos-logos, the metaphysical law become vocal (*logikos*). Such a person was the philosopher-king in Plato's and Aristotle's terminology...the *nomos empsuchos*, the *lex animata*, the law become alive (in a person)." Then, for "the great majority of people" God gave verbal laws, the 3) Decalog and 4) "the positive and negative commands, the "Specific Laws'."]

[44][In a section entitled, "Teilhaber Gottes (θεῖοι ἄνδρες) in der jüdischen Tradition," D. Georgi describes this "divinizing" of Old Testament heroes, *Die Gegner des Paulus im 2. Korintherbrief*, 1964, 145ff. The evidence he gives from other hellenistic Jewish writers shows that their approach is much the same as that of Philo. G. was impressed with what he knew of this book, but had to break off writing before he could make use of it in this article.]

[45][The summary in *Introduction*, 68-71, is perhaps the most succinct; for further bibliography see notes 44 above and 48 below. See also the forthcoming article of H. Köster in *Theologisches Wörterbuch zum Neuen Testament s.v.*'ύσις, and his "Natural Law in Greek Thought" in Neusner (1968).]

become *incarnate,* could become written into the hearts of the few great men of old. The idea was carried on at least through Justin Martyr, who was convinced that Socrates and Plato likewise were incarnations of the Logos;[46] it was so popular in early Christianity that they came near to being canonized as Christian saints.

The background and atmosphere here are platonic: the law, the true law, was a source of platonic reality which could never adequately represent itself in matter. The written law was *ipso facto* inferior to the law of the spirit (to use Paul's word for it). The *nomos empsuchos,* he who was the incarnation of law, had it as his function to formulate law, or rather, to formulate laws in writing. It was essential to have a king who was an incarnation of law, of the spirit-law, so that he could make it vocal, make it λογικός, verbalize it; he himself stands above all the codes, which periodically turn out in new circumstances to be fallible and unjust.[47] The only true justice was in the law of the spirit. According to Philo the great advantage of the Jew with his Jewish tradition and scripture was not that the letter of the law was revealed to him, but that Moses, the supreme incarnation of law, had made verbal the true law and that the Jew had access to it in the persons of these great patriarchs.

This understanding of the true law as a kind of platonic Real, a basic thesis of Philo's whole writing, is carried over directly in Paul's contrast between the law of the letter and the higher law of the spirit. It is this latter law which, in the sphere of ethics, issues in the higher principles of morality which Paul is everywhere and throughout his

---

[46] [See G.'s *The Theology of Justin Martyr,* 1923, especially chapter 5, "The Logos".]

[47] [In his lengthy essay, "The Political Philosophy of Hellenistic Kingship," *Yale Classical Studies* I (1928), 55-102, G. argues that this is "the official political philosophy of the Hellenistic age," 102, and "the philosophy of state which thrust itself irresistibly upon the Roman imperator," 100; "νόμος ἔμψυχος was...a by-word for royalty of great antiquity in the second century of our era," 94 ("*second* century..." is a correction written into G.'s copy of the essay). G. found much of his evidence in neo-Pythagorian texts contained in the Stobaean fragments; his summary of the view of kingship stated there clarifies the present article at this point: "The supreme function of the king is by virtue of his own relationship with deity...to infuse into a man a new power, which is a new recognition by man of his own potential nature...until the logos of the king...like leaven, has transformed man's lumpishness into the divine existence God meant him to be. Thus transformed in his spiritual nature, man will be an imitation of the king as the king imitates God, each in turn self-ruled and subject to no external compulsion. So man will at last have achieved the dream...of all Greek ethical thinking, he will be able to live spontaneously by divine law and dispense with the seriatim compulsion and injustice of the written codes," 90f.]

letters exhorting the Christians to follow. It is not at all an antinomianism which allows one to do whatever one pleases; one follows the higher principles of morality, but as *principles* and not as specific commands.

It is this approach to morality which appears behind much of what is said in chapter two of Romans. For example, verse 10: "Glory and honor and peace for everyone who does the good, the Jew first and also the Greek." *The* good, τὸ ἀγαθόν which Jew and Greek may do, is a Greek philosophical term, not a Jewish expression; it reflects the universal good and, with it, the universal law discussed above. Whoever practices this higher law, whoever reflects it in his character, brings into effect what Plato or a later Platonist might have called *to agathon*, just as Philo did.[48] Some gentiles have put *to agathon* before themselves as their model; they have "done" *to agathon*, says Paul. Such gentiles, who have no Jewish law, have the true law written in their hearts (vs. 15). Paul here shows that he is using "law" in two senses, that revealed by Moses in the Torah and that which can become *empsuchos*.

Again in verse 13 Paul contrasts those who are hearers of law with those Jews and gentiles (cf. vs. 9f.) who are doers of law, οἱ ποιηταί νόμου. "Law" in both cases is singular; "doers of law" does not mean that these wonderful people are doers of *Jewish* law. If they are a "law to themselves", clearly they do have a law; just as clearly, it need not be a written law.

Romans, Ch. 3

Paul has shown that the keeping of the higher law is a matter of the heart, not something external which can be measured by precepts of the written law. The higher moral good which people should practice

---

[48]For example, in *de Posteritate Caini* 85: "(Moses) in a thoroughly philosophical way makes a three-fold division; he says, 'it is in your mouth and heart and hands' (Deut. 30:14 LXX), that is, in words, in plans, in actions. For these are the parts of *to agathon*, and of those it is compacted, and the lack of but one not only renders it imperfect but absolutely destroys it." Philo omits the references to the Old Testament covenant and to the commandments which abound in Deut. 30. He talks instead, para. 86f., of the sophists who do not keep the three parts of *to agathon* united. Then, in para. 88f., he mentions "the boundaries of the good and the beautiful...(which) were fixed not by the creation to which we belong, but on principles which are divine and are older than we and all that belongs to earth." We have left the Old Testament thought-world; *to agathon* here is an object of philosophical speculation. [In his article in Kittel's *Theological Dictionary of the New Testament* I, 1964, s.v. ἀγαθός, W. Grundmann discusses both Philo and Paul but makes no particular reference to the use of *agathon* with the definite article, the point which concerns G. here.]

has of course been reflected in the written law: avoidance of adultery, of stealing, of blasphemy against God – these are all mentioned in the Mosaic code. If however the gentile avoids these, the question is: What advantage has the Jew in having the Mosaic code? What is the value of circumcision? (vs. 1). Because of the way the previous chapter ends, these questions must arise. Though the written law cannot bring the Jew *dikaiosune*, it does at least bring him knowledge of sin – thus verse 20 finally answers verse 1. But verse 2, always mistranslated because literally untranslatable, answers in a deeper way. The Jews were given a share in that great *pistis* [49] (of God) by being given the formulated laws of God, *ta logia*. Most Jews were false to this *pistis*, but this by no means impugns the *pistis* of God (vs. 3ff.).[50] The few who did not betray this *pistis* will in the next chapter be presented in the person of Abraham who, because he had *pistis* was also *dikaios* like God.[51]

Thus the Jewish law is itself a great revelation of the righteousness of God, and of his faithfulness, his *pistis*, his stability, which stands out all the more clearly revealed in contrast to the people who break the law and so becloud everything. While the primary revelation, the higher law, is available to all men, the Mosaic code, a second gift of

---

[49]According to vs. 4, God is "true" and "just", words apparently synonymous with *pistos*. [See following note.]

[50]The word *pistis* is one of the most difficult in the New Testament, because it appears in a great variety of meanings. I suggest 1) that the noun, like so many abstractions, is secondary to the adjective *pistos*, which means trustworthy, reliable or trusting; 2) that "to have *pistis*" and "to be *pistos*" are absolutely identical in meaning. [In his Kittel article on *pistis*, Bultmann agrees that the noun *pistis* and the verb *pisteuo* are secondary to the adjective *pistos*, although both noun and verb are quite early, the verb being in use from the seventh century BC, (English translation in *Bible Key Words* III, s.v. *pistis* 34ff.). As *pistos* is sometimes more active in meaning ("trusting"), sometimes passive ("trustworthy"), so the noun "can mean the trust that a man feels as well as the trust that he inspires, that is to say, trustworthiness," 36. Bultmann also indicates that neither the adjective nor the noun are religious terms in classical Greek; it is not until the hellenistic period that they become part of the religious vocabulary. At that time *pistis* "became the key word in the propaganda of the proselytising religions, not only Christianity", 41. There is perhaps an indication of the distance between Paul and Qumran in the understanding of Hab. 2:4 in Rom. 1:17 and in 1 QpHab viii, 1; in the latter "the saying is made to refer to the 'doers of the Law'...the exact opposite to what Paul finds in the same prophecy," H. Ringgren, *The Faith of Qumran*, 1963, 247 – but see his discussion there.]

[51][Here G. finds the same parallels between the adjective *dikaios* and *pistos* which he drew earlier (pages 143-44 above) between the nouns *dikaiosune* and *pistis*.]

God, was specifically given to the Jews; *this* is their great advantage (vs. 2).

But now (*nuni de,* vs. 21) still a third revelation of the righteousness, the resolute "law-abidingness" of God has been granted; in Christ it has been made freshly available quite beyond anything that men have had before. From this point on indeed no one has any excuse. Now we leave the law of the Jews entirely behind, since through this law comes only knowledge of sin (vs. 20).

Actually all men have been and still are sinners (vs. 23); only as they come into the *dikaiosune* of God can they hope to become righteous themselves (vs. 24). God's *dikaiosune* is available only as a gift, only through Jesus Christ; in his sacrifice he manifested God's *dikaiosune* (vs. 25) by his own faith (vs. 22 & 26). We are made righteous because this faith *of* Christ is given us.

It is crucial to note that "faith" in this passage (vs. 22 & 26) is not faith *in* Jesus Christ but the faith *of* Jesus Christ, πίστις ('Ιησοῦ) Χριστοῦ.[52] There have been many attempts to make this phrase conform to the traditional idea of Christian faith; I see no possible way to do so. Rather, as the parallels between the faith *of* Abraham and the faith *of* Christ in the next chapter will make clear, this faith *of* Christ is simply his trusting that the cross would not be the end, and that God would save him from death because God is *pistos,* God is the righteous one who is absolutely supreme in that he is beyond life and death. As we identify with Christ, become one with him, we ourselves are given the faith *of* Christ. It is not our faith, it is no goodness of ours; it is a free gift. By this faith *of* Christ, transferred to us, we have hope of immortality ourselves.[53]

---

[52][See now the arguments of G.M. Taylor for the translation "faith of Christ," 75f. in the article treated in the following note.]

[53][Here G. states most clearly his understanding of "faith" in Paul as the faith which Christ himself possessed and demonstrated and gives to Christians; while G.'s may be a unique understanding of faith, it is quite in line with the rest of his interpretation of Romans and with his thesis that the key to Paul is to see him against the background of the hellenistic Judaism best known from Philo. G. interprets three major Pauline terms in similar ways: *dikaiosune* (see pages 143-44 above), *nomos* (see page 145ff. above) and *pistis.* (In an article discussed just below, G.M. Taylor gives useful details regarding the interrelation of these three words in the Pauline letters, 59ff.). Just as *dikaiosune* is primarily the stability and trustworthiness *of God,* and just as *nomos* is embodied *in Christ,* the *nomos empsuchos,* so *pistis* is first of all *Christ's pistis,* his own trust in God, a trust which has a preliminary manifestation in the larger-than-life patriarchs of the Old Testament (cf. the discussion of *nomoi empsuchoi,* page 41ff. above). Once G. has said this about the source of faith, he can go on to describe the faith of Christians in a number of ways, e.g. as gift (page 155ff. below) and as

obedience (page 141 above). In the traditional Pauline corpus similar or identical expressions occur in Gal. 2:16 bis, 20 ("the faith of the Son of God"); 3:22; Eph. 3:12; Phil. 3:9.

G.'s "philonic" understanding of *pistis* in Paul might appear so much his own that no other scholar's work bears directly on it; nevertheless, certain references can be given:

1) In the standard reference works: W. Bauer, *op. cit.* s.v. πίστις, 2,b, *b* on "the *pistis Christou* in Paul"; F. Blass and A. Debrunner, *op. cit.* para. 163 entitled, "objective genitive".

2) A detailed study of „die mit *pistis* verbundenen Christus-Genetiv" is given in O. Schmitz, Die Christusgemeinschaft des Paulus im Lichte seines Genetivgebrauchs, 1924, 91-134. Reviewing the debate on the subject, Schmitz points out certain dangers: 1) that of forcing this genitive into any one grammatical category, e.g. the "objective" or the "subjective" genitives; 2) that of defining *pistis* too narrowly, i.e. equating it either with acceptance of historical data, or with the believer's (mystical) union with Christ, cf. 131. He concludes: „Alle diese Schwierigkeiten fallen mit einem Schlage weg, wenn man sich entschliesst, die mit *pistis* verbundenen Christus-Genetiv im Sinne einer ganz allgemeinen Näherbestimmung dieses 'Glaubens' als 'Christus-Glauben', 'Christus-Jesus-Glauben', 'Jesus Glauben' zu verstehen, ohne irgend ein konkretes verbales Verhältnis zwischen den beiden Nomina, sei es nach Art des Gen. obj., sei es nach Art des Gen. subj. durch den Genetiv als solchen ausgedrückt zu finden... So versteht es sich von selber, dass Christus 'Gegenstand' des 'Christus-Glaubens' ist (vgl. Gal. 2:16); aber das ist nicht die einzige Beziehung, die zwischen diesen beiden Grössen obwaltet, vielmehr wird Christus (wie Gott) für Paulus nie in der Weise Objekt, dass er nicht zugleich ihn selber (Paulus) zum Objekt machte und zwar so, dass er (Paulus) mit seiner Subjektivität dadurch an der Objektivität dieses Subjekts (Christus) beteiligt würde...Daher bestehen bei Paulus die objektiv-historischen Aussagen und die subjektiv-mystischen Aussagen immer zusammen wie die Wasserbestände in zwei kommunizierenden Röhren. Dieser gesamte, in vollem Gleichgewicht befindliche historisch-mystische, objektiv-subjektive Sachverhalt liegt den mit *pistis* verbundenen Christus-Genetiven zugrunde," 132f. Schmitz's work is evaluated by A. Deissmann (who argues for his own brand of "mystical genitive") in *Paul: A Study in Social and Religious History*[2], 1927, 162ff. with footnotes; and by R. Bultmann in "Zur Geschichte der Paulus-Forschung," now reprinted in *Das Paulusbild in der Neueren Deutschen Forschung*, ed. K.H. Rengstorf, 1964, 331ff.

3) In an important article "The Function of πίστις Χριστοῦ in Galatians," *JBL* 85 (1966), 58-76, G.M. Taylor argues that in this letter this phrase is "the *fidei commissum* of Roman law; and that Paul uses this concept to explain, in juristic terms, how the inheritance of Abraham is transmitted, through Jesus Christ, both to Jews and gentiles," 58. According to Taylor, *diatheke* in Galatians is not the equivalent of the Hebrew *berith*, but of *testamentum*, the Latin term for "will", 63 note 8. *Fidei commissum* (which is translated *pistis* in Roman legal documents written in Greek) is the only variety of *testamentum* by which a testator could name two successive heirs (the first-named heir being obliged, if he accepts the benefits of the legacy, also to accept the second-named as, in effect, his own heir), or by which a national alien could be named the heir of a Roman citizen, 66. Applied to Galatians, this means that "Abraham and Christ

Before Paul can go on to illuminate this understanding of faith and righteousness from the Old Testament story of Abraham, he must make clear its implications for "law"; the philonic distinction between the higher law and the written law is again essential for the argument. On the basis of "law" our boasting is "excluded" (vs. 27), but "excluded" is the equivalent of the German "verboten"; it implies a law that forbids. By what law is humility enjoined and personal boasting, self-righteousness, excluded? The Mosaic law by no means does so, for there is great satisfaction in obedience, in the law of legal acts, ἔργα. God commands, I obey, and the righteousness is my own. The supreme sin of pride, spiritual pride, is here "boasting" (vs. 27), the inevitable result

---

are successive testamentary heirs, who receive the inheritance in πίστις – *fidei commissum* – because that device is necessary to constitute Christ as successive heir, and because the testament is intended to benefit gentiles as well as Jews (i.e. people of another nation) and to adopt them all as equal heirs through Christ's heirship. The testament can not take effect until Christ, as successive testamentary heir, accepts the inheritance, including its obligations, with the consent of his father, God (4:4f.). Until then the intended beneficiaries are subject to tutelage," 67. While Taylor applies his explanation to the Galatian letter generally, it should be restricted to one section, 3:15-4:7, where Paul is making use of this Roman legal terminology in an explanatory analogy, beginning with κατὰ ἄνθρωπον λέγω (cf. RSV's paraphrase: "to give a human example..."). In 3:26ff. there appear the different and more familiar phrases "baptized into Christ", "put on Christ", and "one in Christ"; these are here paralleled with and "geared into" the legal metaphor, which comes to the fore again at 3:29. Taylor's explanation fits well with the use of *pistis Iesou Christou* (3:22) and *diatheke* (3:15 & 17) within the verses of this metaphor, but not otherwise. Thus, *pistis* in 2:16, 20 would not be taken to mean *fidei commissum* without the "help" of 3:15ff., and *diatheke* is used later in another analogy (4:22-31) in a very different, non-legal way (this in spite of Taylor's denial, 63 note 8). Also, the "entirely new and different juristic personality" effected among the Romans by adoption is quite a distance from the ideas "death to self" and "new life in Christ" in 2:20 and "putting on Christ" and being "baptized into Christ" in 3:27 (compare these verses with the legal text referred to in note 20; see also 66f.). Nevertheless, Taylor's explanation of *fidei commissum*, 65-74, is a valuable commentary on the use of *pistis Christou* in 3:15-4:7; in this "human example" Paul again (cf. page 34 above) appears to be fitting his words carefully to his readers, here the Galatians, since, as Taylor points out, "the Galatian was the only non-Roman legal system" to make use of just this kind of testamentary law, 70. (For an attempt to explain the Galatians passage on the basis of rabbinic law, see E. Bammel, "Gottes ΔΙΑΘΗΚΗ (Gal. iii, 15-17) und das jüdische Rechtsdenken," *NTS* 6 (1959/60) 313-19.).

4) The genitive might be explained as a Semitism whose closest parallel is the "construct state" of the Hebrew of Aramaic substantive. This explanation would find some support in K.G. Kuhn's article, "Der Epheserbrief im Lichte der Qumrantexte"; here Kuhn shows that "die Vorliebe...für Ketten von Genetivverbindungen" in Ephesians is a characteristic of its "semitizing" Greek and has close parallels in the Dead Sea Scrolls, *NTS* 7 (1960/61), 335f.]

of an approach to righteousness by deed, acts, obedience. Psychologically Paul is entirely right. Legalism does bring satisfaction the satisfaction of self-approval; we are sure that God likes an obedient child.

But now, for the Christian, boasting is "excluded". By what law, by what *nomos?* The Jewish law, the law of works? No, but by the law of faith (vs. 27). No more clear statement could be made of the difference between the two laws: one is the higher law, which manifests itself and is achieved through faith; the other is the law of precepts, observed only by human effort and thus never really, thoroughly fulfilled.

The contrast continues: according to verse 27b we are justified "through the *law* of faith", according to verse 28 we are justified "apart from the works of *law* ". Again two laws, two entirely different laws, the law of the Jews and the law of faith. In verse 29f. this contrast between two laws is linked to the theme of the inclusion of the gentiles, just as it was in 2:10ff., 2:25ff. and 3:21ff (πάντες).

"On the contrary, we uphold the law..." (vs. 31). By going beyond the law of Moses to the law of faith, we are not overthrowing the idea of God's law, God's way, but we are coming into a higher version of it; through faith we are able to vindicate the law of God, to live it, to *be* it,[54] once we have realized the incompleteness of the law of precepts and individual commands. When we go on to the law of faith revealed in Jesus Christ, do we then vitiate the old law? Not at all! We are simply going beyond it to a law that is more potent and real, but in essence the same.

Romans, Ch. 4

Paul goes to the Old Testament to prove that justification by (the law of) faith was the only principle of justification from the time of Abraham; his interpretation is philonic as he uses Abraham as the great example of the man who is saved by faith.[55] His text is Gen. 15:6. The faith was very simple: God made Abraham a promise and Abraham believed it. This was all that Abraham had to do (vs. 4f.);

---

[54]According to 2 Cor. 5:21, we *"become* the *dikaiosune* of God" by the fact that God put our sin upon him who knew no sin.

[55][On the relationship between Old Testament and New Testament which is implied in Paul's use of Abraham here, see U. Wilckens, "Die Rechtfertigung Abrahams nach Römer 4" in Festschrift G. von Rad, 1961, 111-27; more generally on the use of the Abraham-story, S. Sandmel, *Philo's Place in Judaism: A Study of Conceptions of Abraham in Jewish Literature,* 1956, and M. Dibelius' excursus "Das Abraham-Beispiel" in *Der Brief des Jakobus*[11] (HNT), 1964, 206-14.]

God did the rest, God reckoned it (ἐλογίσθη) to him as righteousness, *dikaiosune*, i.e. God pronounced him just, gave him righteousness, quite apart from any knowledge of written law, simply because he had believed God.

Paul very much wanted further Old Testament support for this, so Ps. 32:1ff. is made to fit (vs. 6ff.). This text has nothing to do with God's "reckoning" *dikaiosune*; it manifests a traditionally Jewish idea of forgiveness, i.e. God's forgiving a failure to keep the law. But the verb used in the Abraham story also appears here (λογίσηται, vs. 8); following Jewish proof-text methods, this connection was enough.[56]

Afterward came the law and the enjoinment of circumcision (vs. 9f). The faith that made God ascribe righteousness to Abraham was a relation between him and God on a level any pagan could experience (though few ever did) – no laws, no circumcision, and yet God declared him *dikaios*, just.

God's purpose in this was to make Abraham the father of *all* the faithful, of all who believed (vs. 11f.). Descent from Abraham and inheritance of the blessing have nothing to do with the flesh; the descendants of Abraham are those who have such a faith that *dikaiosune* is reckoned to them, imputed to them, whether they have been circumcised or not. The promise was made to Abraham not through law, διὰ νόμου but διὰ δικαιοσύνης πίστεως (vs. 13); this last phrase is puzzling, but I think it should be translated "through the faith that brings *dikaiosune*" since, throughout, Paul has been contrasting *nomos* and *pistis* as means toward *dikaiosune*.[57]

Paul begins to define this faith. It is a gift – this we must not forget – a gift of trust in God, who can make the dead alive and treat what does not exist (because dead) as though it existed (vs. 17). Abraham believed in the steady rule of God, in his reliability, in his existing

---

[56][J. Jeremias has shown that Paul's repeated use of the verb *logizesthai* in this chapter is an argument by analogy along the lines of the *gezera ʾawa*, the second of the seven interpretative rules ascribed to Hillel (cf. H. Strack, *Introduction to the Talmud and Midrash*, 1959, 94, and G.F. Moore, *Judaism*, 3:73 note 14). Jeremias gives the rule thus: "dass identische (oder gleichbedeutende) Wörter, die an zwei verschiedenen Schriftstellen vorkommen, sich gegenseitig erläutern," "Zur Gedankenführung in den paulinischen Briefen" in *Studia Paulina*, in honorem Johannis de Zwaan septuagenarii, 1953, 149.]

[57][In his article "Philo Judaeus," *Interpreter's Dictionary of the Bible*, 3:798, (1962), G. says: "The heart of Philo's message is exactly expressed in Rom. 4:13: 'The promise to Abraham and his descendants, that they should inherit the world, did not come through the (written) law but through the righteousness of faith.'"]

beyond life and death. He trusted in God's promise of descendants even though he knew that both his and Sarah's bodies were dead in so far as their power of reproduction was concerned. He was as good as dead, being a centenarian, and there had long been νέκρωσις in Sarah's womb (vs. 19), so that the miracle worked by God would have to be no less than a "resurrection of the body". Nevertheless, Abraham was fully convinced that God was able to do what he had promised (vs. 21); that is why his faith was reckoned to him as *dikaiosune* (vs. 22).

Paul has drawn his parallels clearly. *Abraham* believed that God was to be trusted even to effect a resurrection; this was the faith *of* Abraham, and it "was reckoned to him for righteousness" (vs. 22). *Christ* believed in his own resurrection – the passage takes that for granted; this is the πίστις Ἰησοῦ, the faith *of* Jesus, which brings righteousness. "But (the words) 'it was reckoned to him' were written not for his sake only, but for our sakes too" – righteousness "*was* reckoned" to Abraham and "*would be* reckoned" to us, for "we" are described as "those who trust in the one who *raised* Jesus our lord *from the dead*" (vs. 24). And God raised him for "our righteousness," ἡ δικαίωσις ἡμῶν (vs. 25). To make his point clear, Paul brings our faith, the faith *of* Christ and the faith *of* Abraham together (cf. vs. 17 & 23ff.): each is a faith in the God who raises the dead, and the result of each is righteousness.

Clearly Paul has had a great experience and discovery; he has found a new life in the crucified Christ – and all this is strangely identified with a gift of *pistis-dikaiosune*, first given to Abraham, then made available to all men through Christ, the Seed of Promise, as we identify ourselves with Christ.

It is inconceivable that the raw experience of Christ should have suggested to Paul this extraordinary rationalization through Abraham, unless he had had considerable association of religious experience with Abraham already. It could not have come simply from the Genesis story of Abraham. How could he have come to think of a *faith of Abraham* which became the *faith of Christ* and so the *faith of Paul*? It would be too much to say that Paul has simply taken over that tradition of hellenistic Judaism, known from Philo, which saw the patriarchs as *nomoi empsuchoi*, possessing great power of salvation for other men. Indeed Paul seldom deals with patriarchs other than Abraham, but (so far as I can see) this is just because Christ, as revealed in the resurrection, was so supremely the *nomos empsuchos*, the incarnation of the higher law, that he had no need of the others and so passed them by. The presence of Christ has made a great change in Paul's theology, but clear traces of the hellenistic Judaism we know from Philo are everywhere to be seen.

Romans, Ch. 5

This chapter adds that *dikaiosune ek pisteos*, righteousness *out of* faith, brings us peace with God. It is through Christ that we have had access to this gift and hope to share in the glory of God (this last is my overtranslation of verse 2, "we have hope of the glory of God"). This is all a free gift; Christ died for us while we were sinners. We contribute nothing, our good deeds purchase us nothing (vs. 8). We atoned for our sins by his blood, indeed we are made righteous by it (vs. 9). This seems at first a contradiction of "righteousness ἐκ πίστεως," righteousness that comes out of faith, Paul's more usual expression; the fact is that the wrath of God had to be appeased before he could begin to give righteousness to us (vs. 9f.). We must be crucified with him before we can have the resurrection in which righteousness is bestowed (6:1-11, see below).

In verse 12ff. a whole new problem opens up. How could the righteousness of *one* be the salvation of the human race? This Paul argues quite after an old Jewish way. The world had always been united in Adam; all men are descended from Adam and all men have to die, because of Adam's sin.[58] Paul leaves the Jewish tradition when he insists that "sin came into the world through one man, and death through sin, so death spread to all men because all men sinned" (vs. 12). The fact of the universality of sin was by no means Paul's invention, but the suggestion that the sin of Adam vitiated Adam's character in such a way that "original sin" came to all men as guilt,[59] and that all men shared in Adam's sin – so far as I know, this is a contribution of Paul himself.[60] I can find no parallels in Philo, or in any other writings; the

---

[58]This basic framework is typically Jewish and will be found worked out in G.F. Moore, *Judaism* 1:460-96. [For a summary of the Pauline understanding of sin and the Jewish background of his thought here, see K. Stendahl, "Sünde und Schuld IV. Im NT," in *Die Religion in Geschichte und Gegenwart*,[3] 6:485f. (1962).]

[59][See *Psychology* 152ff. on the connection Paul makes between human guilt and the death of Christ.]

[60][The manner in which Paul goes beyond his "sources" to a "unique" idea of original has been approached in various ways. A. Dubarle, *The Biblical Doctrine of Original Sin*, 1964, concentrates on Rom. 5:12-21 in discussing "original sin in St. Paul," 142-200. He concludes: "Paul does not form any systematic theory on the origin of sin. According to the object that he has in mind at the time, he draws attention to this or that aspect of the reality. He is not unaware that there remains in every man a personal responsibility (e.g.)...Rom. 1-2...But there is also a collective downfall in mankind...(cf.) Rom. 5:12-19...There is an element of artificiality in these descriptions, which in each case show only one side of the reality," 166. "In conclusion, Paul teaches a handing on of sin from Adam to all men without explaining how it operates. He

Jewish rabbinical teachings definitely steer away from such a conclusion. The rabbis believed that man had indeed become a mortal creature through the fall of Adam, but they make no suggestion of a doctrine of original sin.[61]

is content to take up the thought of Genesis, making explicit the idea that the heritage of the first man contains not only death but also sin," 195, cf. 172, where it is suggested that "perhaps Paul simply brought out and gave abstract formulation to what Genesis described in a concrete way." G. Bornkamm finds in Rom. 5:12-21 a mythological understanding of history containing both Jewish and gnostic elements; its "jüdische Elemente in der Lehre von Erbfluch und Erbtod und im Schema der beiden Aonen erkennbar sind, während die Lehre vom ersten und zweiten Menschen offensichtlich der Gnosis entstammt," "Paulinische Anakoluthe im Römerbrief," in *Das Ende des Gesetzesa*, 1958, 89, cf. 80-90. However, Paul adds two elements of his own: 1) the fact that sin is an action for which the sinner is responsible, the function of the law being to make that responsibility clear and explicit (vs. 13f.); 2) the superiority of grace, whose relation to sin is expressed not by ὡς but by πολλῷ μᾶλλον (vs. 15-7). The effect of these two "Pauline" additions is to break down the mythological view of history and to go beyond it to an understanding of sin and grace which can be traced neither to Jewish nor to gnostic sources. The anacoluthon in vs. 12-21 reflects the intrusion of this new Pauline element: the comparison between Adam and Christ which begins in vs.12 is broken off by vs. 13-7 and then continued in vs. 18ff.]

[61][Paul's Adam-allegory "was in all probability a pure *tour de force* whose consistency with his general thinking had little importance. Philo has scores of such allegories of the moment. But, to the Christian fathers, all that Paul wrote was literally and ponderously true, and so out of this allegory of the fall grew the momentous doctrine of original sin," *Psychology*, 61. Rom. 5:12-21 is a text often investigated, because of what it suggests about the origin of sin (see above note), or because of its use of the figure of Adam; for a recent, detailed examination of the latter, see E. Brandenburger, *Adam und Christus*, 1962. G. will remark that only a Jew could have used *Adam* at this point, but the question remains: What kind of Judaism is the source here, i.e. how heavily penetrated by other influences? Rabbinic elaboration of the Adam-story is summarized by J. Jervell, *Imago Dei*, 1960, 96ff., and by W.D. Davies, *Paul and Rabbinic Judaism*[2], 1955, 44ff.; according to Davies, Paul is familiar both with this speculation (which Davies holds is devoid of hellenistic influence and which results in a glorification of Adam) and with hellenistic Judaism's "distinction between a Celestial and an earthly Adam", 49, a conception which owes much to Greek thought and which occurs, e.g. in the hermetic literature and especially in Philo. But C.K. Barrett holds that Jewish tradition is more unified at this point; he uses Philonic passages to illustrate the tradition "simply because Philo is both more quotable and more intelligible than the Rabbis, and yet proceeds from the same convictions," *From First Adam to Last*, 1962, 7. On O. Cullmann's interpretation, this text contains the two major Christological conceptions of the early Church, Son of Man and Servant of God, which Paul unites "exactly as Jesus united them," *The Christology of the New Testament*, 1959, 171, cf. 170-74. This union solves "the Adam-Son of Man problem which Judaism was actually unable to solve either by tracing man's sin to the fall of

The purpose of bringing Adam in at this point is stated in verse 14: Adam was a type of the "one who was to come," i.e. in Adam all men were united into a single unit, in Adam all men were represented; his deed accounted for the deeds of all subsequent men. So Christ, the "one who was to come," can gather to himself a new "body", a new community or group whose members are "one in him".[62] As the sin of Adam brought condemnation and death for all, so the atoning death and resurrection of Christ brought *dikaiosune* and *zoe* (life) for all (vs. 17f.)[63] Thus we are now in a new dispensation, a whole new order of existence; now we must live by the grace of Jesus Christ.

Romans, Ch. 6

"Are we to continue in sin that grace may abound? By no means!" (vs. 1). We have died to sin, we cannot live in it still (vs. 2). In baptism we partook of the death of Jesus Christ; "we were buried...with him by

---

the angels rather than to the fall of Adam (the Book of Enoch), or by denying the fall of Adam altogether (the Jewish Christians) or by seeking a middle way in presupposing two first men, (Philo)," 170. According to Bultmann, "Rom. 5:12ff. interprets Adam's fall quite in keeping with Gnosticism, as bringing (sin and) death upon mankind," *Theology of the New Testament* 1:174 (1951), cf. 164ff., 251ff.; for a brief summary of gnostic and other speculation about the Anthropos or (heavenly) Man, see S.E. Johnson, *Interpreter's Dictionary of the Bible*, 4:416ff. (1962). It appears that, for this topic at least, it is quite difficult to be precise about what is Jewish, what gnostic, and what from "Greek thought" in general; and it is nearly impossible to separate the "Jewish" themes according to whether they come from "orthodox" or "Palestinian" or "Old Testament-Rabbinic" Judaism on the one hand, or from "hellenistic" or "Philonic" Judaism on the other.]

[62]This new group appears in 1 Corinthians very importantly and in various other parts of Paul's writings. [Cf. the Pauline uses of *soma Christou* to mean the *ekklesia*, e.g. 1 Cor. 12, and the development of this idea in Colossians, where Christ the head *(kephale)* and the Church, the Body, are joined in mutual dependence, Col. 1:18a. For recent summary articles, with bibliography, see H. Schlier, "Corpus Christi" in *Reallexikon für Antike und Christentum* 3: 437-53 (1957) and E. Schweizer in *Theologisches Wörterbuch zum Neuen Testament* 7: 1064ff. (1964). Explanations of the Body-image and of Paul's use of Adam (see note above) are usually closely related e.g. Bultmann refers both to gnosticism, *op. cit.* 177ff., 298ff., while Davies links both to rabbinic speculation about Adam, op. cit. 57. For a brief categorization of sources for the Body-image, see J.A.T. Robinson, *The Body*, 1952 *(Studies in Biblical Theology* 5), 55.]

[63][In an allegory of Noah's ark, Philo says, "because of one righteous and worthy man (Noah), many men were saved" (QG ii, 11, p. 83 of the Marcus translation in supplement volume 2 of the Loeb edition of Philo). G. discusses this allegory in Symbols 8:162ff. and notes that "reminiscences, or premonitions, of Pauline phraseology in Romans are striking" throughout it, note 323.]

baptism into death" (vs. 4),[64] and the result is that we may therefore hope to live with him in the life of glory.

No one can deny that only a Jew could have written such an allegory of Adam (5:12ff.); no gentile would have thought in terms of Adam to explain the power and glory of Jesus Christ. But with 6:5 we begin to swing into the problem in its Greek sense: "For if we have been united with him in a death like his, we shall certainly be united with him in a resurrection like his. We know that our old *anthropos* was crucified with him, so that the sinful body might be destroyed, and we might no longer be enslaved to sin" (vs. 5f.). This passage opens the whole problem of the identification of sin with the body, something as recognizably hellenistic as it is foreign to essential Jewish thought. We are still in our "mortal bodies" even after baptism, and there is always the great danger that sin will run rampant as a result of the body's influence. Paul appears to be introducing a whole new criterion here, a criterion of the corruptability of the flesh, of the subversiveness of the flesh over against the spirit. We are indeed free from the Mosaic law of statutes, no longer does the hoped-for *dikaiosune* come from that law, but we can still yield our members to sin as instruments of wickedness (vs. 13f.) – and this is fatal. It is the old problem brought out in Plato's Allegory of the Cave (Rep. vii: 514ff.): those who have gone outside the cave and seen the glory, seen the truth, seen reality, must still return to the cave and sit on its inner bench again, seeing only the shadows and living the life of the shadows.

Romans, Ch. 7[65]

We have gone through a real death, a death to the Mosaic law and that whole network of theology and ethics which goes with it. The many references to "death" and "mortal" in chapter six are summed up

---

[64][Behind this connection of death with the water of baptism, G. finds a widespread ancient (and modern) equation of water with death; thus the ark or ship becomes a symbol of salvation e.g. in Philo and in the ancient Church. See *Symbols* 8:157-65 for texts and bibliography; this Romans passage is mentioned in note 301.]

[65][This chapter has been the subject of countless studies for the light it throws on e.g. Paul's anthropology or on his view of the law. It has been seen by some as autobiography describing Paul's Christian (*or* pre-Christian) life, and by others as a typical description of a Christian (*or* non-Christian) under the law. Major studies of the chapter include W. Kümmel, *Römer 7 und die Bekehrung des Paulus*, 1929; R. Bultmann, "Romans 7 and the Anthropology of Paul," *Existence and Faith*, 1960, 147-57; and G. Bornkamm, "Sünde, Gesetz und Tod," *Das Ende des Gesetzes*[2], 1958, 51-69. For a recent treatment with which G. strongly disagreed, see K. Stendahl, "The Apostle Paul and the Introspective Conscience of the West," *HTR* 56 (1963), 199-215.]

in 7:1-3 in an argument which turns the Mosaic code back upon itself: once a death has occurred, the obligations of a marriage contract are annulled. We owe nothing to the law any longer, we are free of it and must stop thinking about it: "My brothers, you have died to the law through the body of Christ, so that you may belong to another, to him who has been raised from the dead in order that we may bear fruit for God" (vs. 4). Paul speaks again in terms of the new community, the common existence of all the faithful in Christ.

What has the Mosaic law been doing to us? "What shall we say? That the law is sin? By no means! But had it not been for the law I should not have known sin; I should not have known what it is to covet, had the law not said 'You shall not covet'. Sin, finding opportunity in the commandment, wrought in me all kinds of covetousness" (vs. 7f.). Paul hinted earlier that the law came in to increase the trespass (5:20), but here he makes one of the most extraordinary analyses of the effects of commands upon the human psyche. Every wise parent knows that if children are to be obedient and comply with the wishes and criteria of their parents, they must be given as few actual laws as possible. To give a homely illustration: in the back farms of early New England, toys were almost non-existent, and a handful of dried beans could be a welcome plaything; but wise mothers knew that to give a two-year-old child some beans to play with, while telling him not to put them up his nose, was to invite him to do precisely that. The parent made the suggestion by making the law and prohibition. This is just Paul's point (vs. 7f.): the law, in setting up prohibitions, sets up desires. It is a common saying that the *id* knows no negatives, that every negative command is for the *id* a suggestion; we are coming pretty close to Freud's *id* in this matter of the members and their special life.[66]

"The very commandment which promised life proved to be death to me; for sin, finding opportunity in the commandment, deceived me and by it killed me" (vs. 10f.). The commandment is perfectly all right (the child should *not* put beans in his nose); it is simply that the giving of the command stimulated the desire to rebellion. There is no difficulty about the law itself; it is "holy, just and good" (vs. 12), but it brings death to me because (while the law is spiritual) I am carnal, fleshly, sold under sin.

---

[66]I have no intention of reducing Paul to Freud's categories, but both of them said the truth many times, and one who says the truth is apt to say what others have already said. [In *Toward a Mature Faith*, 1955, G. called this discussion of the *ego* in Romans 7 "one of the most amazing premonitions of later Freudianism," 119, cf. the pages following. For a further discussion of Romans 7-8 in this context, see *Psychology*, 58-63.]

Is the self the person Paul knows he ought to be, the person he feels he should be? Or is the self the person he actually is, the one who sins with or without the law's promptings? "The law is spiritual, but *I* am carnal, sold under sin. *I* do not understand my own actions. *I* do not do what *I* want, but *I* do the very thing *I* hate. Now if *I* do what *I* do not want, *I* agree that the law is good, so then it is no longer *I* that do it, but sin that dwells in me, for *I* know that nothing good dwells within me, that is, in my flesh. *I* can will what is right, but *I* cannot do it, for *I* do not do the good *I* want, but the evil *I* do not want is what *I* do. Now if *I* do what *I* do not want, it is no longer *I* that do it but sin that dwells in me" (vs. 14-20). Paul is lost in the problem of finding his own *ego*, split as it is between idealism on the one hand and the flesh with its desires on the other. What is he, Paul? What am I, Erwin Goodenough? This is the great question we all have been asking ourselves all the centuries since, and we still have no answer.[67]

The array of *nomoi* mentioned in the following verses (vs. 21ff.) will always be the despair of anyone who tries to understand "law" in Paul solely on the basis of the Old Testament and later Judaism. There is an overall law, i.e. that he has a divided *ego:* "I find it to be a *nomos* that when I want to do right, evil lies close at hand" (vs. 21). While Paul calls this a law, it is certainly no part of the code of Moses; it is a law of nature, and we are talking from a Greek point of view which has nothing to do with "codes". "I delight in the law of God in my inmost self" (vs. 22); this could be the law of Moses, but it is more probably the law of the spirit as in verse 25 below. Then "I see in my members another *nomos* at war with the *nomos* of my mind and making me captive to the *nomos* of sin which dwells in my members" (vs. 23);[68] at least one law is introduced here which has not been mentioned in vs. 21f., an evil law which is in the members or in the flesh. Finally Paul closes this extraordinary passage by saying, "I myself serve the nomos of God with my mind, but with my flesh I serve the *nomos* of sin" (vs. 25), a condition of conflict which seems to be according to the first law mentioned, the "law that when I want to do right, evil lies close at hand" (vs. 21).

---

[67]It is true that the Freudians can tell you what the *ego* is, but they do so in their own terms and do not satisfy the rest of us; *ego* is a very mixed-up affair. Philo encountered the same difficulty Paul expresses here, see Spec. iii, 1-6, a passage I have often quoted (e.g. in *Introduction*, 5f.).

[68][In Rom. 7:21-3 "Paul assumes a knowledge of the sort of treatment of law in the inner man preserved to us only by Philo, a knowledge which his readers most probably had, but whose absence has obscured his remarks ever since for later readers," *Light*, 394.]

I read with incredulity the arguments of modern commentators which identify this division of the law of the flesh and the law of the spirit with the *yetzer ha ra* and the *yetzer tob* in rabbinic thought. The sense of inner conflict between an impulse to do right and an impulse to do wrong is universal, and the Jews did express it in this latter form. They did not, in rabbinic circles, express it as the war between flesh and spirit; they did not urge us to get away from the flesh, to die to the flesh in order to escape this conflict. The Jew lived with the conflict, he lived with it nobly, and fought his battle out as best he could. But for Paul, this was not enough. He wanted to be free of the conflict altogether and so turned to the Greek identification of sin with the fleshly element in one's constitution.

In his great work *Judaism*, George Foote Moore has a masterful section on the *yetzer ha ra* and the *yetzer tob*, the evil impulse and the good impulse in man;[69] he makes it clear that this conception is quite different from the hellenistic idea widely held in the time of Paul, i.e. that these two impulses were centered, one in a superior part of man like the soul, and the other in the body. Later, after the publication of Moore's work, I wrote an appendix to my *By Light, Light* in which I elaborately spelled out this Greek idea of the body as the corrupting agent.[70] The theory originally goes back to the Orphics who saw the soul as a fallen particle from God imprisoned in the body (σῶμα-σῆμα,

---

[69][In pages 479-96 of volume 1 and the notes thereto in 3:146-51, especially note 209. The major study of *yetzer* cited by Moore is F.C. Porter, "The Yeçer Hara: a Study in the Jewish Doctrine of Sin," *Biblical and Semitic Studies*, 1902, 93-156. Porter concludes: "The result of our review is that in rabbinical usage the *yeçer* is hardly other than a name for man's evil tendencies or inclinations, the evil disposition which as a matter of experience exists in man, and which it is his moral task to subdue or control. It does not contain a metaphysical explanation of the fact, a theory as to its source or nature...All this, it is evident, has nothing to do with a dualistic contrast of body and soul...It must, moreover, be evident, apart from any positive explanation of Paul's doctrine, that the parallelism between his contrast of spirit and flesh and the rabbinical contrast between the good and evil impulses is remote and insignificant. Of course Paul in Rom. 7 is describing the same experience of struggle between two opposing forces in man upon which the Jewish doctrine rests, but his way of expressing the struggle as a war between the law (of sin) in his members, and the law of his mind (νοῦς), or between that which he possesses and does in his flesh and in his mind, is widely different from the Jewish conception, and seems to rest on a different view of the world and of man," 132-34. The rabbinic evidence is categorized and summarized in the excursus, "Der gute u. der böse Trieb" in H.L. Strack and P. Billerbeck, *Kommentar zum Neuen Testament aus Talmud und Midrasch IV*, 1, 466-83 (1928).]

[70]["Law in the Subjective Realm," 370-443; much of the material in *Light* which is most relevant to the present article will be found in this appendix.]

the body is a tomb). The particle struggled to free itself from the body and those struggles were aided by the Orphic mysteries, the mystic exercises themselves. The idea continues in Plato's *Phaedrus* (246ff.) in the well-known myth of the Charioteer: here the evil horse is the desire for physical pleasure; it pulls the chariot downward, i.e. forces the rest of the soul into an incarnation in the body, where all is lost until man begins to discover the truth again and so orients himself that reason can become master. I will not here review all this material from my book,[71] but I can state positively that the doctrine that sin is a product of the body, that the law of sin is a part of the body, is quite hellenistic. Perhaps its most striking ancient image is the story of the death of Socrates: Socrates' death means that finally he is to escape the body and come at last into the true realm of being; mortal things will trouble him no longer.

Plato and the other Greeks stop short of the iron-clad dualism of the Persians and later Manichees. These are not eternal principles so much as factual descriptions of man's problem. The various members *do* have their own law. It is the law of the sexual organ that it should seek gratification. It is the law of the stomach that it should want food, the law of the body in its weariness that it wants repose. All the parts of our bodies have a law that they should perform their functions, but they are utterly incorrelated, unorganized, and can (any of them) become obsessions, as when the craving for drink takes over a man's reason and he becomes a dipsomaniac. The law of the mind knows

---

[71][In *Light* 395, note 160, G. suggests the following passages as examples of Philo's view of the sinfulness of the flesh: *Gig.*, 12-15; *Immut.*, 142f.; *Agr.*, 89; *Heres*, 239f. In "Philo on Immortality," *HTR* 39 (1946), 96f., he writes: "Often as Philo refers to the 'soul' as the prisoner in the body in the Orphic-Platonic sense, it is strictly (the) higher mind which he means...It is which this correction that we should read all the passages of Philo where he more loosely speaks of the 'soul' as being confined to the prison, the tomb, of the body (*L.A.* i, 107f.; cf. *Q.G.* iv, 152), or where, in terms which alone make Paul's seventh chapter of Romans intelligible, he speaks of the body as a corpse to which we are bound, and of ourselves as 'corpse-bearers': 'The body is wicked and a plotter against the soul, and is always a corpse and a dead thing. For you must understand that each of us does nothing but carry a corpse about, since the soul lifts up and bears without effort the body which is in itself a corpse' (*L.A.* iii, 68, cf. 72, 74). Philo has in this connection the same confusion of figures as Paul, for with both of them the body is simultaneously a corpse tied to the soul, and an active schemer for the soul's destruction." For a brief summary of this point from the New Testament point of view, with relevant texts, see H. Lietzmann's excursus, "Das Fleisch und die Sünde," *An die Romer*[4], *(HNT)* 1933, 75-77. Lietzmann finds Philo to be the ancient writer whose ideas on "flesh and sin" most closely resemble Paul's, and says that this connection of sin with flesh is, for Philo, "das Fundament der Ethik", 75.]

better, but the law of the mind is not strong enough to control our impulses, and we have all sinned, as we all know.[72] The law of the mind is not a matter of precepts, but of the perception of the true religious values; somehow we must have access to a greater realization and acceptance of this higher law.

With their deep hellenistic coloring, Philo's writings run along these same lines: here incarnation in the body is the great tragedy, one is trying always to free oneself from the body, e.g. by ascetic practices or by study. The Greek mysteries were presenting a savior in a Hercules or an Isis; savior-gods were springing up all over. This appealed to Philo and he turned the great patriarchs into incarnations of the higher law, they become his *nomoi empsuchoi*, through whom we could come into the higher law and live lives of value and virtue. He was convinced that the Mosaic law was but a shadow of the higher law; the business of man was indeed to live by the law, but we are not to stop with the precepts and the written law, but go on to the higher law. This higher law was made accessible to man in the patriarchs who had been law-abiding and pleasing to God before, and thus without, the Mosaic code.

In lengthy discussion in *By Light, Light* I called this the "mystery" of hellenistic Judaism.[73] The term received more attention than the idea behind it, an idea which was very familiar to Paul himself, for he has left us a most masterful summary of the real meaning of this mystery: "I want you to know, brothers, that our fathers were all under the cloud and all passed through the sea and all were baptized into Moses in the cloud and in the sea, and all ate the same 'pneumatic' food and all drank the same 'pneumatic' drink, for they drank from the 'pneumatic'[74] rock which followed them, and the rock was Christ" (1 Cor. 10:1-4). I could not have put the essence of the mystery into more compact form myself. Those who had passed through the sea and the cloud were baptized *into Moses*; he was a personal revelation of this higher entity. Baptism *into Moses* exactly parallels Paul's idea of baptism *into Christ*. "They all ate the same 'pneumatic' food and all drank the same 'pneumatic' drink" – Philo says this very often about the manna in the wilderness and the water which issued from the

---

[72][For a description of human nature in these same terms, but in a discussion of Philonic ethics, see *Introduction*, 116f. For an earlier discussion of Paul's "law of the members," see *Light*, 391ff.]

[73][This is the theme of the first nine chapters of *Light*; it is summarized also in *Introduction*, 138-58.]

[74]["I do not see why recent translators make of the 'pneumatic' rock and food something 'supernatural'. That conception is quite foreign to the ancient mind," *Symbols* 12:171 note 44. Both RSV and NEB have "supernatural".]

great rock (Ex. ch. 16-7):[75] the great rock with its stream of water was the Logos which came to relieve them. Paul's change is a simple one: "the rock was Christ."

Behind these verses in 1 Corinthians lies a hellenistic Jewish tradition which Paul has Christianized only by making the rock and its flow not Sophia or the Logos, but Christ. Paul certainly did not invent the idea that the passage of the Red Sea was a baptism *into* Moses. Here is indeed a survival from his earlier thoughtways. The cloud, the rock and the superhuman Moses are all depicted in the Dura Europos synagogue, in a fresco which might well be used among Christians to illustrate and explain Paul's text.[76] Baptism "into" Christ and existence "in" him would be instantly understandable to these familiar with this hellenistic Jewish "Moses" tradition.

Romans, Ch. 8

The same theme continues: "There is now no condemnation for these who are *in* Christ Jesus, for the law of the spirit of life in Christ Jesus has set you free from the law of sin and death" (vs. 1f.).[77] As they were baptized *into* Moses, we are now *in* Christ Jesus;[78] the effect is very similar: we can rise from the lower law to the higher law which Christ embodies as Moses did. Christ has done away with the law of the flesh (vs. 3); the result is that we can fulfill the just requirement of the law by walking not according to the flesh but according to the spirit (vs. 4f.).[79] This "just requirement" is surely *not* the Mosaic law; Paul has not gone through all of his experiences (his death with Christ in baptism, his emerging as a new creature in Christ) just so that he can more faithfully keep the Jewish law. Such an understanding he would have

---

[75][For a further discussion of "spiritual food and drink" see *Symbols* 6:198-216, where G. summarizes the Philonic material.]

[76][This paragraph is based on *Symbols* 10:135. Chapter 16 of *Symbols* 10 (105-39) is G.'s thorough discussion of the Moses-Exodus-Red Sea typology as it applies to the Dura fresco mentioned here; he entitles it "Moses Leads the Migration from Egypt" and prints it as color-plate XIV in *Symbols* 11. For the relevant New Testament and early Christian material, with bibliography, see *Symbols* 10:134ff.]

[77]Cf. 2 Cor. 3:6-18, which describes the giving of the spirit-law which *is* the Lord. [For an ingenious analysis of the source of this text, see Georgi's excursus, *op. cit.* 274-82.]

[78][In *Psychology*, 152ff., G. discusses some uses of "in Christ" imagery in the later Church.]

[79][G. points out that Paul's language here (e.g. living "according to the spirit" and "the mind of the spirit," 8:6) comes close to Philonic terminology, since "Philo often prefers to use the word Spirit when he speaks of the Logos in relation to man, how it comes in at inspiration, and abides in him as the higher mind," *Introduction*, 117 with note 5.]

repudiated altogether. The Jewish law is something past and gone; instead there is a higher law which we obtain through Christ as did those Jews who were baptized into Moses before Sinai had issued a single commandment.

We are no longer in the flesh, but in the spirit, if the spirit of God really dwells in us – so says verse 9 in the peculiar, allusive speech of the mystic; we are in the spirit if the spirit is in us. One cannot press these mystic figures too closely; their purpose is to express union, without a concern for firm, logical terminology. The spirit is the spirit of Christ; if we lack this in us, we do not belong to him.[80]

The major part of this chapter is a peculiarly Pauline mixture of mysticism, eschatology and the doctrine of election, themes which appear again in chapters 9-11; Paul is working at the difficult task of describing Christian existence until the Parousia. Law-observance in the sense of pre-Christian legalism is an impossible solution, yet we are not to live according to the flesh (vs. 12); we must set our minds upon the spirit. The spirit dwells within us (vs. 11, 13ff.) but our bodies are still mortal bodies (vs. 11); the final glorification (vs. 17) and the final gift of life (vs. 11) are still ahead of us, the whole creation sharing our "in-between" state (vs. 19-22).

We have the gift now only partially, only the first-fruits[81] of the spring (vs. 23); in our present struggle for obedience to the higher law, the law of the spirit, we will frequently fail, but the spirit helps us in our weakness, interceding for the saints according to the will of God (vs. 26).[82]

---

[80][For an exhaustive study of the conception of "indwelling deity" in the ancient word, see J. Haussleiter, "Deus internus," *Reallexikon für Antike und Christentum* 3:794-842 (1957), especially the sections on Philo and Paul, 815-20.]

[81][In *Symbols* 5:86 G. suggests that this term "seems in itself to indicate Christ" at work within us. He further points out that Paul sometimes uses $\dot{\alpha}\pi\alpha\rho X\acute{\eta}$ of Christ, and at other times, of certain Christians, e.g. the first converts in Asia (Rom. 16:5) and Achaia (1 Cor. 16:15). This "double implication" of the term occurs already in Philo, and, presumably, in the tradition upon which he draws. According to Philo "the Jews...had been set aside as the first fruits of the human race to the Creator and Father, a prerogative they attained...through the righteousness and virtues of the Patriarchs, 'which endure like immortal plants bearing an everblooming fruit that for their descendants is saving and profitable in every way' (*Spec.* iv, 180f.)...Just as the Christians become first fruits through the merits of Christ, the Jews had become first fruits through the merits of the Patriarchs. Christ as the saving first fruits has his prototype in Philo's Jewish saviors, the Patriarchs who are also first fruits," *Symbols* 5:89. For G.'s discussion of the other instances of *aparche* in the New Testament, see *Symbols* 5:84-91 and 12:104f.]

[82]The distinctly hellenistic character of vs. 29 is usually obscured by translating it: "Those whom he fore-knew, he also predestined to be conformed to the

We have entered a new legal regime, a new order, a new way of life. It is not yet perfect; *dikaiosune* in its fullest form is an attribute of God himself, and we shall not come into it in full perfection until we are rid of our bodies, or until our bodies have been transformed into spiritual entities. But through Christ we come into an entirely different order: in their blundering the gentiles have missed this and gone over to idols; the Jews thought they could win it by trying to obey with ever-increasing nicety the commandments of the Mosaic code. Neither of these will work. We have to die to our whole selves, die to our material nature, die to the flesh and come to live in the law of the spirit which is in Christ Jesus (vs. 2);[83] only in this way do we approach the final *dikaiosune*.

Romans, Ch. 9-11

In these chapters Paul turns to the heart-breaking problem of Israel's rejection of Christ. He finds his consolation in the whole history of Israel, for all the people who are fleshly descendants of Abraham by no means belong to Israel (9:6-8). Over and over again the people have rejected God, while whoring after other gods; God has had to reject them, but he has always kept a remnant. He is keeping a remnant now. There seems to be no way to distinguish between those who obey and follow, and so become a part of the remnant, and those who do not. Even in a family so exalted as that of Isaac, Jacob is accepted and Esau rejected (9:9-13). Why? That is a question we must not ask. Salvation is to come as an act of God, an act of mercy, and not by men's efforts. But why should some have this grace and others lack it? Again, this question we must not ask. Who are we to talk back to God

---

image *of* his son," but what Paul is saying is rather: we are going to be "conformed to the image, i.e. his son," not to an image *of* Christ, but to Christ who *is* himself the image of God. "Image" (*eikon*) is frequently used by Philo in this fashion e.g. *Conf.* 97, *Fug.* 101, *Som.* i, 239 and ii, 45. In Col. 1:15ff. the two chief functions of the *eikon* are "creating" and "ruling", exactly those of Philo's Logos [see the brief discussion in *Introduction,* 104ff. This topic is dealt with in two recent studies whose approach is indicated in their subtitles: J. Jervell, Image Dei: Gen. 1, 26f. im Spätjudentum, in *der Gnosis und in den paulinischen Briefen,* 1960, 271ff.; and E. Larssen, *Christus als Vorbild: eine Untersuchung zu den paulinischen Tauf- und Eikontexten,* 1962, 293ff. Larsson works chiefly with comparative material from the Old Testament, later Judaism and Qumran, while Jervell brings in gnostic texts, e.g. 122-70. For a brief summary of the Philonic and Pauline uses of *eikon* (*tou theou*), see the article by G. Kittel in *Theological Dictionary of the New Testament* 2:394ff. (1964).]

[83]["By simply omitting the reference to Jesus Christ in Paul's Romans viii, we have all been familiar from childhood with a description of the higher spiritual Law which can set one free from the law of the flesh and of sin, a description with which Philo would heartily have agreed," *Light,* 398.]

(9:14ff.)? God does as he pleases with his own; he is a potter who may make vessels of honor and vessels of dishonor at his will. It is not for the clay to question the potter (9:20-23). The gift of grace and with it the gift of faith and with that the gift of righteousness – all these God has finally bestowed upon Jews and gentiles alike (9:24ff.).

Philo's idea of Israel is quite similar. The true Israelites are those who live not by the laws of the commands, but by the Logos and the powers in the higher law. But unlike Paul he does not say that those who are doing the best they can (the ordinary Jews with the Mosaic code) are rejected people. He would have been utterly impatient with Paul's taking this position. For Philo there was the true Israel, and there was the mass of Israelites – what could you expect? The mass of people is not spiritually minded, not capable of the higher experiences, the higher ideas; consequently, they are mercifully given the law of Moses by which they live. Philo saw no cleavage or warfare between these two kinds of Jews. He himself wanted to live the life of the higher, unwritten law of the Logos and the powers, but he was a close fellow-worker with the Jews and would have nothing to do with those who rejected observing the law of Moses.[84] But Christ had made the higher law so vivid, so accessible, so real for Paul that he took the step which Philo would never have taken; he rejected those who tried by their own efforts to be saved. For Paul, salvation must be a matter of abandoning our effort and being given the grace, the gift of faith and of *dikaiosune* (10:3). The Jews who were ignorant of the righteousness that comes from God as his gift[85] sought to establish their own righteousness; they attempted to make themselves righteous by their own effort, and this was their fatal mistake. They could not and did not submit to God's true righteousness, the righteousness by gift.

It is not difficult to receive this gift; "the word is near us, on our lips and our hearts, that is, the word of faith which we preach" (10:8). We must cease our own efforts and pray to God for the gift, "for everyone who calls on the name of the Lord will be saved" (10:13). For this reason we spread the gospel as rapidly as possible by preaching, because no one can confess and believe what he has not heard (10:14f.).

We will not attempt to reconcile chapter 9 with chapter 10. Paul believes in preaching, in telling people, and yet everything is the work of God, foreordained and predestined.[86] Fortunately, for our purpose,

---

[84][Cf. note 43 above.]

[85][On righteousness as a gift of God, see the Käsemann article cited above, note 36.]

[86][The same tension is apparent in the Dead Sea Scrolls; H. Ringgren suggests that "it is probable that the Qumran community itself was not aware of the

the analysis of Paul's thought for hellenistic elements, the settlement of this controversy is not required. I suspect that Paul was a predestinarian very like most predestinarians; in some moods he submitted to God and felt that God did everything, in other moods human effort (even if only the effort of giving up and praying for God's help) seemed of some avail and God did listen. If predestinarians were not of this sort, the Calvinist churches would not have gone on with their preaching. They were carrying the gospel to the people but (by strict logic) if God did this directly for the elect, preaching and churches were quite supernumerary. The problem seems to me not specifically Jewish or specifically Greek; it is rather a problem which has arisen out of Paul's own experience of Christ.[87] He received the great gift *as* a gift, with a sense that his effort was absolutely nil, that only when his efforts ceased was the gift bestowed. But did his own election mean that God turned a deaf ear when others piously asked for salvation and *pistis?* Paul could not say that, and the resulting contradiction is one within his Christian thinking. I see nothing comparable in Philo or in rabbinic texts.

Chapter 11 continues this theme: God has by no means rejected the whole of his people (11:1). Paul himself is proof of that, he himself is a Jew; all Jews have not been rejected. God has hardened the hearts of most Israelites however, so that the gospel will be spread among the gentiles, a thing which would have been most difficult had the Jews all eagerly accepted it and made it a part of their Judaism. Jews have been broken off, branch by branch, from the great olive tree, and gentiles grafted in their places (11:17ff.) But someday the broken-off branches will be taken back and put into the great, true olive tree. If you who have been grafted in begin to feel superior for that fact, you too will be torn off (11:21). The only superiority is in God himself; it is fatal for you to have any pride or sense of accomplishment in yourself.

Romans: the Final Section

Paul's great exposition of the essentials of the Christian faith has come to an end. Chapter twelve brings us into the letter's final section, a

---

contradiction, or in any case did not try to express its belief in a form which was free of contradiction," *op. cit.* (note 51 above) 111.]

[87][The doctrine of predestination "was a natural and logical conclusion from the experience that Paul himself had... but logical conclusions are as dangerous in religion as they are in most of life," *Toward a Mature Faith*, 1955, 147.]

combination of instruction and exhortation directed to specific issues and problems within a Christian's everyday life.[88]

Particular ethical statements in the Pauline letters are often quite like those of Jesus, e.g. in the Sermon on the Mount. Jesus too wanted men to live with neighborly love, as did the rabbis; he too was ready to disregard Mosaic proscriptions for the principles that lay behind them, thus, e.g. he goes beyond "Thou shalt not kill" to forbid even anger and words of derision (Mt. 5:21f.). There is to be no adultery, even in a look (Mt. 5:27f.); no resistance, even under attack (5:38ff.).[89] But Jesus was a Palestinian in that he came to the higher meaning by generalizing the laws of the code themselves; Paul, on the other hand, worked to establish a morality that rises above specific precepts altogether, one that is based instead on the higher perception of right and wrong, on the higher immaterial law.

This difference between the ethics of the Sermon on the Mount and that of Paul is the result of the fact that Paul thinks in hellenistic terms; this becomes clear when we compare him with Philo.[90] In his *de Specialibus Legibus* Philo approaches the specific laws of the Mosaic code much as Jesus does, but his *de Virtute* has interesting similarities to these last chapters of Romans. The *de Virtute* is a summary of the second major section of Philo's writings, the very long "Exposition of the Law,"[91] which details God's giving of the law in the Old Testament, beginning with Creation. Philo's object here is to clarify God's law, the law which could be called the law of nature, since for theists nature is God. In the creation the law of nature[92] is manifest; that is nothing less than the first great revelation of God's law. The second comes in the

---

[88]I include in this section chapters 12-15, since chapter 16 is generally recognized as a piece from another letter altogether. [In the article summarized above, note 31, T.W. Manson rather calls chapter 16 a "covering note" sent to Rome with the summary of Pauline theology now called Romans 1-15. G. probably would not have quarreled with Manson on this point.]

[89][For a detailed comparison of Jesus' view of the commands of the Torah with the views of later Judaism, primarily Qumran, see H. Braun, *Spätjüdisch-Häretischer und frühchristlicher Radikalismus*, 1-2, 1957.]

[90][There are several useful comparisons between Pauline and Philonic ethics in *Introduction*, 112-33. On Philo's ethics, see also E. Bréhier, *Les Idées philosophiques et religieuses des Philon d'Alexandrie*[3], 1950, 250-310; G. once mentioned that it was the first edition of this book which caused him to begin his study of Philo.]

[91][G. characterizes the different groups of Philonic writings and lists those treatises which make up this "Exposition" in his article "Philo Judeus" in Interpreter's Dictionary of the Bible 3:796f. (1962). His book *Jewish Courts in Egypt*, 1929, is an exhaustive treatment of *de specialibus Legibus*.]

[92][See note 46 above.]

giving of the law to the *nomoi empsuchoi*,[93] and then (since these were
not enough) the giving of the law in the Ten Commandments, and
finally the elaborate regulations of the Torah which Philo explicates
in the four books of the *de Specialibus Legibus*.[94] Paul has done nothing
comparably elaborate; the whole of Romans is smaller than the little
de Virtute. Philo, however, never lost his reverence for the Mosaic code
in its literal form, as commandments; consequently he is driven to a long
exposition of these regulations.

But once the specifics of the law have been explained, Philo leaves
detailed laws behind altogether; he is writing for gentiles, for Romans
who ave their own ideas of morality and so, in the *de Virtute*, he
summarizes the special laws under the general topics Courage,
Humanity, Repentance and Nobility.

Here the commands are elevated into reminders of the universal
laws. In his discussion of the commands to kindness, he transforms
specific laws into a general principle. Many laws are quoted to show
how kindness and consideration are required within the tribe; kindness
is due also to proselytes and even to animals and plants. But then Philo
summarizes: "With such instructions he tamed and softened the minds
of the citizens of this commonwealth, and set them out of the reach of
pride and arrogance, evil qualities grievous and noxious in the highest
degree" (*Virt.* 161) – that is, all these many laws of Moses were
actually established to teach the dangers of the great Greek sin *hubris;*
they are to keep us humble and make us realize our own limits.[95] We
must never lose the remembrance of God; that is the one thing which
will help us keep from falling into sin and pride, "for as when the sun
has risen, the darkness disappears and all things are filled with light,
so when God the spiritual sun rises and shines upon the soul the gloomy
night of passions and vices is scattered and virtue reveals the peerless
brightness of her form, and all is purity and loveliness" (*Virt.* 164). As
Philo reminds us frequently in this book, this higher estate of the soul
is called *dikaiosune,* righteousness. It alone will keep us as we should
be, and it comes to us as we turn to God and let the brilliant sun of his
person rise and shine upon the soul. When this happens, "the gloomy
night of passions and vices scatters."

---

[93][See page 41ff. above.]
[94][See note 44 above on the four levels of "law" in Philo.]
[95][For a detailed examination of the hellenistic conceptions present in Philo's
approach to the Torah, see I. Heinemann, *Philons griechische und jüdische
Bildung: kulturvergleichende Untersuchungen zu Philons Darstellung der
jüdischen Gesetze,* 1932. G. evaluates this book in *Introduction,* 11-13.]

Paul's view is recognizably similar; for him the only way to avoid the sins of the flesh is to let the light of God so shine into us that the body with its desires and passions fades out of existence. This is our only hope. This is the way we will come into virtue, virtue pure, virtue unified, the virtue of God.[96]

When Romans 12-15 is compared to the Philonic writing in this way, it becomes clear that Paul's approach to the problems of ethics is as much like the *de Virtute* as his teaching (at its best in Romans) is *unlike* that of Jesus.[97] Indeed the evidence from Philo and Paul strongly suggests that there was a general tendency (among gentiles as well as among hellenized Jews) to admire the Jewish law for its reflection of general principles of morality;[98] both men often appear to me to be capitalizing on such a situation.

While Paul and Philo thus approach the problems of ethics in the same way,[99] Paul's great difference is that he has been so engrossed,

---

[96]Paul and Philo might well describe this result in the same terms; compare the "catalog of virtues and vices" in *Virt.* 182 with those in Paul [e.g. in Rom. 1:29-31, 13:13. See O.J.F. Seitz, "Lists, Ethical" in *Interpreter's Dictionary of the Bible* 3:137-39 (1962) and add to the bibliography there, S. Wibbing, *Die Tungend-und Lasterkataloge im Neuen Testament*, 1959).]

[97][On the use of non-Christian elements in early Christian parenesis and the place of Romans 12 in early Christian ethics, see E. Käsemann, "Gottesdienst im Alltag der Welt," *Exegetische Versuche und Besinnungen* II: 198-204 (1964) and the literature cited there.]

[98][Jewish apologists in the Diaspora were compelled to (and often eager to) relate and recommend their law to the gentiles around them. G. here discusses Philo's approach; other frequently mentioned examples are Ep. Aristeas 128-71 and Josephus, c. Apionem 2:151-235, cf. E. Schürer, *A History of the Jewish People in the Time of Jesus Christ*[2], 2:311-27 (1891). D. Georgi argues "dass das Medium der jüdischen Propaganda vor allem der Synagogengottesdienst und die hier dargebotene Gesetzesauslegung war," *op. cit.* 87, cf. 83ff. and his discussion of Juvenal and Horace, 105ff. The evidence indicates two things: 1) Many Jews realized that their law had to be taken with them into the gentile world; it was important to make Judaism attractive and available to gentiles, but if this were done by rejecting the Torah, the result could no longer be called Judaism. 2) As G. here suggests, the law-ordered life of an observant Jew was often highly attractive to his gentile neighbors. For both of these reasons, the law was a major element (perhaps the chief one) in the contacts between gentile and "apologetic" Jew, with both parties interested in stressing its general principles and universal scope rather than its Jewish particularity.]

[99][The similarity which G. stresses here extends to the literary forms used by Philo and Paul; both employ a common form of hellenistic moral exhortation, the diatribe, which has been characterized as follows: "Eine philosophische Unterweisung volkstümlichen Charakters mit vorwiegend ethischem Inhalt...In ihrer Anlage ist die D(iatribe) ein fingierter Dialog mit einem anonymen Gesprächspartner...(Sie) bedient sich der einfachsten u(nd) ausdrucksvollsten

encompassed, engulfed by the vision of Christ that he no longer needs to defend the specific commands; indeed he rises above them altogether and looks toward a state where the higher mind, the higher vision, the higher self illuminated by God, is governing us, so that the body has become dead.

Paul's vision of Christ leads to many differences between his statements and those of Philo, but it is clear that both of them are trying to lead man into a life in which the higher part, the part engulfed by God, takes over and the fleshly impulses are no longer in control.[100]

Kunstmittel der klassischen Rhetorik...Die Verfasser von D. lieben es, ein bestimmtes Repertorium von Themen aus der philosophischen Elementarethik abzuhandeln," H.I. Marrou, "Diatribe" in *Reallexikon für Antike und Christentum* 3:998 (1957). Marrou, 999f., finds the following examples of particular elements of the diatribe style in Romans: ethical exhortation, chaps. 12-15; imaginary dialogue or *apostrophe*, 2:1, 9:19; interjected protests, 9:19, 11:19; question and answer, 6:1-19; personification of abstractions, 10:6-8; *parataxis*, 2:21f., 13:7; parallelism, 12:4-15; catalogue of vices, 1:29(-31); imperatives, 12:14f. On the diatribe in Philo, P. Wendland, "Philo und die kynisch-stoische Diatribe," in *Bieträge zur Geschichte der grieschischen Philosophie und Religion*, 1895, 1-75; Wendland indicates (cf. 66) that Philo's attacks on gluttony, sexual license and other contemporary evils owe much to the Diatribe, his *de Vita Contemplativa* being one of the clearest examples of this influence. H. Thyen relies heavily on Philonic examples to demonstrate the similarities between hellenistic-jewish preaching and the Diatribe, *Der Stil der jüdisch-hellenistischen Homilie*, 1955. On Paul, see R. Bultmann, *Der Stil der paulinischen Predigt und die kynisch-stoische Diatribe*, 1910; Bultmann argues that the Diatribe has a limited but definite influence on Paul, cf. his conclusions, 107-09.]

[100][Both for Philo and for Paul "the only possible solution is that the higher mind conquer the lower members...The permanent adjustment is not, during this life at least, disembodied existence, but complete regeneration, the goal which Paul called 'the redemption of the body' but which he more commonly, like Philo, called by the legal-ethical terms, *dikaiosune* or justice. This term with both men still has the meaning which Plato gave it in the Republic: namely, a perfect regimentation of the state, civic or subjective, by which the higher faculties are in command, and the lower members perform their functions freely and fully, but keep each to its own business according to the laws fixed by the proper governor...Nothing distinguishes both thinkers more sharply from Stoic ethics than the refusal to build up the inner ethical harmony from within...Philo like Paul despaired of achieving the end without a new union with the Universal Spirit: the fragment or extension (of that Spirit) within him was helpless against the forces of his lower nature unless it was freshly united and augmented in the divine Spirit or Logos as a whole," Introduction, 118. "On no point is the thinking of the two so similar as on the ideal adjustment of the soul and body for one who found the higher reality," 116.]

General Index

175

Index to Biblical References

Brown Judaic Studies